Brahman

Jayaram V

Second Edition 2025

Published by
Pure Life Vision LLC
New Albany, Ohio

Brahman

Copyright © 2010 & 2025 by Jayaram V. All rights reserved.
Published and Distributed Worldwide by Pure Life Vision LLC., USA.
First edition 2010, Second Edition: 2025

No part of this publication may be reproduced, stored in a retrieval system, or transmitted in any form or by any means, electronic, mechanical, photocopying, recording, scanning, or otherwise, now known or hereinafter invented, except for quotations in printed reviews, without the prior written, express permission of the publisher or the author. This strict copyright protection is meant to ensure the respect and integrity of the author's work. Requests to the publisher for permission to print portions of this book or for bulk purchase of the book should be addressed to Pure Life Vision LLC, PO Box 1003, 102 W Main St, New Albany, OH 43054.

NO AI TRAINING: Without in any way limiting the author's and publisher's exclusive rights under copyright, any use of this publication to "train" generative artificial intelligence (AI) technologies to generate text is expressly prohibited. The author reserves all rights to license uses of this work for generative AI training and development of machine learning language models.

Pure Life Vision LLC is a registered company in the U.S.A. Pure Life Vision books and E-Books are available through numerous bookstores, online websites, and our online store. For inquiries, please visit https://www.purelifevision.com.

Cover Design © Jayaram V, 2025

Library of Congress Publisher Cataloging-in-Publication Data

V, Jayaram, (Vemulapalli)
Brahman
    p. cm
    Includes bibliographical references
    LCCN: 2025930837
    ISBN- 13: 9781935760191
    ISBN -10: 1-935760-19-X

Printed in the United States of America
10 9 8 7 6 5 4 3
First Edition 2012. Second Edition 2025

Contents

Preface	11
Author's Note	12
Brahman, in the Vedic Tradition	15
Brahman as Power and Potency	19
The Symbolism of Food as Brahman	31
The Ritual Brahman We Have Forgotten	39
I Know Him, and I Know Him Not	48
Thou Art That	54
The Creator and the Created	58
Brahman as the Sacred Sound	62
Brahman in Temple Worship	67
Brahmavidyas – Ways to Realize Brahman	75
The Creator God of the Upanishads	91
The Attributes of Brahman	100
Brahmopasana – The Paths To Liberation	109
Brahman as Isvara, the Personal God	121
Brahman and Brahma Prajapati	127
Why Brahman is Not Ritually Worshipped	139
Nidhidhyasana – The Contemplation of Brahman	145
Brahman and the Brahman Priest	157
The Difficulties of Knowing Brahman	166
Aspects of Brahman	171
Hinduism and the Belief in One God	184
Elements of Monotheism in the Early Vedic Tradition	188
The Paradox of Knowing Brahman	208
The Duality of Brahman and Atman	212
Bhagavan – The Glorious God	221
Brahman in Advaita and Dvaita Schools	225
The Glossary of Brahma(n) and Related Words	233
Bibliography	239

To Brahman, all the Divinities, Gurus, and Guardians of Dharma

About the Author

Jayaram V has authored over 3000 articles and 16 books, which include such notable works as Brahman, The Awakened Life, An Introduction to Hinduism, Bhagavadgita: Unveiling Gita's Secrets, Essays on the Bhagavadgita, Brahman, The Awakened Life, Hinduism, an Introduction, Selected Upanishads, Brihadaranyaka and Chandogya Upanishads, Shiva Sutras: Mystic Knowledge Explained, The Hindu Caste System, etc. His writings are appreciated all over the world for their originality and quality of information and his analysis and interpretation of ancient texts. Jayaram V has studied Hinduism and related religions for over 40 years and writes regularly about various aspects of Hinduism, Buddhism, Jainism, spirituality, yoga, and self-improvement. Through his writings, he brings out the knowledge found in the ancient texts, their hidden symbolism, and the significance of various key concepts found in them and interprets them objectively with modern insights and without sectarian biases. His scientific and spiritual background helps him examine the subjects analytically with an open mind and maintain objectivity in his writings and interpretations. He combines the mundane and finite aspects of life with the mystical and transcendental without losing sight of their spiritual and practical value in today's world. Inspired by Swami Vivekananda, Sri Aurobindo, and several other spiritual masters of the past and present, he founded Hinduwebsite.com in 2000 to counter negative propaganda and share authentic information about Hinduism and related religions. He believes in religious tolerance and the fundamental freedom of everyone to choose their faith or belief system according to their nature, needs, and preferences. He believes that atheism is also a part of one's spiritual journey. His efforts have helped make ancient Hindu texts more accessible to the world audience and appreciate the teachings found in them. His work has helped bring the wisdom of India's oldest religious and spiritual traditions to people around the world and educate and inspire them. You can explore more of his writings on Jayaramv.com and Hinduwebsite.com.

Books By Jayaram V

The Bhagavadgita: Unveiling the Gita's Secrets, 2024

Shiva Sutras: Mystic Knowledge Explained, 2024

The Awakened Life: Spiritual Knowledge from India's Sacred Traditions, 2024

Brahman, 2025

Essays on the Bhagavadgita

The Bhagavadgita: A Complete Translation

The Bhagavadgita: A Simple Translation

Introduction to Hinduism, 2024

Selected Upanishads

Brihadaranyaka Upanishad, Revised 2024

Chandogya Upanishad, Revised 2024

Think Success: Essays on Self-help

Being the Best: Practical Advice for Peace and Happiness

Thoughts and Quotations

Sadhana Panchakam - The Fivefold Spiritual Practice

The Hindu Caste System, 2025

Abbreviations

Katha. - Katha Upanishad

Mand. – Mandukya Upanishad

Mund. – Mundaka Upanishad

Isa. – Isa Upanishad

R.V – Rigveda

Brihad. – Brihadaranyaka Upanishad

Ait. - Aitareya Upanishad

Note: The verses or information quoted in this book are noted by the scripture's name, chapter number, section number, and verse number in the same order. For example, Brihad.1.2.4 refers to Brihadaranyaka Upanishad, Chapter 1, Section 2, and Verse 4.

Preface

The first edition of this book, published in 2010, has been well received by our readers. We are revisiting it after 15 years. Jayaram V has agreed to review and update his previous work, which is unique in several respects. Perhaps this is the first of its kind. We have made several improvements in the second edition while keeping the same basic format and information. Importantly, the core content remains unchanged, ensuring the book's reliability. Under the guidance of Jayaram V, the author, the first edition has been meticulously revised. New information and a new chapter have been added.

Jayaram V has corrected spelling and grammar errors in addition to enhancing the layout by updating the cover page, adjusting font sizes, and reworking the line spacing and page numbers. Chapter titles and the book's title have been added to the headers on each page, and the text has been updated appropriately wherever necessary to improve the style or clarify certain points previously discussed. Most chapter headings and overall content of the book remain the same as in the first edition. However, we did not include a preface for the first edition. We corrected that mistake and added a preface to the second edition.

The Vedas, which are themselves thousands of years old, are the basis for the knowledge of Brahman. The subject itself is such that the basic knowledge of Brahman always remains the same. We hope that these changes make the book not only more useful but also easier to read and understand and that you will enjoy reading this revised edition. Happy reading!

Publishers
February 2025

Author's Note

I wrote much of the content for this book several years ago, partly due to inspiration and partly based on my study and exploration and the realization that He is relatively unknown to even Hindus, which often leads to the allegation that Hinduism is a polytheistic religion with too much emphasis on rituals. I noticed that we have many books about gods and goddesses and various other subjects but hardly any notable work on Brahman, the highest Deity of Hinduism. Lord Krishna himself mentions him in the Bhagavadgita, but somehow, we revere Lord Krishna as the Godhead, ignoring that Lord Krishna himself spoke to Arjuna in oneness with Brahman in the first person, which is the natural state of all self-realized yogis and incarnations. Brahman is the Supreme Deity of all the Upanishads, Tantras, and other sacred texts of Hinduism. Bhagavadgita is no exception.

If the Vedas are the heart of Hinduism, Brahman is the heart and soul of the Vedas and other sacred texts. Indeed, He is the oldest Supreme Deity in the history of human civilization. Therefore, I wished to fill this gap and draw the readers' attention to this Secret Deity, who remains in the background as the Universal Witness, the Self of all, and the ultimate source and goal of all. We may worship all the deities of the Hindu pantheon to our hearts' content, but without ignoring that each of them is a manifestation or representation of Brahman only. In this regard, Lord Krishna's statements are apt to remember that those who worship the gods go to them, but those who worship Him, the Supreme Lord, go to Him only. He would take care of His dearest devotees who worship him exclusively with unwavering devotion and offer their actions to Him without desire.

To all those who are engaged in spiritual practice and are interested in their spiritual growth, here is my advice. Regard Him as the all-pervading universe because it is the nearest approximation of Him you can ever find in your wakeful consciousness. No image, sacred symbol, or object can justify His universality and immensity as much as the universe in which we all live. If you persist in this thought with faith and devotion, you will remain always connected to Him and inseparable from Him. You will not feel the need to worship Him in any other way. As an integral part of the gross and subtle universe, you become an aspect of Him because you are a part of the same universe and contain the essence of the universe both physically and subtly, just as a drop in the ocean. The Upanishads compare Brahman to space (Akasa), which pervades and envelops all and yet remains unaffected by all that happens in it. You are an aspect of Him and an integral part of Brahman. He is in you and outside you. The universe personifies Him. It represents His universal form or universal body, the one that Lord Krishna had shown to Yashoda and later to Arjuna. Therefore, know that He is so close to you that you do not have to shout to Him for help. You just let Him know what is in your mind or what you are thinking. He will hear you and respond to you appropriately according to what is best for you.

This book of mine is a theistic representation of Brahman, the highest God of Hinduism, based on my study and understanding of the Samhitas, the Upanishads, and various schools of Hindu philosophy. Brahman is not a God in the traditional sense. To describe Him as a God from the narrow and simplistic perspective is to diminish His immensity and unconditional universality. Nor is He a mere Creator in the traditional sense of a magician or a miracle worker. He does not entirely fit into the traditional dualistic views of God with which we are familiar. At the most, God is His manifested form, whom we call in our scriptures Isvara, the Lord of the Universe, and whom we worship as Brahma, Vishnu, Shiva, and other deities.

Even when we use all such descriptions for study, understanding, or contemplation, we should not forget that He is above all and represents all possible realities, aspects, consciousness, energies, and dimensions one can ever imagine. He has both finite and infinite realities, finite and infinite forms, manifested and unmanifested states, and known and unknown aspects. As the Bhagavadgita declares, all this is just a little fraction of Him, which He supports with a little fraction of His energy. Yet, He is attainable to the indefatigable devotees. He reveals Himself to the extent you unwind yourself and give up yourself or all that you love and cherish and cling to. He manifests when you disappear into yourself. He is the ultimate and absolute principle, who is the source of all sources. He is the God of gods and creator of the creator gods. He is the mysterious force that moves everything yet remains incognito.

Our words are inadequate to describe Him, and our intellect is insufficient to understand Him. Although He is the highest God of Hinduism, He is relatively unknown and rarely spoken about except in spiritual circles as the inmost Self or the universal Self. The Vedas are all about Brahman. The knowledge of the Vedas is traditionally deemed the knowledge of Brahman. Its secrets are hidden in the subtle nuances of sounds coming from the heavens rather than the intellect of the human mind. Hidden within the Vedas are the mystic sounds filled with the power and presence of Brahman. Through those sounds, He can be reached.

However, few people know that the Vedas are not about gods but about Brahman. They do not know that the Vedas are divided into four parts to be consistent with their basic worldview, which revolves around Brahman, who is both immanent and transcendent with both material and spiritual aspects. Hence, they suggest a way of life that places equal emphasis on balance and order and pursuing both material and spiritual goals for fulfillment and complete satisfaction in life. From this work, I hope readers will get a brief glimpse of the supreme Brahman, His importance, and His absolute nature in the continuity of the eternal tradition we know as Hinduism.

Jayaram V
December 2010
February 2025

Brahman, in the Vedic Tradition

Brahman is the indescribable, inexhaustible, omniscient, omnipresent, original, first, eternal, and absolute principle, who is without a beginning, without an end, who is hidden in all, and who is the cause, effect, source, material, support, and manifestation of all creation known, unknown and yet to happen in the entire universe. He is the most incomprehensible, inexhaustible, unapproachable, and radiant being, who is beyond the mind and the senses. He is the mysterious Being of vast dimensions who attracts the attention of intellectual and scholarly minds of all ages and yet eludes their understanding, intelligence, illumination, and imagination. The nearest thing in our objective world, with which we can compare Him, is the indefinite space (*akasa*) or the void (*sunyam*), which stretches indefinitely into the infinite universe and envelops all. However, Brahman is neither space nor void, but the active, intelligent, self-willed, self-directed, independent, Supreme Being who upholds, inhabits and envelops the worlds and the beings as their only source and support. Our imagination is not adequately equipped to envision His vast dimensions or recreate the qualities and aspects with which the scriptures extol Him.

The Upanishads describe Him as the one, indivisible, eternal universal Self, who is present in all and in whom all are present. He resides in the human body, as the individual Self, behind the golden sheath (*anandamaya kosa*), without blemish, and without parts (Mand. 2.2.10). He is beyond the phenomenal world, where neither the sun nor the moon nor the stars shine and where He alone shines by His own power. When a seer sees Him as golden-hued, he attains supreme equality with Him. The Vedic tradition holds the belief that the human body is made up of five distinct sheaths, namely the gross physical body (annamaya kosa), the breath body (*pranamaya kosa*), the mental body (*manomaya kosa*), the intelligence body (*vijnanamaya kosa*) and the bliss body (*anandamaya kosa*). The last one envelops the Self and reflects its golden hue. Although the Self is held within the city of nine gates (body) and is subject to the cycle of births and deaths, it remains pure and resplendent, unaffected by the events of the phenomenal world.

It is difficult to know when the Vedic people actually stumbled upon the idea of Brahman. It should have happened in the very early stages of the development of the Vedic tradition because Brahman was (and still is) central to the Vedas and the Vedic tradition. The knowledge of the Vedas is synonymous with the knowledge of Brahman. Brahman is their author and their subject. Brahman literally means that which expands, uplifts, or goes forth. The Vedic people considered it the power of manifestation hidden in the mantras, which manifested as one chanted them loudly according to a specific rhythm, accompanied by specific rituals. The priests regarded themselves as Brahmanas because they thought that they alone had the knowledge to invoke It. In the performance of the sacrifices, they laid great emphasis on the procedure as well as the correct pronunciation of the chants because they believed that Brahman worked wonders when they followed the rules strictly and maintained ritual purity. In sacrifices, correct pronunciation of the subtle sounds and syllables in the mantras was of vital importance because the power hidden in the speech (*vac*) manifested correctly when the breath hidden in the mouth was released properly with sound.

They also believed that the same power, which moved through the sacrifices, also rested in the heavens and gods and connected them with humans through space and time. The same power that regulated the universe regulated their minds and bodies and held the five life breaths in their respective channels. The source of that power was Brahman. According to the Purushasukta of the Rigveda (10.100), it was set in motion when Brahman, as Purusha, the Cosmic Male, performed a great sacrifice of universal proportions upon Himself, in which He sacrificed His own energies and materiality to manifest creation. The Purusha of thousand eyes and thousand feet who performed that sacrifice was so mighty that He spanned across the earth, heaven, and much beyond, and the whole manifestation was just a fraction of Him. According to the hymn, from Him Viraj (warrior, first son of

Brahman, phenomenal world) was born. From Viraj, Purusha was born again. This second Purusha was a replica of the original Being, except in dimensions. He is described in the Vedic scriptures as Brahma or Prajapathi (Lord of Beings). The ancient rishis and gods (*sidhyas*) used him to perform a great sacrifice, from which emerged all the beings of the three worlds, the celestial objects, justice (*dharma*), time (*kala*), and many phenomena, including the knowledge of the Vedas. According to the Purushasukta, therefore, Brahman is both the efficient and material cause of the universe. He created the worlds and beings out of Himself using His own energies.

The knowledge of Brahman increased further during the emergence of the Upanishadic thought, which coincided with the internalization of the Vedic rituals and the proliferation of ascetic movements. The Vedic seers questioned the preoccupation of the people with rites and rituals at the cost of their spiritual welfare. They wanted people to lead balanced lives and look within themselves to experience the power of sacrifice unleashed by Brahman lying hidden within them. They wanted them to use that power to escape from the consequences of their actions (*karma*) and attain immortality rather than relying upon the unsteady boats of worldly sacrifices to go to the world of gods and ancestors and return again to experience old age and death (Mund. 1.2.7).

In the later Upanishads, we see a further development of the same thought process. In transcendental states, Vedic seers realized that Brahman was the highest, eternal, inexhaustible, and universal Self, who transcended all limitations and stood above all as the central and connecting principle of the entire creation. He was not just the source of power and energy (annam) but the Self of all, who, as the inhabitant of the entire universe, enveloped whatever moved in this moving world (Isa.1) and yet remained free from change and instability.

As the mover of heaven and the earth, He was the source of the dynamism and liveliness (*chaitanyam*) that was characteristic of all life forms. The Upanishads do not envisage Him as mere prayer power, sacred chant, or the uplifter of sacrifices that moved through the worlds and the invisible spaces on the strength of the speech (*vac*), as the Vedic priests believed. Nor was He just a Brahman priest who sat through the rituals and supervised their performance with the eyes of an eagle. He was the sacrifice, the sacrificial altar, the priest, the sacrificer, and the recipient of the offerings on a scale that was never imagined before. They found Him to be the all-pervading phenomena that existed in all and that controlled the movements and destinies of all life forms. He was not the subject of the senses but their source. He was not the known but the knower, the power behind all sensory perceptions, thoughts, and actions.

The Upanishads abound in the superlatives and, sometimes, contradictory and confounding descriptions of Brahman to denote His inclusiveness, universality, indeterminism, and completeness. However, they do not give us an intellectually satisfying picture of what Brahman is and how we may relate to Him mentally and spiritually. One may read the Upanishads a thousand times and yet may feel troubled with doubts and questions about His enigmatic essential nature. Even after years of study, scholars find Brahman beyond their intellectual grasp. Knowledge becomes inadequate and redundant when we contemplate upon Brahman of vast dimensions. The best way we can gain insight into Brahman is through personal experience, which comes only after years of dedicated practice and inner transformation. The knowledge of Brahman does not increase by knowing more about Him, nor does it diminish by not knowing Him. It is the sacred knowledge that manifests by itself when the mind is asleep, senses are withdrawn, and we are no longer bound to the boundaries of our waking consciousness. Since neither the mind nor the senses nor the intellect goes there, we do not know whether we know Him or not. If we think that we know Him, we probably do not. As the Katha Upanishad declares (1.2.23), He is attained only by those who are ready for the journey and whom Self chooses.

Brahman as Power and Potency

Brahman is the highest, supreme, universal power having the potential to manifest, transform, transpose, and conceal reality. One may call Him God because it is a familiar term. However, the word, with its traditional meaning, may not adequately describe His essential nature. Brahman is a more complex and enigmatic Supreme Being who does not actually fit into the simple and stereotypical definition of God. People may think about Him as a personal God having a name and a form and some human characteristics. However, it is doubtful whether anyone will ever really know Brahman at all or relate with Him mentally and intellectually. The Vedic people looked upon Brahman primarily as a manifesting, galvanizing, and activating power. They relied upon that power to propel their prayers heavenwards during the sacrificial rituals and invite the gods to the ritual place. Even now, many Hindus mistake Brahman for a priestly person (Brahmana) or for the creator god, Brahma, who is mentioned in the Vedas as the Creator and in the Puranas and epics as one of the Trimurthis (Trinity). Those who have studied Upanishads know Him usually as the absolute reality from which manifests the Supreme Being or the Lord of the Universe.

The word Brahman is said to be derived from the root word "brah," meaning to grow, exceed, strengthen, extend, or spread out, and "man," which may denote either movement or a thing. Some scholars tend to connect it with the root, "brahat" or "brahati", meaning large or "extensive." From a historical and ontological perspective, the former meaning seems to be more plausible and acceptable. According to Griswald [1], the name Brahman refers to "(1) a class of priests, the Brahmanas; (2) a department of ancient Sanskrit Literature, the Brahmana texts; (3) the Ultimate Reality of the Vedanta, Brahman; (4) the first person in the later Hindu Trinity, Brahma; Indian religion before the Buddhist disruption, Brahmanism, and (6) the modern theistic movement known as Brahma Samaj. To these, we may add many others [2]. Griswald also states that according to Grassmann's

Index Lexicon, the word Brahman appears in the Rigveda about 240 times and is used interchangeably for mantra, mati, manman, mansa, dhi, stoma, arka, ric, gir, vachas, uktha, vac, etc.," in conjunction with the names of the Vedic hymns. He, therefore, believes that the word was used to denote a Vedic hymn or "a brief utterance of the priest in worship." According to some scholars [3], etymologically, the Baresman of Zoroastrian scriptures and Brahman of the Vedas originated from the same root word with a common meaning as "thing extended, lifted up, presented, or offered." Both of them might have originally meant a religious offering. While we are not sure to what extent these words are interrelated, it seems there is a definite correlation between the words mantra and Brahman. Both are the heart and soul of the Vedas, and it is difficult to conceive the scriptures without either of them.

Mantra (man + tra) is that which uses (tra) or unleashes the power of the mind (man), and Brahman (brah + man) is the invisible and inexhaustible power hidden in the endless universe (*brah*), which can be connected through the mind (man) and harnessed with the speech or the sounds arising from the chanting of the mantras to connect to gods and seek their help to manifest thoughts or fulfill desires. According to Purva Mimansikas, that power rested in the yajnas (sacrifices) and could be harnessed with speech by using the right methods, procedures, and instructions as prescribed by the Vedas. They did not believe that Brahman was a Being or a Deity who would act or react independently. He represented the hidden power of the sacrifices. Hence, the right way to invoke that power was through sacrifices only.

Whether you believe in the ritualistic philosophy of Purva Mimansa or the spiritual doctrines of Vedanta, and whether you believe Brahman as a Being or a Universal Power, harnessing that power through speech, sacred sounds, or spiritual practice (*yoga*) is the central theme of the Vedic sacrifices. The Vedas are said to have originated from Brahman through his speech (sound). Vedic seers who heard them from Brahma in their meditative states rendered them into verbal form. Subsequently, they identified two fundamental aspects of Brahman: Purusha representing His pure consciousness or the Self, and Prakriti representing His universal energy and form. This duality does not manifest (*sambhuta*) in Brahman's absolute state but manifests in Brahma and creation. One is self-illuminated (Viraji), and the other is illuminated (*Viraj*) by the Self. In humans, they are represented by the Self and the body.

Whatever the truth, Brahman is central to Vedic theology. The Vedas suggest how the power of Brahman can be manifested through sacrificial rituals, speech, and righteous actions. Therefore, the tradition they represent is known as Brahmanism or Vedism. The knowledge that aims to harness His power through sacrifices is known as Purva Mimansa, the path of the ritualists who engage in Karmakanda. The spiritual philosophy or the knowledge (Jnanakanda) that speculates on Him and aims to realize Him through transformative practices and transcendental states is known as the Vedanta or Uttara Mimansa.

Brahman is pronounced in two different ways: Brahman and Brāhman (with a long vowel). Each has a specific meaning. The first one, used in a neutral sense, with short vowels, represents the supreme, universal Self, which is extolled in the Vedas as the secret power hidden in the chants and the entire creation. The second one, used in a masculine sense, with a long first vowel, represents either a Brahmana, a Brahman priest, or a divinity (Brahmanaspati), who is filled with the sacred power of Brahman or possesses the sacred knowledge of the Vedas or any Brahmana text. Brāhmanas belong to the Brahmana caste. Traditionally, they perform priestly duties in temples and know how to invoke and make use of the power of Brahman hidden in the Vedas or other sacred texts. Such power emanates from their ability to remember and chant the sacred verses of the Vedas or from the experience of oneness with the inner Self. The law books clearly distinguish between the former and the latter, stating that a true Brahmana is the one who knows Brahman and has realized Him without duality. Brāhmana, with an additional "a" at the end, denotes 'Brāhmana' the second section of the Vedas, which deals with the proper techniques and procedures to invoke the magical power of Brahman through rituals and spiritual practices. The Vedas, which are four (*Rigveda, Samaveda, Yajurveda,* and *Atharvaveda*), are revelatory texts consisting of lengthy hymns composed by the Vedic seers in Sanskrit, the language of the gods after they probably received them in trance or subtle states from Brahma, the creator god, who is described as the source and the teacher of all knowledge for the humanity. Since Brahman is their ultimate source and they are revealed at the beginning of every cycle of creation through Brahma, the teacher of gods, asuras (the wicked ones), and humans, they are considered eternal. They are rightly known as Shruti (the heard ones) in contrast to the Smriti texts that are based on memory or human intellect.

Therefore, it may be incorrect to say that the Vedic texts evolved over a long time. The Purva Mimansa School, which holds the Vedas as the source of all, goes even a step further and claims that not only the words in the Vedas but also their meaning and pronunciation are fixed and remain the same eternally. In other words, according to them, the hymns of the Vedas are not subject to varied interpretations or speculations. To understand them and use them in rituals, one must know them and their meaning and pronunciation correctly. For these reasons, the Vedas have been guarded rather zealously by several ancient lineages of Brahmanas since the earliest times, treating them as inviolable texts of revealed knowledge (shruti) and the personification of Brahman in speech form. Hence, curators of Vedic manuscripts agree in principle that all four Vedas have remained unchanged throughout the subcontinent even after centuries. Our understanding and interpretation of them may change, for better or worse, as the world progresses and as Hinduism and its traditions pass through different ages and phases of expansion and transformation. Concurrently with those changes, our understanding of Brahman may also change. However, the composition and the essence of the Vedas remain unchanged.

In the Rigvedic period, the knowledge of Brahman remained confined to the priestly class, who kept it a secret because their livelihood depended upon it. They used the knowledge of the Vedas to perform rituals and nourish gods using the transformative and creative power of Brahman hidden in the mantras. However, they did not treat Brahman like a deity who depended upon humans for nourishment through sacrifices. Hence, the Vedas, as a rule, do not instruct humans to worship Him ritually through sacrifices while suggesting that He is the final object and recipient of all offerings and worship. They look upon Brahman as the secret Deity and the ultimate power hidden in the sacred chants and prayers of the Vedas. By invoking that power, they can secure favors from gods and patrons alike and fulfill their desires. For the knowledgeable worshippers, Brahman denotes auspicious and infinite power that can be invoked and harnessed by chanting the hymns and performing sacrifices as prescribed by the Vedas. With the knowledge and purity gained from their study, austerities, and the blessings of Brihaspati or Brahmanaspati, the lord of the prayers and the leader of gods, as personified by their teachers, one can attain liberation and reach His immortal world. However, to produce correct results from the sacrifices upon which their reputation depends, those are engaged in priestly duties or daily sacrifices must master the art and craft of performing them strictly as ordained by the Vedas and their derived texts, such as the Grihyasutras, Vedangas, etc. Nowadays, such rigidity and obduracy are rare to find, but the Brahmanas in the Vedic period practice it.

Because of such beliefs, the gurukulas of the Vedic period imposed rigorous standards upon the students who wanted to study the Vedas and perform sacrifices. They had to learn and memorize the Vedas correctly by living with their gurus for at least two decades under their personal care. Once they graduated, they had to work a few years as apprentices and excel in using that knowledge effectively for the righteous ends for which it was intended. Vedic teachers, aware of their obligatory duty to preserve the knowledge and uphold the Dharma, subjected their students to rigorous discipline until they were proficient and ready to stand on their own. They had to master and excel in the Vedas, grammar, phonetics, the subtle nuances of the vocal and guttural sounds hidden in the sacred chants, their correct pronunciation, and the rules, restraints, and procedural aspects of performing the rituals as specified in the Vedas or instructed by their teachers before they could return to their home and start their lives as young householders (*snatakas*).

The sacrificial rituals are elaborate affairs. Some of them, which are, of course, not practiced nowadays, take months just for planning and preparation. In the Vedic period, the officiating priests took great care to ensure their efficacy, sanctity, and purity, spending considerable time in choosing an auspicious date, time, and place, sanctifying the altar with purification rites, selecting the right kind of priests, building the altar, and preparing the participants to participate in the rituals. Several priests participated in elaborate and complex rituals, dividing duties among themselves according to their knowledge, seniority, family lineage, and experience and working in harmony. While they performed their tasks with utmost care and caution, one priest, with years of experience behind him, sat silently, keeping an attentive watch over the entire proceedings to ensure that the ritual went according to plan and procedure. He was known as the Brahman priest. His main duty was to make sure that the potency (Brahman) of the ritual remained intact, and it established a connection between the host of the sacrifice and the gods through prayers and brought them to the ritual place to receive the offerings and fulfill their part in concluding the sacrifice. It was his duty to ensure that the injunctions of the Vedas were strictly followed, mistakes were avoided, and the objectives of the sacrifice were reached without complications and negative consequences.

Outwardly, it may seem that the sacrificial rituals are meant to secure favors from the divinities in return for the sacrificial food offered, but inwardly, what happens is that they generate and channel that power of Brahman hidden in the sacred sounds of the Vedic hymns. By participating in them, the priests, as well as the host of the sacrifice, participate in an act of creation. By performing their obligatory duties and nourishing the gods, they participate in the welfare of the world and their families and ensure order and regularity. The Vedas do not explicitly mention the hidden presence of Brahman in the hymns but allude to it symbolically as the power that illuminates the sun and the moon and keeps them revolving in their respective spheres. They describe that it is the same power that shines objects in the eye, reaches the ear as sounds, moves the mind and senses towards the objects they desire, makes fire burn, water flow, wind blow, and the five vital breaths (pranas) move in the body in their respective upward, downward, or lateral channels. We presume that it is all-pervading and all-enveloping. It is hidden in all aspects of creation: in humans, divinities, and mantras alike, which makes them so potent and excellent. It separates the worlds, becoming the space between them, creates order amidst chaos, and provides the beings and the divinities with food, intelligence, illumination, and consciousness (chaitanyam). It is an auspicious and vigorous power that can expand and grow indefinitely beyond our thoughts and imagination or contract and become imperceptible to the senses. As a binding force, it connects the worlds and holds them together on a single thread.

Vedic priests believed in their divine right and authority to study the Vedas and invoke this auspicious power hidden in the Vedas, which the Vedas themselves proclaim that they were born from the mouth of Purusha, the Cosmic Being. No one created them. No one knows who created them. Whoever knew them heard them from someone, a teacher, a father, a seer, etc. Hence, they are known as the heard scriptures (shruti). Their source is speech, more specifically, the speech of God (*Brahmavac*), because he is the earliest, the first, and before all. Therefore, the assumption is that if they have a source, that must be God Himself. They are meant for humans to perform their obligatory duties, one of which is to nourish the gods, the personifications of Brahman, and help them protect the world. Vedic people who engaged in these duties regarded themselves as Brahmanas. The name was justified since they had the knowledge of the Brahman hidden in the Vedas, and they knew how to invoke His power through sacrifices and extend their reach to the heavens through their speech. They believed that with that knowledge, they could secure divine help and control some aspects of their lives and the world around them. They did not make offerings to Brahman because He was independent and, unlike gods, did not depend upon humans or anyone for anything. Besides, He was the source of everything, including the sacrifices, and was also their ultimate recipient. As the Bhagavadgita affirms, He represents and is hidden in every part of a sacrifice. He is also the power hidden in the chants and the sacrifices that propel the gods to descend to the ritual place and accept the offerings. Vedic priests knew how to manifest that power through chants and rituals and obtain desired results. They also knew that, in His highest manifestation as Isvara, He represented every aspect of the sacrifice: the sacrificer, the sacrificed, the divinities and the Brahmanas, the sacrificial pit, the sacrificial fire, and the object of the sacrifice.

Physically, sacrificial rituals ordained by the Vedas are believed to radiate certain aspects of Brahman (as the sacrifice) into the surrounding atmosphere, such as the flames from the sacrificial pit, the sounds that come from the chants, the light and the heat radiated by the sacrificial fire, various smells and aromas arising from the burnt oblations, and the smoke that rises from the sacrificial pit and joins the mid-air. The flames denote the sun and the immortal path of gods, and the smoke represents the moon and the gray path by which ancestors go to the ancestral world. Together, they create an aura of purity, religiosity, solemnity, and sanctity around the ritual place, filling the minds and hearts of the worshippers and onlookers with a sense of wonder, faith, and devotion. Equally important are the vibrations from the chanting, which spread in all directions and fill the space around the ritual place. Their potency is augmented further by the chanting of the Riks or the singing of the Samans at the beginning, middle, and end of the rituals and by the prefixing of auspicious and mystic syllables such as Aum, which also personify Brahman. Vedic people regarded Aum as the mantra of all mantras and believed in its purifying and uplifting power and its equation with Brahman (*Aksharabrahma*). Subsequently, it became the most sacred word of not just Hinduism but many other traditions, including Buddhism, which opposed the Vedic rituals and did not believe in Brahman.

As Vedism grew in complexity with the development of the Upanishadic philosophy and the growth of several ascetic traditions, Vedic seers and scholars realized that the same power, which was hidden in the sacrificial rituals and the sacred chants, was also present universally as the resultant force of an ancient ritual, which Brahman performed using the waters of life as the sacrificial altar and a portion of Himself as the sacrificial material. In the depths of their minds, they recognized that Universal Priest and the power hidden in the universal sacrifice He performed as Brahman, the Cosmic Person of universal dimensions, who was without a beginning and an end and who was the highest of all. While some historians tend to view these developments sequentially as phases in the development of Vedic thought, it is quite possible that they developed concurrently, unknown to each other, since many traditions existed in ancient India and within Brahmanism, each led by a seer, sage or genealogy, which kept their secrets mostly to themselves, as is evident from the descriptions and conversations we find in the Brihadaranyaka and Chandogya Upanishads.

Vedic seers, who acted as the trustees of the knowledge contained in Upanishads, extolled Brahman as the source and origin of everything and as the real architect who carved the worlds and weaved the web of reality as He spread forth like a spider in all directions from His own being. They thought that as the inviolable power of infinite dimensions, He, that ultimate and Absolute Self, sprang into action out of a desire to manifest alternate realities and dualities and experience them objectively as the other or the second. Arising from the cosmic ritual, as the sacrifice and the sacrificer, He unleashed His manifesting power to create divinities, demons, worlds, beings, laws, knowledge, celestial phenomena, social order, elements, modes, primal parts (tattvas), universal laws, births, deaths, joys, and sorrows. They envisioned Him as the absolute and infinite universal sacred power that spread across all the spheres, inhabiting the entire universe as its enjoyer and controller. Just as He was hidden in the sacred syllables of the Vedic hymns as their inexhaustible (*akshara*) potency, He remained concealed in the entire creation as its immortal Self.

They believed that when people meditated upon Him or His

forms intently, withdrawing their senses and their minds, regulating their breath, performing austerities, and practicing celibacy, He manifests in them as spiritual heat or pure energy (*tapas*). Just as the potency of the prayer spreads in all directions through the sound and reaches the divinities, the accumulated power of austerity (*tapah*), arising from the internal sacrifices such as yoga, self-control, renunciation, and contemplation, gives the meditating seers a supernatural ability to communicate with gods and obtain boons from them. It also enables them to manifest things and invoke the power of Brahman. If they persist in their efforts, overcoming their desires and shortcomings, it leads them on the path of immortality, the illuminated path of Gods, to the world of Brahman.

Vedic priests believed that the inviolable power of Brahman made everything possible. In their belief system, it was the sheer power of His inviolable will that brought forth the worlds, their objective reality, and life forms. Whether the senses moved among the objects or the vital breath moved in the body, it was because of "That." They referred to it often in neutral terms as It, That (tat), and often in personal terms as the mysterious Being, who controlled all the bodily functions and supported the life breaths. They defined it in roundabout ways as not speech, but That by which speech was expressed; as not thought by the mind but That by which the mind was thought; and as not seen by the eye, but That by which the eyes were seen. In other words, in their worldview, Brahman was the center and the substance who moved everything in the microcosm of the human being as well as in the macrocosm of His Cosmic Personality (Purusha). He controlled all the worlds, and all created things and beings at all levels, with great indifference as their sole Seer, Support, and Enjoyer.

Whether the Vedic scholars arrived at such an expansive vision of Brahman by themselves because of their growing awareness or found a new meaning and purpose in the hidden symbolism of the Vedic scriptures, we do not know. It appears that there was a coming together of diverse traditions within the Vedic religion and an integration of complex philosophical views derived from various other sources, which resulted in the complex worldview that we find today in Hinduism. We also know that during the post-Vedic era, Vedic priests lost sight of the hidden symbolism of the Vedas and sacrifices and focused on their mechanical and outward observation. They also faced growing criticism from other traditions, ascetic movements, and new schools of Vedic and non-Vedic philosophies and theistic systems, who not only challenged the emptiness of superficial ritualism but also emphasized the need for contemplative approaches, selflessness, and self-purification to discern the truths of life hidden beyond the apparent reality and the physicality of human nature and resolve the problem of human suffering. Because of the influx of new ideas, the Vedic religion underwent structural changes and incorporated many new concepts and philosophies with far-reaching consequences.

However, the vision of Brahman found in the Upanishads remained its most compelling and potent force and enabled it to survive many challenges in its long history. They are considered, to this day, the most profound discoveries in the spiritual realm, which can help us connect to the universe, experience oneness with it, and see it from the heights of that singularity as one's own projection or extension, using our consciousness as the bridge. Of course, the consciousness must be stable and free from impurities to achieve it. In the Samhitas, Brahman is the sound hidden in the hymns. In the Brahmanas, He is the sacred ritual itself. He represents its structure as well as its content. In the Aranyakas, He represents the power of austerity and self-control. In Upanishads, He becomes the Self of all. As the sound, He is hidden in all the sounds that reach our ears, especially in the sacred sounds hidden in the Vedas. As the power of the ritual, He is hidden in every aspect of it, like the energy (shakti), liveliness (chaitanyam), and consciousness (*chitta*) hidden in the human body. In the meditating hermits and forest dwellers, He becomes the contemplative and spiritual power (*tapas*) arising from their internalization of the Vedic rituals and purification of their minds and bodies. Finally, in the minds of those who study the Upanishads and strive for liberation, He appears as the universal

Supreme Self and the inner Self, representing the highest and absolute reality.

Footnotes

1. Griswold, Harvey D., A Study in the History of Indian Philosophy. A Dissertation presented to the faculty of Cornell University for the degree of doctor in philosophy.

2. Please refer to the glossary of Brahma (n) and Related words at the end of this book.

3. Baresman means a bunch of twigs. Griswold states that the equation was suggested by German scholars Dr. Haug and Wackernagel in 1868.

The Symbolism of Food as Brahman

By the power of contemplation, Brahman expands. From that, food is produced. From food (come) life, mind, the five elements, the worlds, the rituals, and immortality. Mundaka Upanishad (1.1.8).

From food only, all beings, whoever dwells upon the earth, are produced. Further, by food only, they live, and, into food only at the end, they pass. Food is indeed the eldest of all beings. Therefore, it is spoken of as the healing herb of all. Taittiriya Upanishad (2.2.1).

Do not despise food. That shall be the rule. Taittiriya Upanishad (3.8.1.).

Vedic people viewed Brahman as both knowledge and power and regarded Him with high esteem as the source of health, wealth, and immortality. They thought that He was the mysterious power hidden in space and sounds and, through them, connected the worlds and the beings and facilitated their interdependence and nourishment. By contemplating upon Him as the Universal Self or the Self with concentration and self-control, they believed that one could gain spiritual powers (*tapas*), knowledge, and immortality (Kena 2.4). They did not view Purusha and Prakriti as two separate eternal entities, as some native traditions subsequently came to hold, but as aspects of One Supreme Reality, Brahman. In their worldview, Brahman was the First Cause and the material and efficient source of all creation, and gods, unknown to themselves, derived their strength and power from Him by virtue of their close proximity with Him. Their supernatural abilities were His gifts. The Kena Upanishad illustrates the relationship between gods and Brahman and their inability to recognize Him when He appeared before them during a chance encounter with Indra, Vayu, and Agni.

According to this story, once Brahman secured a victory for the gods against the demons. The gods were unaware of it and assumed that they won the victory because of their own prowess. Therefore, when Brahman, as the story goes, appeared before Indra, Vayu, and Agni as a Yaksha (an ethereal being), and when they saw Him from a distance, they did not know who He was. They requested Agni to go near Him and enquire. When Agni went and stood before Him, He asked Agni to identify himself and his power. Agni replied that he was Agni and that he could burn anything on earth. Brahman placed a blade of grass before him and asked him to burn it. Agni used all his power to burn that blade of grass, but before Brahman, his firepower did not work. Next, Indra sent Vayu. Again, Brahman asked him to identify himself and his power. Vayu replied that he was Vayu and that he could blow off anything in the world. This time also, Brahman placed a blade of grass before him and asked him to blow it. Vayu tried with all his might but could not move the blade of grass a little. Finally, Indra himself came to inquire who He was. As Indra approached Him, He disappeared. Maybe He did not want to humiliate him, or maybe because he spent thousands of years learning from Brahma about the nature of the Self. According to the Upanishad, after Brahman disappeared, Uma Haimavathi, the Mother Goddess, appeared in the sky and told the three gods who the Being they saw and because of whom they secured their victory.

The moral of this story is that Brahman is the source of all, and whatever we have or achieve arises in our lives from Him only. Even if you have all the wealth and strength in the world, you cannot accomplish anything unless you have His support and unless He works through you as your very energy and the mover of your will and consciousness. He is the power and potency from which everything in the creation derives its sustenance and direction. He is the one who moves your life, desires, and actions and makes possible your existence, continuation, and liberation. Even to perform mundane actions such as seeing, hearing, eating, sleeping, etc., we depend upon Him since He is the source of all the energy in our bodies. He is the power hidden in all five elements, all our organs and our consciousness.

Hence, the Upanishads identify Brahman with food, the source of all vital energy (*prana*) for the jivas. For the jivas, food (annam) is the main source of energy. The Vedas declare it as an aspect of Brahman [1]. The Upanishads make frequent references to food as the source of vigor and life [2]. In this context, food does not mean just the food we eat, the food we serve to gods in sacrifices, or the food all the other jivas, such as plants and animals, eat [3]. Symbolically, it represents the energy of Brahman or all the energy that flows in the whole creation, including the energy that is present in food and our minds and bodies. It is the very vitality (*chaitanyam*) that characterizes life itself. The same energy plays an important role in the sacrificial rituals as their igniter, mover, and nourisher. Vedic people believed that on the cosmic scale, this universal food (energy) of Brahman sustained and regulated the order and regularity (*Rta*) of the whole creation, from the smallest atom to the vast and expansive universe one sees in the night sky. In their worldview, food was not just food in the physical sense but the source of all the gross and subtle energies of our bodies and the whole creation. They knew that it was imperishable [4]. Their concept of food also included the vital energy (prana) that flowed in the body or in the breath, the sense objects (*vish*) one desired to enjoy or possess, and the knowledge, thoughts, prayers, gifts, and actions one offered to the divinities as the sacrifice. For them, whatever one could give, receive, reciprocate, or exchange mentally or physically in ritual worship or spiritual practice counted as food only. In other words, all mental objects, such as thoughts, emotions, passions, feelings, desires, and attachments, constituted food only, and giving them up was an act of sacrifice and penance in the quest for liberation.

Food is central to all Vedic rituals. They are incomplete if food is not offered to the deities or those who participate in them. This is true about both external and internal sacrifices. In the internal sacrifices, worshippers offer food mentally to the presiding deities of the organs before eating. By that, it is believed that food will become purified and does not lead to the predominance of tamas. When a person dies, the officiating priests perform sacrifices in which they use balls of cooked rice to build the subtle body of the deceased ritually, believing that it will help the departed soul to travel to the ancestral world with a subtle, causal body and survive there until they return. With further offerings made periodically by the descendants, the causal body is replenished regularly so that the soul remains in the ancestral world for a longer period and exhausts more of its karma before it returns for another birth. Therefore, the Vedic tradition encouraged people to make periodic offerings of food to their ancestors to invigorate them and help them stay nourished and return safely for a better life in the next birth. For the Vedic seers, Brahman was the ultimate source of all energy and, therefore, all food. Through the sacrifice of life and creation, He uses parts (tattvas and gunas) of Himself as the sacrificial food to create all animate and inanimate things as the remains of the sacrifices. As Death Himself (*Kala*), He consumes all that exists here as His food so that he can ensure the progression of the worlds and the continuation of the time cycle (*Kala Chakra*).

The entire material universe owes its existence to this universal sacrifice, which He performed at the beginning of creation, with parts of Himself serving as the sacrificial food (material and energy). He performed it to set in motion the wheel of creation and manifest the worlds and the beings. To this day, Hindus follow His example and perform sacrifices (*yajnas*) as the ideal means to fulfill their desires or manifest the reality they want to enjoy. Vedic priests also follow the same example He set in motion. They use sacrificial materials secured from the body of Brahman (the world) as the solid and liquid offerings of food and offer them to the deities to secure their cooperation to achieve peace and prosperity or fulfillment for themselves and their patrons. The more enlightened ones use their actions, possessions, minds, and bodies as sacrificial material. They pour their thoughts, actions, knowledge, egoism, desires, and attachments into the fire of renunciation to become empty and attain oneness with Him. In the penance of life, they give up everything and dedicate themselves to the knowledge and attainment of Brahman.

As the mover of all things, Brahman also facilitates the interconnectedness and mutual dependence of all existence. During the sacrifices, when the hymns of the Vedas are chanted, the energies that are hidden in them as the presiding deities of those chants wake up and ascend through space to the heavens. When gods hear those pleasing sounds, they feel inspired and visit the sacrificial place and accept the food offered to them. Nourished by the sacrificial food, they gain strength and help the worshippers by fulfilling their desires or protecting them from adversity or the evil forces who are always intent on disturbing others and creating chaos.

Whether it was in the world of the mortals, gods, or on a cosmic scale, food was, therefore, central to the Vedic conception of life and its preservation in various forms. Vedic people saw it as the power of Brahman that regulated the worlds and the world order and sustained the beings of the four worlds, namely the earth (*bhur*), the ancestral world (*bhuh*), the heaven (*svah*), and the world of immortals (*maha*). Human beings alone, especially Brahmanas, or the knowers of Brahman, had the knowledge of how to perform the rituals and nourish themselves and others through them. Therefore, they thought that they had the obligatory duty of studying the Vedas, performing sacrifices, nourishing the gods and the ancestors, and upholding Dharma for the sake of creation and Brahman. These early ideas subsequently led to the concept of Prakriti as the governing principle of all life, such as the one expounded by the Classical Samkhya School.

The Upanishads describe how food is transformed into energy in the body and how it sustains life. They contain passages according to which, upon digestion, food, having transformed into energy (prana), enters the various parts of the body through nerve channels (nadis) and becomes the moving and sustaining force (*ojas*). A part of that energy transforms into semen (*retas*) and helps in the procreation, transmigration, and continuation of embodied souls, birth after birth, according to their karma. When people practice yoga, austerity, and self-control for self-purification, it transforms into spiritual energy (tapas) and intellectual brilliance (*tejas*) and makes the body pure and fit for attaining liberation or developing spiritual powers (*siddhis*), such as the power to manifest or change the order of things.

Contrary to popular opinion, in the early Vedic society, both the priests who performed the sacrifices and the seers who contemplated upon Brahman aimed at the same goal: the realization of the supreme power of Brahman through sacrifices. The former did it for worldly ends, using various sacrificial materials and actions as food in the fire of karma yoga, and the latter did it for spiritual purposes, using themselves as sacrifices in the fire of knowledge and renunciation. With the help of internal and external sacrifices (*yajnas*), they thought that they would be able to establish peace and prosperity on earth and protect themselves from evil desires and influences. Although they used different means, their aim was the same: to invoke the power of Brahman for the welfare of oneself and others and serve the aims of creation and liberation. Since Brahman was the source of all energy, actions became important on both fronts, and from it gradually emerged the ideas of karma and karma-sannyasa, or the renunciation of desires and the fruit of actions. If people made the right use of food (the energy present in material things and living forms), performed obligatory duties, and followed the injunctions of the Vedas strictly and dutifully, they reaped rich rewards and went to the immortal world of Brahman, never to return. Otherwise, they went to the world of ancestors and returned from there after becoming food to gods[5]. Having exhausted their causal bodies, they fell to the earth along with rain and reentered the world of mortals first by becoming food to plants and animals and later by entering the human bodies through food and becoming semen. All this is His play. As the Creator and Controller who rules the mortal world, He creates all this as food for the sacrifice of creation. As the Lord of Death with insatiable hunger, He consumes all this as the offering he makes for Himself in the sacrifice of destruction and dissolution.

The Vedic texts affirm Brahman as the personification of consciousness and energy (*chitshakti*). They identify Him as the real power (*shakti*) and the source of dynamism (*chaitanyam*) in all moving things and describe Him as the highest and supreme power, in whose fear everything works and moves in a regulated manner. He is not dependent upon the mind or intelligence, but they work for Him and because of Him. He is independent of the senses, but the senses depend upon Him. He is independent of Time (*Trikalathita*), but Time is under His control and moves by His command. He ensures the orderliness of creation (rta) and the orderly progression of events (niyati). He is the hidden force behind the movements and actions of the mind and the body. He moves, without moving, the celestial bodies, the wheel of creation, the wheel of Dharma, breath (prana), speech, senses (*indriyas*), chakras, days and nights, the progression of events, and the manifestation of things. He is responsible for all actions, movements, and movements within movements. Hence, the Vedic seers instructed that in order to achieve liberation and resolve their karma, human beings must live on earth selflessly without desires and attachments, renouncing the ownership and doership of their actions (Isa. 2). Otherwise, they would enter the dark hells [5] ignorance and delusion and prolong their suffering. By saying this, they were indirectly hinting that one should not look upon Brahman as pure consciousness only but also as the power that moves everything and is the source of all manifestation.

Some schools of Vedanta that draw inspiration and essential teachings from the Vedas identify Brahman as the First Cause and the source of all creation. They refute the contrarian notion that Prakriti (Nature) exists as an eternal, independent entity. According to them, Prakriti becomes the sacrificial food in Brahman's creation, from which comes the material, energy, and activity necessary for the manifestation of beings, objects, elements, modes (*gunas*), primordial parts of the body (*tattvas*), the impurities, and the order and regularity of the whole creation. The material universe is Brahman's Field of Energy manifested by Himself and from Himself during a universal sacrifice. Since it is a sacred aspect of Him and is filled with His dynamic power, the scriptures exhort us to use it responsibly and selflessly to perform our obligatory duties and fulfill our obligations to Isvara, ourselves, gods, ancestors, our families, other humans, all other beings, and the world. They also advise us to cultivate purity by practicing rulers and restraints and living righteously so that we can let the Self shine through us like a lamp that shines brightly through the lamp's clean glass. Besides, with the purity arising from the predominance of sattva, we can improve our chances of attaining liberation and immortality.

Footnotes

1. Annam parabrahma svarupam.

2. The subject of food is mentioned in several Upanishads. Food also represents the earth element and the subtle sense of touch. For example, the Taittiriya Upanishad warns, "Do not speak ill of food. It is the rule. Life verily is the food." The Upanishad concludes with a mystic chant, which says, "I am food... I am the eater of food... I, who am the food, eat the eater of food."

3. A Comparative History of the World Philosophy From the Upanishads to Kant by Ben-Amii Scharfstein, 1998, Chapter 1: The Beginning of Metaphysical Philosophy (page 59).

4. Brihadaranyaka Upanishad, 1.5.1.

5. The Upanishads speak mostly of the world of mortals, the world of gods, and the world of ancestors. The concept of hell ruled by Yama, the Lord of death, is not mentioned in many Upanishads. However, Yama, the Lord of Death, appears prominently in the Katha Upanishad as the teacher of sacred knowledge.

The Ritual Brahman We Have Forgotten

He said to them, "Two kinds of knowledge should be known, declare the knowers of Brahman, the transcendental and the worldly. Of these, the worldly is the Rigveda, the Yajurveda, the Samaveda, and the Atharvaveda, and the knowledge of Phonetics (Shiksha), Ritual (kalpa), Grammar (Vyakarana), Etymology (Nirukta), Metrics (Chandah) and Astrology (Jyotishya). And the transcendental is that by which the indestructible is overtaken." Mundaka Upanishad (1.1.4, 4-5).

Having attained Him, having attained the Self and become satisfied with their knowledge, free from passion, peaceful, having attained the omnipresent from all sides, the seers, the stable ones, with concentrated minds enter the All. Mundaka Upanishad (3.2.5).

In Vedic parlance, every action we perform and every process of the mind, body, and life amounts to a sacrifice because all actions have the same characteristics as a sacrifice: a subject who makes an offering (of energy, etc.), the intention or purpose for which the offering is made, a recipient or object who receives that offering and fulfills that purpose, and the result or consequences that manifest from it as the remains or the result of that sacrifice. Thus, living is a sacrifice. Dying is a sacrifice. Breathing is a sacrifice. Eating is a sacrifice. Digestion is a sacrifice. Sleeping is a sacrifice. Bathing is a sacrifice. Perception is a sacrifice. Thinking is a sacrifice. Worshipping is a sacrifice. Marriage is a sacrifice. Indulging in a sexual act is a sacrifice. Giving birth to a child is a sacrifice. Cooking food is a sacrifice. Learning is a sacrifice. Listening is a sacrifice. Teaching is a sacrifice. Helping others is a sacrifice. Seeking the help of others is a sacrifice. Meditation is a sacrifice. Fighting a war is a sacrifice. Every action that we perform or in which we are involved for our benefit or the welfare of others is a sacrifice. In fact, the English word sacrifice does not adequately convey the meaning of the sacrificial rituals (*yajnas*) of the Vedic religion. In common usage, sacrifice means giving up something, giving away something, or killing an animal, ritually or symbolically, for some specific purpose. In Vedic parlance, you make a sacrifice or a ritual offering with the intention of reaching out to the gods or the Supreme Lord, Isvara. You do it either due to a particular desire or with a specific intention to convey your love and devotion, unburden yourself of your past sins, achieve some goal, overcome adversity, etc. Sacrifice is the means to communicate with the supernatural to overcome your natural barriers and limitations and achieve some goal or objective for selfish or selfless reasons.

In each act of sacrifice, you have an intention or purpose, a sacrificer who acts as the subject or the host, the material that must be sacrificed, the act of offering, the receiver or the object of the offering, one or more witnesses, and the result of the sacrifice. In that sacrifice, you convert, purify, elevate, or transform your gross and subtle energies. Each sacrifice is essentially an act of creation in which you spend (sacrifice) your energies to manifest your thoughts or desires or realize your dreams. Hinduism is called a way of life because it rests on the foundation of sacrifice. Every action that you perform in life, good, bad, high, or low, is perceived as a sacrificial offering to yourself or God, who, due to ignorance and delusion, many fail to realize as the real sacrificer, the sacrificed, and the receiver of the sacrifice. Those who ignore this fundamental truth and live for themselves, assuming ownership of things and performing their daily sacrifices with egoism and selfish intentions, must pay dearly for the consequences of their actions. This is the law of Dharma well-explained in Bhagavadgita and several other scriptures. Each sacrifice is also an act of karma. Hence, the ritual knowledge of the Vedas, found in the Samhita and Brahmana sections, which deals with the sacrifices, is known as Karma Kanda, the ritual part. The concept of karma is rooted in the idea of sacrifice and is very closely related to the idea of a jiva's life as one big sacrifice that goes on continuously, starting from birth until death. It is essentially a Vedic concept that is rooted in the ritual model and the hidden symbolism of Vedic sacrifices. Those who argue that the concept of karma came to Vedic people from other traditions do not know or understand how closely and conceptually karma and yajna (sacrificial ritual) are interrelated and how they influenced the various schools of Hindu philosophy and devotional theism.

From the beginning, two streams of thought coexisted in the Vedic tradition. From the perspective of the Vedas, there is no conflict between the two as they both work for the same ends. One focuses on the ritual aspects of divine worship, and the other on the possibilities of self-realization and immortality. On the surface, both approaches seem to be divergent. However, in the Vedic conception of human life, they fit perfectly as two complimentary paths that enable people to live in peace and harmony with gods and fulfill the four major aims of their lives, namely performing obligatory duties (*Dharma*), earning wealth (*Artha*), fulfilling desires (*Kama*) and achieving liberation (*Moksha*).

With the help of elaborate sacrificial rituals, Vedic people performed their obligatory duties and sought material wealth and enjoyment. The rituals gave them a sense of control over the seemingly uncontrollable aspects of life, under the belief that everything originated from the magical and supernatural power of the rituals, including gods and the highest heaven itself. However, they were not satisfied with the temporary gains of this world. They also wanted to secure a better place for themselves in the higher worlds. Therefore, they developed a whole range of philosophies around the concept of internalizing the rituals and making use of the ritual powers and the cosmic structure hidden in the human personality. By withdrawing into themselves and probing into the deeper aspects of human life and contemplating upon them, they tried to internalize the rituals with which they were very familiar so that they would be able to transcend the limitations of human life and secure for themselves a place in the world of immortals. The Purva Mimansa followers believed in the efficacy of external rituals to fulfill one's desires and achieve the four aims of human life. The followers of the Uttara Mimansa (*Vedanta*) school believed in the efficacy of internal rituals to attain Brahman.

We can see the importance of both the approaches in the basic structure of the Vedas and the conception of the ideal human life envisaged by the Vedic tradition. Each Veda is divided into four parts, namely the Samhita, the Brahmana, the Aranyaka, and the Upanishads. The first two constitute the ritual segment (*karmakanda*) and the last two the knowledge segment (*jnanakanda*). The Samhitas contain invocations, which the priests chant loudly to release the power of Brahman hidden in them to propitiate the various gods. The Brahmanas deal with the procedural and technical aspects of the rituals, by which the purity and efficacy of the rituals can be maintained and its purpose realized. They were called Brahmanas because they suggested the means to secure the power of Brahman through the rituals to the maximum effect. The Aranyakas and the Upanishads contain the esoteric knowledge of Brahman, the hidden meaning of sacrifices, and the means to attain immortality and self-realization. They encourage contemplative methods to explore the transcendental truths of Brahman and realize Him as one's pure Self.

Vedic people believed in the importance of both branches of knowledge to achieve balance and fulfillment in life. They were often torn between the two paths, but overall, there was an honest attempt to reconcile both. The karma-sannyasa yoga of the Bhagavadgita finely combines both approaches into an integrated approach in which householders can continue to perform their obligatory duties without renouncing worldly life or abandoning their families. From the Isa Upanishad also, we learn how important it is to follow both paths for achieving happiness in this life and liberation hereafter. The Vedic seers did not want people to give up their obligatory duties and family responsibilities in the pursuit of liberation. At the same time, they did not want them to become overly distracted by them and ignore their spiritual welfare. They wanted them to look at their lives as sacrificial offerings in the sacrifice of creation and participate in it as Isvara's replicas, using their minds and bodies to fulfill the purpose for which they were born. Of the six schools of Hindu philosophy, the Purva Mimansa deals with the ritual aspects of the Vedic religion, while the Uttara Mimansa, also known as the Vedanta, deals with the spiritual aspects of the nature of Brahman and the means to self-realization. While differences exist between the two divergent approaches, they complement life in their specific ways.

This is well evident in the manner in which the Vedas portray the ideal of Varnashrama Dharma, which envisages human life in four successive phases, starting from birth to death. They are Brahmacharya (celibacy), Grihastha (householder), Vanaprastha (forest dweller), and Sannyasa (ascetic). During Brahmacharya, one goes to a school to acquire the knowledge necessary to perform one's obligatory duties and achieve liberation. In the Grihasta stage, one marries, raises a family, and performs obligatory duties for peace, prosperity, and happiness of oneself and others and for the sake of God. In the third phase, one retires from active duties and goes to a forest or a secluded place to live like a hermit and cultivate the right mindset, practicing austerities, self-control, and various yogas. As we can see, in the first two phases, the emphasis is mainly on rituals and obligatory duties (karmas), while in the last two phases, as people retire from active life and work for their liberation, the attention shifts to knowledge, self-control, self-purification, devotion, and renunciation.

Evidently, Vedic people used the power of Brahman hidden in the chants and rituals of the Samhitas and Brahmanas (karmakanda) for worldly gains and the knowledge of Brahman found in the Aranyakas and Upanishads (*jnanakanda*) for spiritual development and self-realization. In the worldly life, they externalized their worldly desires by actively pursuing them with the help of gods and sacrifices and in the mental plane, they sublimated them with the help of yoga and other spiritual methods. The rituals gave them a sense of power and control over the world around them and an opportunity to seek the help and protection of gods. The spiritual methods helped them look at themselves and their lives in a much broader framework, with Isvara or Brahman as the center and circumference of everything, in which they had a rare opportunity to channel the power of Brahman into themselves through internal sacrifices and purify themselves for attaining His auspicious state. In both approaches, righteousness, ethical conduct, purity of intention, faith, and devotion to duty, as well as the Deity, occupied a central place. As Brahman's true representatives, humans have the right to enjoy the pleasures of life without ignoring their temporal and spiritual duties and responsibilities. Karma Yoga, Jnana Yoga, Atma Samyama Yoga, Bhakti Yoga, and Kama Sannyasa Yoga were products of this great synthesis. They are meant for householders only to achieve peace and happiness here and hereafter.

It is not true that the early Vedic religion was merely a religion of sacrificial rituals and magical chants. Its central theme was Brahman hidden in the sacrifice, which the Vedic priests believed was the key to both peace and liberation. According to them, everything emerged out of sacrifice only: the gods, the eternal law of duties and morals (*Dharma*), truth, day and night, sea, sun and moon, heaven and earth, and the regions of air and light (R.V 10.190). The power that manifested them came from Brahman in the cosmic plane and from the sacrificial rituals performed by the Brahman priests in the earthly plane. In the Vedic world, life revolved around Brahman both spiritually and materially. The ritual and spiritual practices complemented their lives and made them complete. They fitted perfectly in their conception of the world order and the duties of humankind, according to which nourishing the gods and seeking liberation were both the prime duties of each human being and neither of them could be ignored without attracting negative consequences (Isa.).

Subsequently, many changes took place in the Vedic religion, as the traditional priestly families, who were privy to the knowledge of the Vedas, migrated to different places in ancient India for various reasons and had to find new patrons for their survival and continuity. In the process, they made peace with other religious groups and their beliefs and practices. Ultimately, it appears they compromised more than what they bargained for since, by the time the Buddha and many ascetic traditions emerged on the religious scene of ancient India, it had lost much of its vitality, purity, and originality. The knowledge of the Upanishad probably remained confined to a few esoteric groups, who preferred to keep it as secret knowledge and teach it to qualified students only. Even those teachers were rare and difficult to find as they mostly lived in the forests away from the civilized world.

As a result, what remained was the outer shell. The Brahmanas in this phase, who were supposed to be the guardians of the faith, lost the original meaning of the Vedas and even that of rituals. Those who learned the Vedas recited the hymns without knowing what they actually or symbolically meant. People performed rituals for worldly reasons to fulfill their selfish desires without knowing their true value and hidden symbolism. Many Vedic deities faded into the background, while new gods emerged on the scene, who were relatively unknown in the Rigvedic period. Although rituals and sacrifices continued to dominate the religious lives of the people, many looked for other alternatives to secure peace and prosperity. The decline of the importance of sacrificial rituals was perhaps the most unfortunate development of the later Vedic period, which led to the decline of Brahmanism and the ascendance of rival traditions, some of which were opposed to purely ritual practices and everything they signified.

The Varna system also played an important role in the decline of the Vedic religion. It sealed the fate of Vedic society, as the Vedas were taught to students based on their varnas and family status rather than their individual merits. Students learned the Vedas by rote, memorizing them mechanically, mostly without knowing what they memorized. As a result, the Vedas and several other texts survived in their original format, but both their original meaning and hidden symbolism were lost. This decline in knowledge coincided with the emergence of new schools of philosophy, devotional movements, and the rise of ascetic sects, which undermined the practice of rituals and the pursuit of worldly goals. Instead, they encouraged spiritual and contemplative methods and exclusive devotion to attain peace and liberation. While the people in earlier ages embraced life and sought the assistance of divinities for peace and prosperity, ascetic movements of the post-Vedic period favored the renunciation of worldly life and attainment of peace and liberation through austerities and self-denial. What remained of the Vedas was memories of its past glory, a semblance of faded aura that emanated not because of their content, which few people understood anyway, but their antiquity and respect for tradition. The aftershocks of these developments were felt for a long time in Hinduism and its social and cultural aspects.

Even today, Hinduism carries the scars of its past. People generally do not show much preference for elaborate rituals compared to devotional and spiritual practices, gurus, and their teachings, which they hold in great esteem. Still, many people express their devotion through domestic rituals, celebrate sacraments (*samskaras*) and festivals with great fanfare, worship gods in temples, and go on pilgrimages. They also celebrate Puskaras and Kumbh Melas, which occur periodically. These practices may have their roots in the Vedas but bear very little resemblance to the ancient Vedic sacrifices and penances. Hardly anyone worships Indra, Varuna, Soma, or Vayu or performs daily (*nitya karmas*) and occasional sacrifices. This does not make them any less religious. While rituals may not satisfy the intellectual curiosity of educated minds as much as the spiritual and contemplative practices, the ritual aspect of Hinduism is still as important and relevant as it was before. Rituals are essential for cultivating discipline and purity, serving God and His creation, nourishing the gods, humans, and other creatures, and ensuring order and regularity. They also pave the way for one's purification and liberation.

Despite the progress we have made in all these centuries, we still need to nourish the gods and obtain their help and support because there are certain things we cannot do, such as containing the spread of evil in human society and keeping our minds and bodies pure. Both are essential for the spiritual evolution of humanity and for establishing peace and order in society. Presently, our gods are vastly underfed and malnourished since not many people perform sacrifices or make offerings. They are victims of our apathy and ignorance. Most of them have already withdrawn from the earth's consciousness, which is why our Dharma is on the decline, and most of our prayers remain unanswered.

Similarly, Hindus have an obligatory duty towards their ancestors. Hinduism is essentially an ancestral religion. The scriptures affirm that you are not alone in your transmigration but connected to a long line of ancestors through your karma and destiny. Some of them will be born as your family members and some as your friends and relatives. Therefore, as their descendant, you have an obligatory duty to ensure their peaceful transmigration by nourishing them regularly and ritually and helping them in their rebirth. Besides, for the continuation of the ancient Dharma, the transmigration of souls, and the preservation of life on earth, ritual practices should not be abandoned. They represent the visible aspects of Hinduism and should be practiced without falling into superstition and obscurantism to revive and reestablish the holistic and divine-centered life, which was characteristic of the Vedic period. We need to make proper use of the power of Brahman with a sacrificial attitude and without assuming its ownership or putting it to misuse. If gods are happy, the Dharma will prevail and the violence and evil that we are seeing today will gradually decline.

I Know Him, and I Know Him Not

Knowing belongs to the field of duality. In the absolute state of Brahman, knowledge exists but not our objective methods of knowing. Knowing requires a subject, an object, and a process or action that connects them both. Brahman, the absolute Self, does not depend upon any of these agencies. Knowing, if at all, must happen internally, inherently, or spontaneously in the absolute state of Brahman because Brahman is without a second, and there is nothing other than Him. Knowing implies time and space, memory and recollection. In Brahman's absolute dimension, knowledge exists by itself and does not have to depend upon the support of any physical or mental organ or faculty. The process of knowing is made possible in our case by mediating agencies: our senses, intelligence, and our accumulative, analytical, and conditioned minds. The Self (*Atman*) does not depend upon them. It is independent, self-existing, self-knowing, free of accessories and dependencies, and beyond the mind and the senses. Therefore, even if you realize Brahman, after years of contemplative and austere practices, it would be difficult for you or anyone else to explain intellectually the nature of Brahman based on such experiences because they would not take place within the confines of your mind but outside of it. If you can remain awake in a deep sleep, then perhaps you are qualified to know Brahman consciously. However, the important question is how many can really manage to do it. A seer is awake when others are asleep and asleep when others are awake. The seers are, therefore, known but not really well understood. As far as I know, only in some tantras do some esoteric techniques exist that suggest how one can experience the absolute and blissful state of Brahman consciously in Turya, the transcendental state.

The paradox of self-realization is that when you are one with Brahman, you have no idea what happens inside you because your mind and senses do not participate in it. After experiencing the transcendental oneness in the self-absorbed state of nonduality, when you revert to your ordinary consciousness, you do not remember what happened because your transcendental state of unity does not depend upon memory to sustain itself. Neither is it a mental, imaginative, or cognitive process. Therefore, unless you develop some intuitive mechanism that can express itself through a silent and passive mind, bringing the knower of things into the field of your awareness, you will not be able to recall your transcendental experiences or recreate them mentally to feel that experience, and, if necessary, to prolong it. In most cases, transcendental experiences are beyond the reach of ordinary consciousness. Through a vague intuitive process, you may know what might have happened, but in your wakeful consciousness, you may still experience the duality and the distinctions of the objective world.

However, when you purify your mind and body and balance the modes (*gunas*) of Nature in your physical self, your transcendental experiences, by repeatedly recollecting and reliving them, may become a part of your existential reality and your essential nature, and others may see in you signs of superior consciousness expressing itself profoundly and perceptibly. When you interact with people in that state, they may see in you a reflection of God, Isvara, in your words and your actions due to the harmonious union of Purusha and Prakriti without the barriers of impurities. However, this is rarely achieved. Self-realized yogis are complete, stainless, and perfect in all respects. They represent the state of Brahman, even during wakeful hours, by restraining their senses, stabilizing the mind, and staying free from the influence of the ego. However, even they may not know much about Brahman or articulate Him other than what they might have read in the Vedas or heard from their masters. Some may feel internally that they are awakened and connected to their divine nature and the Turya state because they are always happy, contended, peaceful, and blissful, independent of what they perceive or experience. Even after you are awakened and attained the transcendental state of oneness, Brahman may still not reveal Himself to you to the extent He reveals Himself to His physical nature in an incarnation or emanation. However, He will shine through you and your consciousness to the extent you are pure and to the extent you have transformed and integrated the diverse and contradictory aspects of your personality into a harmonious whole.

Transcendental states can be attained through effort, and with further effort, they can be experienced consciously or memorially. Indeed, if you can fill your consciousness with the presence of Brahman through persistent practice by establishing your mind in Him, having overcome all the obstacles and resolved all the contradictions, and if you can bring His light and power into your wakeful consciousness, it will open a door inside you and help you perceive things from a broader perspective with sameness and without judgment and the interference of your ego and your habitual and preconditioned mind. It gives others who interact with you an opportunity to communicate with that pure state and benefit from that interaction. It is difficult to say what exactly happens to them on such occasions. We learn from the accounts left by others that when they meet enlightened people in whom the light of Brahman shines, they may gain knowledge, experience déjà vu or deep feelings of devotion or exhilaration, feel purified, uplifted, or inspired. We also hear that sometimes something in them opens and prompts them to seek liberation for themselves. In some cases, because of karma or impurities, nothing may happen.

The absolute state of Brahman is complete (*purnam*) and inexhaustible. You may add something to it or take away something from it. Yet it remains full. When the Upanishads say that space (*akasa*) is Brahman, Aum is Brahman, intelligence is Brahman, the Self is Brahman, or the sun is Brahman, it does not mean that Brahman does not exist in other things or that He represents a limited or specific reality. Vedic seers used these statements to convey the infinity and the all-pervading and all-encompassing state of Brahman in human terms and the indisputable truth that Brahman is indeterminate, indefinable, and one and only, without a second.

To understand Brahman intellectually, we have to rely upon words and concepts that our minds can comprehend and visualize with some clarity. We have to know objectively how an absolute principle can manifest itself and function independently in a relatively limited and impermanent world like ours without diminishing itself. Very appropriately, Vedic seers tried to define and describe Brahman, using the concepts, objects, analogies, symbols, qualities, and relationships they knew. In the language they knew, they described His essential nature, infinity, supremacy, and universality. They explained His mystery, infinity, essence, and absolute state symbolically in terms of Vedic sacrifices, rites, and rituals and the parts of the human body so that seekers of liberation could use them to practice austerities and meditate on Him to produce with their minds and bodies the same conditions that personified Him. They also relied upon their transcendental experiences to enhance and enrich their knowledge and understanding of their hidden states of consciousness that brought them closer to His pure state. If they compared Brahman to the vital breath (prana), it was to denote His universality, expansiveness, vigor, and life-sustaining quality. If they compared Him to the lightning, it was to denote the power, brilliance, and His ability to destroy the darkness of our minds. The Upanishads abound in such comparisons, inferences, and cryptic symbolism couched in ancient Vedic ritual terminology, with which we are not fully conversant. However, the seekers of Brahman who followed them knew that they were but scratching the surface of an infinite body of knowledge to know the unknowable, to explain the unexplainable, and to define the indefinable state of transcendental reality that was beyond the reach of their minds and senses. The tradition continues even today. Those who pursue Brahman know that they are on an adventurous journey full of mysteries and surprises and that the path to Him is never set in stone but reveals itself to them at each point as they progress. The path to Brahman is as mysterious and indeterminate as Brahman Himself. The Bhagavadgita suggests that it becomes easier for those who take refuge in Isvara, His manifested aspect as the Supreme Lord and Controller of the Universe.

One of the greatest strengths of Hinduism is that it is less dogmatic about the interpretations of the scriptures or the intellectual and theological discussions about the nature of God or the reality of life. The six Darshanas or philosophical schools of Hinduism affirm the conviction that Hinduism is an open-ended tradition that accepts with great tolerance the diversity of thought and the contradictions that arise in our awareness as we pursue the knowledge that is beyond the grasp of our minds and senses. Such inclusiveness and open-mindedness are rarely seen in other traditions, except perhaps in some schools of Buddhism. Hinduism accommodates a whole diversity of thought and encourages speculation, debates, and discussions to settle matters of dogma and philosophical disputes because truths of metaphysical realms are complex and multidimensional and do not fit into a rational framework. Further, we cannot fit them into our rational mindset and logical thinking without approaching them from different perspectives. Therefore, Hinduism acknowledges that even if we have revelatory texts like the Vedas, which are proclaimed to be inviolable and authoritative, we may still experience incongruity and difficulty in understanding the truths of Brahman and may still make mistakes in our conclusions and interpretations. The seers and scholars of ancient India, therefore, preserved and studied diverse schools of thought found in the six Darshanas, even if they did not concur with them.

The Upanishads affirm that Brahman is other than the known and above the unknown, and if people think that they know Him, they probably do not. What this means is that one should not be certain about their knowledge of Brahman, even if they are self-realized yogis or attained oneness with Brahman. The knowledge of Brahman (*brahmajnanam*) is indeterminate, and so is our knowledge of Him. Hinduism, therefore, calls for humility and tolerance in exploring and understanding transcendental truths. It encourages open debate and discussions about the interpretation of theological truths as both a contemplative and intellectual practice and a learning experience, without losing sight of the highest and the absolute truth we identify with God, which is absolute, holistic, indefinable, and inexpressible. In the objective realm of the human mind and its limited perspective, truth is hidden somewhere between the pairs of opposites and behind a plethora of confusing distractions, illusions, and appearances masquerading as facts. You will not know one side of reality without being aware of the other, and you will not arrive at any truth correctly or completely if you wrap your mind in rigid dogmas, half-truths, and preconceived notions that stifle your freedom and impair your reason.

For centuries, Indian scholars interpreted the wisdom of the Upanishads variously, according to their beliefs and in support of their philosophies and dogmas. They did not change the scriptures to support their arguments. They did not shut down opposing views or persecute those who disagreed with them. Rather, they used their knowledge to justify their beliefs and opinions and refute those of others. In the same Upanishads, Vedantins, Mimansikas, Vaishesikas, proponents of Dvaita and Advaita, yogis, Tantrikas, and many others, including some Buddhists, found evidence or opinions to validate their beliefs and philosophies. Despite their fundamental differences, they accepted the testimony of the Vedas as reliable proof (*pramana*) without ignoring the importance of logic, discernment, experience, inference, doubt, and inquiry to evaluate metaphysical truths and determine the nature of reality.

Thou Art That

Conditioned by the belief that God is above all, it is human nature to condemn as blasphemous if anyone claims that he is God or a divine entity. In some religions, it is a mark of disrespect to God and a violation of the divine law and the code of conduct they uphold. However, in Hinduism, it is not taken that seriously or considered an abomination. Indeed, from a spiritual perspective, it is an ideal the aspirants are expected to attain, not falsely, but through oneness with Brahman. The Upanishads encourage seekers of Brahman to identify themselves with Him and develop oneness and a universal vision through the destruction of the ego and related impurities. They ask you to consider yourself as an embodiment of the highest Brahman and acknowledge your pure Self (Atman) as your true Self. You must contemplate upon that Truth and the possibility of realizing your divine nature, cultivating divine qualities, transcending your duality and natural barriers, and saturating your mind and body with the thoughts of the Self or Brahman. You must also withdraw into yourself and find Brahman or Isvara within in the depths of your own being. However, the Upanishads also caution you to be careful about your ego and your true intentions and restrain them so that you will not fall into temptations and misuse the knowledge and power of Brahman for evil purposes. To realize Brahman and immerse yourself in your divine nature, it is necessary to cultivate purity (*sattva*) [1] and sameness (*samatvam*) and sanctify your life with the wisdom of the Vedas and the knowledge of the Self.

Logically speaking, we live in the womb of the material universe. We are an integral part of it and are never separate from it. The energy that resides in your body belongs to the universe, and when your body is shed, it returns to Mother Nature. Indeed, everything around you and in you belongs to the universe only since it is the source. Our consciousness may vanish upon our death, but the energy that moves it and upholds it returns to the universe dutifully. The consciousness itself may return to the universe since it is a form of energy particularized by your personality and memories. Indeed, it is said that when a whole galaxy is swallowed by a black hole, all the data contained in it remains stored in the black hole. Whatever may be the truth of such events, we are never free from the reality that surrounds and envelops us from all sides. Just as we cannot escape from the space that surrounds us, we cannot escape from the universal Self that is present everywhere. We may exist individually as separate entities within a larger system. However, from the universal perspective, we belong to one absolute reality. The individuality of each being that lives on earth is but a temporary construction that is subject to change and decay. It never goes away from the universe since there is no place for it to go. No matter what happens, the universe is always complete. Hence, the peace mantra from the Isavasya Upanishad, "Aum! That is full, and this is full; from the full arises the full; when the full is taken from the full, the full still remains full. Let there be Peace, Peace, Peace."

If a seer says that you are God, most probably, you will not agree with him because you are brought up with a belief system that conditions you to deny your oneness with God and acknowledge yourself as a limited and imperfect human being. You will perhaps feel more comfortable with the notion of treating yourself as an ordinary mortal stuck in samsara, a devotee, or a follower of God rather than as God's creation or a divine entity in your own right. This attitude is embedded in our consciousness because we are conditioned to submit to authority, fear the unknown, and hold our meekness as a virtue rather than an impediment to our exploration of truth. When you submit to the authority of scripture, tradition, or popular opinion, you try to fit in the system and deny yourself an opportunity to explore the truth on your terms or experience life according to your convictions and perceptions. You become a conformist rather than the protagonist of truth. It is the price most people pay to make peace with the world and avoid unnecessary attention and criticism.

The earliest Upanishads were composed before devotional (bhakti) movements appeared in the post-Buddhist era. Vedic seers encouraged students to assimilate the knowledge of Upanishads and meditate on Brahman as their inmost Self and

Self of all. They instructed them to reflect upon the great statements (*mahavakyas*) found in them, such as "I am That" or "you are That," to transcend their natural limitations and identify themselves with the expansive states of Brahman. It was a simple and practical approach, which helped them break the habits of their minds and bodies and surrender to the highest and absolute Reality, transcend their ego-consciousness, and live with a divine-centric attitude. At the same time, Vedic priests of those times called themselves Brahmanas since they believed that they descended from Him through a sacrifice and had the exclusive right on earth to invoke Him through sacrificial rituals and further His creation.

The Upanishads, at least the earliest ones, as the belief goes, are not speculative works but revelations that flashed in the human consciousness during serene moments of deep reflection as sacred sounds. Vedic seers treated them with great respect as embodiments of inviolable truths and used them for their contemplation and spiritual transformation. They encouraged students of Brahman to contemplate the truths hidden in them and know their essential nature and the nature of their existence without the weight of authority or fear of dogma. They led them on an inward journey of self-discovery to find the Truth hidden in the deepest layers of their own consciousness and experience oneness with it.

From the Upanishadic point of view, the statement that you are Brahman (*tattvamasi*) [2] is neither a conviction nor a dogma but a self-evidentiary reality, which the seekers can experience by withdrawing into themselves and realizing their essential nature. For them, it is a provable fact, not objectively as a scientific truth, since scientific methods can only validate objective truths, but subjectively in one's own field of awareness in which objectivity and otherness have no place. It is a universal truth anyone can experience by following certain disciplines and making necessary sacrifices (*tyaga*) to undergo self-transformation. Self-realized yogis, who have silenced their egos and cultivated divine virtues, give us an opportunity to see the presence of God in them and convince ourselves about such possibilities. When we are in their presence, or when we hear their words of wisdom or listen to their discourses, our objections, doubts, fears, and resistance drop away.

Spiritual gurus and enlightened masters are venerable because they are fully awakened and free from the ignorance and bondage of their limited nature to samsara. They channel the self-existing higher knowledge through their thoughts, words, and actions. Through them, God, Isvara, the Lord, speaks to us as they silence their minds and desires and radiate His light like pure crystals that are untainted. By emptying themselves and renouncing all that keeps them separate from Him and by yielding to Him in oneness, they let those who come into their presence discern His hidden presence. They give them an opportunity to interact with their fully awakened Selves and experience nearness and devotion to God, which is otherwise possible only for a few enlightened masters and awakened ones. Self-realized yogis, the jivanmuktas, who achieve liberation in the embodied state, are truly living incarnations of Brahman, who is otherwise unknown and unattainable to the ordinary mind.

Footnotes

1. Sattva, one of the three primordial qualities, is the essential nature of Isvara, the Lord of the Universe and the manifested Brahman. Because of its luminosity and plasticity, sattva is believed to play an important role in perception.
2. There is an argument that according to the rules of Vedic grammar, the expression 'That you are' is not acceptable because we cannot join a neutral noun 'that' with a masculine pronoun 'you.' Therefore, the expression may actually mean, 'that is how you are.' Source: A Comparative History of World Philosophy From The Upanishads To Kant by Ben-Ami Scharfstein.

The Creator and the Created

Although the seers of the early Vedic civilization described Brahman as one supreme, eternal, and transcendental principle, they also perceived Him as the sole inhabitant of the manifested universe, hidden in all His living creations as their inmost Self. Therefore, they described Him as the indweller (*Antaryami*), the Self of all (*sarvabhutatma*), the One and the many, the finite and the infinite, the center and the circumference, the enjoyer and the enjoyed, the sacrifice and the priest, and so on. Integrating within Himself such contradictions into one harmonious whole, He stands above all as one incongruous and indeterminate reality that is mysterious, remote, and yet communicable through personal experience and inner awakening. The Vedas declare that the one universal Self appears as many out of the desire to experience duality and companionship.

Braham has two aspects, one without form and qualities and the other with form and qualities. The former is His original, undifferentiated state, referred to in the scriptures as the non-being (*asat*), formless (*amurtam*), and unmanifested (*avyaktam*). It is the indeterminate state of latency, the seed state, from which arises, out of an impulse, the Primal Being (*Adi Purusha*), who is also the Lord of the Universe (*Isvara*). Assuming myriad forms, for His pure delight, He becomes the Lord of Creation (*Brahma Prajapathi*) and manifests, out of Himself, numerous worlds and beings. At the same time, He veils Himself behind the forms and appearances of His creation and becomes hidden (*nigudham*). Thus, as the creator and concealer, He becomes visible yet invisible, known yet unknown, immanent and yet transcendent. He creates pairs of opposites, such as heat and cold, day and night, light and darkness, knowledge and ignorance, rivers, and oceans, the sky and the earth, noise and silence, joy and suffering, and freedom and bondage.

His attributes are many, and repetitively, they are suggestive of His universality, control, and overlordship. The duality and the myriad contradictions that are inherent to His essential nature are the riddles that His followers are expected to know, understand, and assimilate until the confusion and contradictions that assail their minds are reduced into one harmonious and holistic truth consciousness, which neither confirms nor contradicts but accepts everything as an aspect of the same effulgent truth. In the Katha Upanishad (2.3.1), we find a description of Manifested Brahman as the Tree of Life (the Asvattha tree) in reverse, whose roots are above, and the branches spread down below [1].

For over three thousand years, scholars and philosophers debated, discussed, and argued whether Brahman and His creation are the same and whether the One and the many that arise from Him represent the same fundamental truth or are different. The Advaita schools argued that the apparent diversity was but an illusion, a mistaken notion of reality created by the senses but actually unreal and has no existence in the transcendental, eternal, and absolute state of Brahman. Just as you realize upon waking up from a dream that the dream was unreal, when you wake up from your current state of ignorance and delusion into a deeper awareness in which the mind and senses are inactive or silent, you will realize that what you considered real was actually an illusion or a projection of your mind and does not really correspond to what exists outside. It is just like you mistaking a rope for a snake or a mirage for water for a brief second. When the truth dawns upon you, you will realize that there was no snake, there was no water, and what you saw was an illusion created by your own expectations, fears, desires, or ignorance. Similarly, when you wake up from ignorance and see the world with the eyes and mind of an enlightened seer, you will realize that there was no duality, no diversity, and that everything was but one supreme indivisible Brahman.

Followers of the Dvaita (dualistic) schools argue that God and His creation are eternally different but real. The apparent reality of the material universe is as real as the hidden reality of the Self or God. The world is not an illusion because you live in it every day and experience it continuously in different states of consciousness. According to them, God is multi-dimensional and exists in different conditions and states of reality. Therefore, the multiple realities and things He creates, which constitute His manifested diversity, are as real as the highest Brahman. However, we cannot equate them because they belong to different states of reality and possess different characteristics. For example, God is omniscient, omnipresent, and omnipotent, but His creations are not. That includes even gods and other celestial beings. They possess some of His powers and divine qualities but are not the same. They also depend upon Him, just like everything else. Even though the individual Selves, which are numerous, are absolute, they do not have the universality and omniscience of God. While He is eternally free and independent, we depend upon Him and exist in Him in different states of bondage and liberation as eternally free souls, liberated souls, temporarily bound souls, and eternally bound souls. All that He creates exists because of Him and His enjoyment. Therefore, followers of this school suggest that humans should acknowledge God as the Supreme Being and worship Him with devotion, seeking our liberation.

Indeed, both schools agree that the Creator and His creation are different. Advaita says that creation is an illusion and unreal, whereas Dvaita says that both are real and permanent. Other schools fall in between these two basic philosophies and take a middle stand. We do not know which of them is correct. Probably, duality and diversity exist in the outer aspects of creation, while unity exists in its deepest core. Individually, the parts are different, but collectively, they represent one system and one reality. In the ultimate analysis, the component aspects of the manifest universe represent but one reality and theoretically, we may even reduce them into a unified and undifferentiated state of pure energy. The primordial golden egg (*Hiranyagarbha*) represents such a state. When we reduce things to their essential elements, the diversity of the universe resolves itself into a unitary structure.

We see this happening every day in our own case. When we are awake, we know who we are, and we see the distinction between others and us clearly. However, such distinctions disappear in the deep sleep state when we do not know whether we exist or not and whether we are different from others or not.

Footnotes

1. So goes the verse, "With the root above and the branches below is this eternal tree. That is pure; that is Brham. It is immortal. All the worlds take their shelter in it, and no one ever goes beyond it. This truly is that." The tree of life is also comparable to the sun. Its base or support is in the world of Brahman above, and its rays spread downwards in a thousand directions like the branches of a tree.

Brahman as the Sacred Sound

Aum is Brahma. Aum is all this. Taittiriya Upanishad.

Brahman in the Veda signifies ordinarily the Vedic Word or Mantra in its profoundest aspect as the expression of the intuition arising out of the depths of the soul or being. It is a voice of the rhythm, which has created the worlds and creates perpetually. Sri Aurobindo

Thus, it has been said elsewhere, "Two types of Brahmans should be meditated upon, sound and soundless. By sound alone, the soundless is manifested. Now that sound is Aum. Moving upward by it, one reaches into the soundless. This is the path to immortality, complete union, and transcendence." Maitri Upanishad.

There are two Brahmans, the sound Brahman and the transcendental. Those who know the sound Brahman reach the transcendental Brahman. Maitri Upanishad

Vedic people believed that the efficacy of sacrificial rituals depended upon the purity of the sounds and the performance of the sacrifices. The sounds arising from the mantras depended upon their chanting, and their performance depended upon how truthfully and sincerely they followed the procedures and injunctions of the Vedas. If everything went well, the gods descended to the ritual place and accepted the offerings, granting in return the wishes of the people who performed them. To ensure that they obtained the right results, upon which their reputation rested, the Vedic priests spent considerable time learning the Vedas and associated texts, including pronunciation, grammar, etymology, and the subtle nuances of the sounds hidden in the chants. They spent years perfecting their knowledge as apprentices under experienced priests to master the intricate details of the rituals.

However, despite these precautions, there was always the chance of mistakes happening during the performance of the sacrifices because someone was negligent, made errors in singing the Samans or chanting the Riks, or failed to follow the code of conduct or personal purity. Since they were performed collectively by a number of priests who specialized in different branches of the Vedic knowledge, it was difficult to expect everyone to comply with the same level of sincerity, discipline, and moral commitment. Therefore, to safeguard the rituals from such lapses and ward off evil and negative consequences, the priests sang a special set of initiatory prayers at the commencement of each sacrifice to purify the place, the object or utensils used in the sacrifices, and the people who participated in them. We do not know exactly what songs or chants they chose for the purpose in ancient times, but we know from the texts that some of them belonged to the category of songs known as Udgita or the high chants, which were sung according to the melodies and meters of Samaveda.

"Ud" means superior, upwards, expanding, opening, power, etc. "Gita" means song. Udgita means the song that moves upwards or heavenwards or the song that makes prayers superior and divine. A special class of Vedic priests, known as Udgatirs, used to sing them to sanctify the rituals and enhance their power and purity. They believed that when the Udgita was uttered in conjunction with the Vedic hymns, it moved the prayers heavenwards with multiplied vigor. For a long time, the priests did not mention the Udgita in public, nor did they sing it publicly, except during the rituals. However, from the Upanishads, we know that the priests attached a great significance to it as it sanctified and uplifted the Vedic rituals and brought them closer to the gods.

The Chandogya Upanishad identifies the Udgita with the Sun, with the breath in the mouth (speech), and with the diffused breath (*vyana*), which suggests that its sounds have the same tendency to move or reach distant places as the sun rays and prana. In another verse, it compares the three syllables hidden in the Udgita, namely 'ut,' 'git,' and 'ta,' with the three worlds, with the sun, air, and fire, and with the three Vedas. It further says that whenever breath is suspended in the chanting or whatever action requires exertion and the holding of breath, there is Udgita. The Upanishad actually begins with the declaration that one should meditate on Aum, which is the Udgita. Its essence is Saman, the song that expresses it. The Upanishad also proclaims that speech is Rk, breath is Saman, and the syllable Aum is the Udgita. Symbolically, it describes Udgita as that which upholds life, which connects things or brings them together, and which makes things pure and bright. These statements suggest that Aum should be hummed like a Saman with long intonations and deep breaths.

Aum is identified as Udgita in many verses of the same Upanishad, which points to its growing importance and the increasing assimilation of many ascetic traditions into the Vedic religion. One verse declares, "Now what is the Udgita is Pranava (*Aum*) and what is Pranava is Udgita. So, really, the Udgita is the distant Sun, and the Sun is continually chanting Aum." We find a similar passage in the Maitri Upanishad, "The Udgita is Pranava, and the Pranava is the Udgita, and the Udgita is that Sun (*Aditya*) and he is Pranava." Pranava is another name for the sacred syllable AUM. It is a combination of 'prana' and 'ava' or 'va.' 'Prana' means the vital energy that flows in the body and keeps it alive. 'Ava' means protect, defend, or promote, and 'va' means wind, air, or auspiciousness. This confirms that the Vedic priests used Aum to protect and purify the sacrifices, chants, and worshippers.

The Mandukya Upanishad speaks about Aum's significance. It compares the four sounds hidden in Aum with the four states of consciousness. The syllable 'A' represents the waking consciousness (*jagrata*). 'U' represents the dream state (*taijasa*). 'M' represents the deep sleep state (*prajna*), and, finally, the combined sound of 'AUM' represents the indeterminate transcendental state (*turiya*). Aum is described as the very Self, which "has no elements, which cannot be spoken, into which the world resolves, and which is benign and nondual."

In the Taittiriya Upanishad, we find the declaration that Aum is Brahman (*aum iti brahma*) and Aum is all (*Aum it idam sarvam*). It further states that Aum is used for various purposes because any activity that starts with the utterance of Aum comes to fruition. Vedic priests used Aum to purify and energize their chants so that they reached the gods and beckoned them to the ritual place. They used Aum when they sang the Rigvedic Riks (hymns) to the tune of the Samans and when they recited the prose parts (*Shastras*) of the Vedas. The Adharvayu priests used Aum to signal permission to the Hotr priest to chant the Rigvedic hymns. The supervising Brahman priest, who usually remained silent during the whole sacrifice, uttered Aum to give his approval. He also used it to give his consent to the Agnihotri priest to pour the oblations into the sacrificial fire. Students of the Vedic period began their study of the Vedas by uttering Aum with the belief that by studying them with that auspicious beginning, they would attain Brahman. Aum was also the secret mantra uttered in the ears of the young children during their Upanayana (initiation) ceremony. These practices continue. Aum is not the only sacred syllable. There are others. However, Aum is the most potent and important of all, at least so in the Vedic tradition and mainstream Hinduism.

Sound played an important role in the Vedic ritual and spiritual practices, and Aum highlighted it. It added sanctity and solemnity to the sacrificial rituals and meditative practices and worked like a subliminal message to alert the mind and bring it to attention and the present moment. As time went by, it assumed even greater significance not only in Hinduism and its sectarian traditions but also in Buddhism, Jainism, and several ascetic and monastic traditions of ancient India. The Vedas identified Aum as Brahman in sound form (*Sabda Brahma*) and Brahman in word form (*Akshara Brahman*), a belief that is still prevalent in Hinduism. Even now, in all Hindu sacrificial rituals and methods of worship, Aum is invariably used in conjunction with the use of mantras, prayers, and the chanting of the divinities' names and epithets. It is also used in the practice of yoga and before undertaking any important or auspicious work. The Upanishads loudly proclaim that by chanting Aum repeatedly one purifies the mind and body and stabilizes them in the contemplation of Brahman. The chanting of Aum is also used to regulate breathing and the flow of prana, control thoughts, overcome desires, and restrain the mind and senses. By meditating upon Aum, it is said that one can hear the subtle sounds that exist in the higher mental or subtle planes of our consciousness.

However, despite all the praise, awe, and mystic aura surrounding it, no one knows exactly the true meaning of Aum. Maybe we have lost its true meaning. Maybe we were never meant to know it since it is a part of the Srauta tradition. Everyone heard it from someone else, and no one exactly knew what it meant or signified. The mystery, therefore, continues. We have assumptions about it but we are not sure whether such assumptions are correct. We know that it is a sacred word and that it has a great symbolic significance; but we do not know what it actually means and how it came to occupy such a central place in the ritual and spiritual practices of Hinduism.

Today, AUM, or OM as it is sometimes pronounced, is one of the most popular words, along with God or Amen. It is known all over the world and in various traditions. It is used in both yoga and meditation and in conjunction with many rituals and methods of worship. Many companies, people, and products are named after it. People claim to have heard it in their subtle minds and equate it with Nada, the sound of prana flowing in the subtle channels (*nadis*) of the body. It is uttered by millions of people every day all over the world in temples, at homes, and elsewhere. Yet no one knows what it actually means, apart from the speculative theories that we have. Some believe that it was the first sound that followed the Big Bang or the creation of the universe, or it was the first sound that manifested and heralded the beginning of creation or life itself. It is also compared to the sound of a flowing river, rolling thunder, bellowing wind, burning fire, or ocean waves. According to some, it is the sound of breathing or the sound of the flow of vital energy in the body, which yogis often hear in deep meditative states as the eternal sound, Nada. Whatever it is, a few utterances of Aum stabilize the mind and prepare it for Pratyahara, the withdrawal of the mind and senses into oneself, Dharana, concentration, and Dhyana, meditation.

Brahman in Temple Worship

The Self cannot be known intellectually nor by instruction. He is attained by one whom the Self chooses. Mundaka Upanishad 3.2.3.

I do not think that I know it well. I do not think that I do not know it either. He, who among us knows it, knows it, but he also does not know that he does not know. Kena Upanishad 2.2.

In ancient India, religious knowledge was imparted only to those who qualified for it and met the expectations of their teachers, who followed the strictest standards in recruiting students. They looked for students who had the faith (*sraddha*), devotion (*bhakti*), humility (*bhayam*), interest, inclination, readiness, and patience to go through the rigorous discipline required to master it. Different traditions kept their knowledge to themselves and imparted them to a select few. Vedic seers followed the same tradition with regard to the Vedas and the Upanishads. Caste became an important factor in the later Vedic period, but in the early Rigvedic time, knowledge was probably taught to students according to their merits and qualifications. Some of the early Vedic scholars and seers belonged to the lower castes, which points to this possibility. For example, Satyakama Jabala did not come from a priestly family. His mother worked as a maid in many households and confessed to Satyakama that she could not be certain who his father could be. Yet his teacher found him fit for the knowledge of Brahman because of his truthfulness and humility, which were characteristics of a true Brahmana, and accepted him as his student. Women also received sacred knowledge in those times if they were qualified. Yajnavalkya taught the knowledge of the Self to his wife, Maitreyi. Women scholars are also mentioned in some Upanishads. The Chandogya Upanishad mentions Raikva, the man with the cart, who came from a lower caste but possessed great knowledge and wisdom. According to the Upanishad, when King Janasruti heard about him, he went to him personally with gifts to learn from him the knowledge of Brahman. He carried as gifts a gold necklace, a thousand cows, a chariot with mules, and his daughter. Upon seeing the girl, Raikva accepted the gifts and agreed to teach Janasruti. Caste was, therefore, not a major issue in the ancient Vedic society to qualify for the esoteric knowledge of the Upanishads. Perhaps caste was a deciding factor for learning the Samhitas and Brahmanas but not so much for the Aranyakas and Upanishads since they were taught by many outlier groups and Kshatriya masters.

The Upanishads were taught to those who were spiritually ready for liberation, dispassionate and indifferent (*vairagyam*) to worldly enjoyments, and well-prepared and determined to face the hardships of ascetic life, a trend that many ascetic traditions continued to follow for a long time. The same trend continues in Hinduism even today. Castes and family lineages do not carry much importance in the ascetic traditions of Hinduism even now since one cannot become an ascetic or a sannyasi without renouncing these external criteria, along with all desires and attachments. Renunciation is a personal decision. The desire to renounce worldly life and take up sannyasa must arise voluntarily. No one should feel forced to renounce their duties and obligations to join an ascetic movement. It should also not happen because you want to escape from problems, duties, and responsibilities. In Hinduism, householders have a choice. They have the option to pursue their worldly goals (*Dharma, Artha,* and *Kama*) without losing sight of their moral obligations (*Dharma*) and their liberation (*moksha*). They can renounce worldly life and their obligatory duties only if they develop a genuine distaste for worldly enjoyments and an irresistible desire to seek liberation. However, even then, sannyasa or asceticism is not the only option available to them. They still have ample choices to pursue liberation, such as karma-sannyasa yoga or bhakti yoga.

Vedic seers were not inclined to teach the knowledge of the Self to everyone and displease the gods, on whose benevolence they believed they depended. The gods are opposed to the idea of humans knowing Brahman and bypassing them (Brihad. 1.4.10) in the pursuit of liberation. They do not want humans to break the chain of command and go directly to Brahman. The Upanishads declare that knowers of Brahman surpass the gods and go to the world of immortality, from which they will not return. The gods do not appreciate it. They desire humans to perform sacrifices and nourish them regularly with offerings so that they will remain strong and active in their heaven and perform their obligatory duties (dharma) vigorously to uphold the order and regularity of creation (*Rta*) and protect themselves and humans (rta) from the demons, who are intent on dethroning Indra, the leader of the gods, taking over the heaven and creating chaos. Knowing this, Vedic priests focused on appeasing the gods to obtain their help and cooperation for the welfare of the worshippers. They remained loyal to the gods upon whose benevolence they believed their lives and the world depended. Therefore, they guarded the knowledge of Brahman with utmost secrecy (nigudham) and revealed it to a few aspirants who, in their estimate, deserved it because of their character, conduct, intelligence, and readiness.

The Upanishads state that Brahman is a mysterious Being unknown even to gods. Even the gods, who know Him somehow, know Him incompletely. If this is so with the gods, we can imagine how difficult it must be for humans to know Him correctly without doubt and confusion. With our limitations and surface consciousness, we may know Him relatively and objectively in a dualistic state of mind and in a language and imagery with which we are familiar. However, it would be like knowing the details of a painting, scenery, or image without seeing it or the melody of a song without hearing it. We may know Brahman intellectually and conceptually through self-study (svadhyaya), imagination, inference, etc., or from others. However, it will not help us much in our effort to know Him. While it may strengthen our aspirations or prepare us mentally, it will not grant us the direct experience of oneness, the state of transcendence, or self-absorption.

We find the reasons and the validation for this in the Upanishads. According to them, one cannot know Brahman intellectually because He is "other than the known" and "above the unknown." "If you think that you have understood Brahman, you know but little." The seers of the Kena Upanishad (2.1-2) admit this incongruity and difficulty in these words, "I do not think that I know it well; not do I think that I do not know it. He, who among us knows it, knows it, and he also does not know that he does not know." The inference from this is that we cannot know Brahman fully ever. Hence, we must have the humility to acknowledge and accept that as a universal truth.

Brahman is both transcendental and immanent. He is hidden in every aspect and dimension of the material universe. The reality we grasp with our senses in the objective realm is an aspect of Him only, but one cannot know Brahman through perceptions only. One may perceive a reflection of His auspicious qualities and hidden presence in His manifestations but cannot see Him or know Him based on those perceptions or inferences. According to the Brihadaranyaka Upanishad (1.4.7), breathing, speaking, seeing, hearing, and thinking are "merely names of His acts." You may meditate upon them individually, but you do not know Him by them unless you "meditate upon them all as the Self." What you perceive through the senses is not Brahman but the "differentiation," which Brahman manifested as names and forms. To know the Self, you must perceive the unity hidden in the diversity of existence. When the perceiver, the act of perceiving, and the perceived are known together, one knows Brahman. The monistic schools of Hinduism consider that Brahman is formless, and the forms of Brahman, to whichever hierarchy they may belong, are temporary and unreal. The dualistic schools believe that the manifested forms of the formless Brahman are real and distinct. However, even they acknowledge that they are not the same as Brahman.

The Upanishads surpass the other scriptures and traditions that we know in projecting uniquely and comprehensively the vastness and greatness of the Supreme Lord of the Universe, who is popularly known in Hinduism as Isvara, the manifested Brahman or Brahman with the qualities and modes of Prakriti (Nature). They provide us with a vision of God, whose descriptions are as enigmatic and multilayered as the descriptions of the material universe we find in the textbooks of modern astronomy. Most of them are also couched in symbolism and cryptic statements, which make them difficult to understand even after years of study. To a reader who is not familiar with the Vedic tradition and does not know much about the sacrifices and other forms of worship, many long verses, such as the ones we find in the Brihadaranyaka or Taittiriya Upanishad, do not make much sense. Therefore, unless we spend considerable time studying them and know the sacrifices and ritual symbolism thoroughly, we do not grasp the essential knowledge of many Upanishads. It is also important that we study them in the context of the Samhitas and the Darshanas so that we may grasp their full meaning and understand the symbolism hidden in them.

Even when we read the Upanishads selectively, which is what most people do, it is difficult to know Brahman. It is difficult for the human mind to conceptualize Brahman and express the inexpressible, which is why since ancient times the subject of Brahman remained vastly unknown to the public. Brahman is not like the other deities we know. He is the God of all gods. He represents the entire reality, with all the dualities, conflicts, and contradictions, excluding nothing. He is indeterminate. There is nothing certain about Him. We cannot say that this is Brahman, and this is not Brahman. Even that which we think is not Brahman (asat) is also one of His numerous states or dimensions only. In modern terminology, He is the universe as well as the quanta, which the Upanishads succinctly put as the largest of the large and the smallest of the small.

The Upanishads reflect the duality, which is often confounding. In one verse, we find that He is unchangeable or immutable, and in another, we learn that all things emerged out of Him. If He is unchangeable, then how do things manifest from Him, or how can He be the source of any effect? To a mind that is stuck in categorizations, logical thinking, and generalizations, such contradictory expressions are very perplexing, but for the enlightened minds of the Upanishadic seers, they represent His all-inclusive and all-encompassing absolute reality and essential nature. They represent His wholeness, completeness, or perfection. He is one and only, and everything, the good, the bad, all in between. Hence, He contains and resolves within Himself all the conflicts, extremities, and contradictions. He represents both the higher and lower knowledge. He is near and yet far away. He is immanent as well as transcendent. He is beyond the senses and yet moves among the sense objects. He is both 'is' and 'is not,' the Self and the not-self, the subject, the object, and what connects them.

The human mind finds such apparent contradictions too difficult to resolve and His qualities too abstract, remote, contradictory, and impersonal to relate with Him or worship Him devotionally without suffering from doubt and enigma. Therefore, although He is acknowledged as the indweller of the animate and inanimate objects and the master of the senses, He is not worshipped ritually in the temples. In the Bhagavadgita, Lord Krishna clearly says it is difficult to worship the unmanifested (*avyakta*) Brahman (12.6). The Vedic priests do not worship Him directly or ritually because they consider Him to represent every aspect of the ritual: subject, object, offering, ritual place, sacred fire, and so on. Therefore, when the make offerings to gods and chant the hymns, they know that Brahman is already an integral part of them and participates in the sacrifices as their presiding deity (*Adhi Daiva*) and the Chief Witness. He is also the source of sacrificial food and the food itself used in the offerings.

The meditating yogis usually do not contemplate upon Brahman directly but upon a symbol or a personal deity whom they equate with Him. There are no temples for Brahman, even though He has been the highest God of Hindu tradition for nearly four thousand years. While we do not know clearly why it has been so, I have tried to present below a few plausible explanations.

1. As an impersonal and universal power, Brahman is responsible for all life and dynamism (chaitanyam) in the universe. So whatever way you may worship and whomever you may choose to worship, you worship Brahman only.

2. In Vedic rituals, Brahman is the sacrificer as well as the sacrificed. The material for the sacrifice comes from the body of Brahman since all matter and energy belong to

Him only. The power that is invoked and the power that emanates from the rituals are also the power of Brahman, which connects men with gods and brings them together. Brahman is, therefore, the means rather than the object of ritual worship. It is why the scriptures do not justify worshipping Him either ritually or in an image form.

3. Brahman has no corporeality. He is self-existent and independent. He personifies food and is the source and consumer of all food. He is also complete and satisfied within Himself. Nothing diminishes Him or completes Him. Unlike the gods, He does not depend upon humans for nourishment. Therefore, in Vedic sacrifices, worshippers do not directly invoke Him or offer Him the sacrifice.

4. Brahman is the universal Self. He can be reached only by knowing the individual Self (*Atman*) that is hidden in all. The Upanishads, therefore, encourage contemplation of the individual Self (*Adhyatma Yoga*) rather than the ritual worship of Brahman.

5. The unmanifested and formless Brahman does not participate in creation. He does not respond to the calls of individual worshippers. It is Isvara or Brahman with form, who is dynamic and self-willed. He initiates creation and actively responds to the calls of His worshippers. The tradition, therefore, encourages the worship of Isvara or His many forms rather than the unmanifested, formless Brahman.

6. According to the scriptures, Brahman should be worshipped internally through contemplation and austerities rather than ritual worship. You qualify for His worship only when you are free from all attachments and seeking. Rituals are usually performed out of desire and with specific intentions. Therefore, they are not the right means to worship Brahman.

7. Brahman is formless and transcendental. For worship, we need an object, image, or form. Brahman, in his absolute

aspect, is none of these. Besides, the moment you objectify Brahman, attribute a form, name, or notion to Him, and try to worship Him, He ceases to be the absolute, supreme Brahman and becomes one of His manifestations. Therefore, worshipping Brahman ritually as an image or idol is practically impossible.

In Hindu tradition, Brahman is the ultimate destination. Even if you worship other gods, eventually, you will reach Him only because He is the Supreme Lord, and the world is verily Brahman only. By worshipping other gods, one moves higher and higher in the worlds, and when all things perish in the dissolution of the worlds, one attains unity with Him (Maitri. 4.6). The same idea is expressed in the Bhagavadgita also. Therefore, it is up to the devotees whether they would like to approach Him directly by practicing yoga and other spiritual methods or indirectly by worshipping personal gods and other deities, accepting them as Brahman in their purest state. Hindu tradition does not impose any restrictions upon its followers how they worship Brahman. It is left to the practitioners whether they like to choose the difficult and outlier paths that rely upon knowledge, intellect, and severe penances or follow the less demanding paths that rely upon devotion, worship, sacrifices, and surrender.

Brahmavidyas – Ways to Realize Brahman

We have already discussed how it is difficult to grasp Brahman mentally or intellectually because He is beyond the mind and the senses. The Upanishads offer various techniques and theories to resolve this problem. They suggest that one may become established in Him by meditating on His universal form (*visvarupam*) or His particular aspects and manifestations. According to the Vedic tradition, one may acquire the knowledge of Brahman in any or all of the following ways. While there may be many, these are proven and reliable ones. They all can be practiced simultaneously. However, while practicing them, one must give up egoism, desires, attachments, and delusion.

- Listening to the adepts
- Studying the scriptures
- Contemplating upon the truths of Brahman
- Remembering Him or His names and manifestations
- Experiencing the truths of Brahman without duality
- Through sacrificial actions and devotional worship
- By providence or divine grace

There is a big difference between knowing Brahman intellectually and experiencing Him truthfully. Experiencing the absolute state of Brahman comes from self-transformation and purification attained by persistent effort, sincere aspiration, and unconditional surrender, not through egoistic striving and seeking or the delusional and tortuous methods of tamasic resolve. Knowledge of Brahman is considered Vidya, the true knowledge. It is also known as Brahma-jnanam. The various methods and symbols used to know Brahman or acquire transcendental knowledge are traditionally known as Brahmavidyas. They are proven methods, paths, or approaches by which one gains knowledge of Brahman intellectually or experiences His auspicious and absolute state.

Vidya means knowledge as well as study. It is derived from the same root word (*vid*) as the Vedas and is closely associated with the Latin "videre," meaning to see, and the more popular English word "video." The Vedas declare Vidya as knowledge and Avidya as ignorance. Indeed, their practice application depends upon the users. For example, for the Upanishadic seers, knowledge of sacrifices or worldly knowledge constitutes Avidya or ignorance because they do not liberate the souls from bondage. Brahmavidyas are the specialized studies, which provide an insight into the nature of Brahman or His aspects. The total number of vidyas is said to be 32. One does not have to know or practice them all because, in the end, they all point to the same truth and lead to the same goal. The following discussion about the Brahmavidyas is based mostly upon the information available in the Brahma Sutras and the verses found in the Upanishads concerning each. To provide an idea of what they mean, I have discussed some in detail and the rest briefly. The Vidyas are helpful in stabilizing the mind in Brahman and setting it free from its habitual ways, desires, and attachments so that it mentally prepares one for liberation. If you are creative, you can create your own vidyas to establish your thoughts in Brahman and dissolve your mind so that the nondual state of oneness becomes your natural state (*sahaja vidya*).

Prana Vidya: In Hinduism, prana should not be mistaken for the simple air we breathe. It is also prana. However, in the spiritual context, it refers to the vital energy or the life energy present in the body in gross and subtle forms. The flesh in the body is a form of energy only. So are the food we eat, the energy that circulates in the body and keeps it alive, and the nourishment the organs in the body receive after digestion. They all constitute prana. Prana is an aspect or form of Shakti, and thereby Brahman. It is a purifier when controlled. When its circulation in the body is obstructed, problems arise, and the body becomes enervated or sick. Prana Vidya is about the study or knowledge of prana, its role in sustaining life as an aspect of Brahman, and its importance in purifying the mind and the body for liberation. In Prana vidya, we study the various types of energies to know how they flow in the body and what role they play in sustaining our lives and purifying our consciousness so that we can attain mental absorption, which will eventually lead to the nondual state of self-absorption. The importance of breath is mentioned in various Upanishads, especially the Brihadaranyaka (6.1.1) and Chandogya Upanishads (5.1.1). The following account of prana and prana vidya is gleaned from them.

Prana is Brahman, the oldest (*jyestam*) and the greatest (*srestam*). Whoever knows it thus also becomes the oldest and the greatest. Life depends upon prana. The various parts of the body, such as the speech, the senses, and the mind, depend upon it, and therefore, they make an offering to it. Prana uplifts all (*ukta*), unites all (*yajus*), and rules all (*kshatra*). People come into the world with breath, and they depart from here with breath. Wise men (*dhira*), therefore, purify their breath with water before and after eating food. Breath has different names depending on how it circulates in the body. Prana is the inward breath, Apana is the outward breath that goes out through the apertures in the body, Vyana is the diffused breath present in all the limbs, Samana is the middle breath, and Udana is the breath that moves upwards from the heart region towards the head. At the time of death, it gathers all other energies (pranas) in the body and leaves the body from the top of the head. According to Chandogya (3.13.1), the five breaths are the five openings of the heart to reach the gods. Meditating upon them results in distinct benefits. Meditating upon Prana leads to luster and health; upon Vyana leads to fame and prosperity; upon Apana leads to wisdom and health; upon Samana leads to fame and beauty; and upon Udana leads to strength and greatness.

The Prasna Upanishad (3.7) describes where the five breaths are located in the human body.

- Prana is located in the eye and ear as well as in the mouth and the nose.
- Apana is located in the organs of excretion and reproduction.
- Samana is in the middle. It equalizes whatever is offered as

food. From it also arises seven flames.

- Vyana moves in a hundred arteries of the heart where the Self is located.
- Udana is located in the head and the limbs. At the time of death, it moves upwards into the head through one of the arteries coming from the heart, and from there, it goes either to heaven or hell according to one's actions.

As stated before, prana is not just the air we breathe, although we call it also prana. It is the energy or the force that sustains life, movement, and consciousness. It connects us with the world around us and with others through food, speech, the senses, and breathing. It is the only visible way in which we all are connected to each other, to gods, other living creatures, and the rest of creation. It is why our scriptures emphasize the significance of nonviolence (*ahimsa*). They do not want us to cause prana-hani, the destruction of prana. We all exist in the ocean of prana, described in the scriptures as the waters of life. Whatever we do leaves its ripples in the ocean and affects others. Just as Brahman uplifts and expands the whole creation, prana also expands and uplifts all the jivas. Hence, Upanishads often describe the senses as breaths only. In the mouth and throat, it becomes speech. From the speech are born the Vedas and the sacrifices. In the mind, it becomes consciousness, memory, and perception. In the eyes, it becomes light. In the ear, it becomes sound. Therefore, Upanishads, such as the Kausitaki Upanishad, rightly identify prana with Brahman, the source of all.

Panchagni Vidya: Fire (*Agni*) and its various forms are central to Hindu rituals and spiritual practices. In sacrifices, priests kindle the ritual fire (*yagajni*). In spiritual practice, ascetics kindle the bodily fire (*tapa*) internally through austerity. The warmth we feel in the body is also an aspect of fire. Prana, or the vital energy in the jivas that keeps them alive and gives them their characteristic movements, awareness, and liveliness (*chaitanyam*), is also a form of fire only. Semen and eggs in the body are produced from the fire (vigor) in the body. They facilitate the transmigration of embodied souls and help the householders attain the chief aim of happiness and fulfillment (*kama*). When yogis practice self-control and celibacy (*Brahmacharya*), the internal fire (*tapa*) of the body transforms into bodily vigor (*ojas*), mental brilliance (*tejas*), and bodily luster (*varchas*). Finally, at the time of death, a part of it joins the funeral fire, and a part of it joins the causal body (*karana sarira*) and accompanies the soul.

The sacrificial fire was central to the practice of Vedic religion. Vedic people kept different types of fires in their households, such as the Ahvaniya, Garhapatya, and Dakshinagni fires, to perform different types of sacrifices. These fires reminded them of their daily obligatory duties and moral and social responsibilities. Each of them also had the obligatory duty to keep the fires burning continuously for as long as possible. If they were lost or became extinguished, they had to rekindle them ritually to ensure that their sanctity and continuity were not lost. The Vedas recognize Agni, the fire god, as the most prominent deity after Indra. He is often extolled as the highest of all who is found in the brilliance of the sun and illumination of the mind. He is the first recipient of all the sacrificial offerings and distributes them among the other gods according to their due share, which varies depending upon the type of sacrifice and the presiding deities. He is also known by different names, each named after a sacrificial fire or the purpose for which it is used.

Panchangni vidya is the knowledge of how to meditate on the five aspects of fire and the fate of people when they die. It describes where they go, what happens there, who goes to the immortal world, who returns from the ancestral world, in what form, and so on. The reference to it is found in the Brihadaranyaka Upanishad (5.2) in a conversation between Prahavana Javali, the king of Panchala, and Gautama, a Brahmana of great repute. It is also mentioned in the Chandogya Upanishad (5.10). It also contains the knowledge of the events associated with an embodied soul's existence after death and their correlation to five principal types of fire, which manifest during a sacrifice as fuel, smoke, flame, coals, and sparks. The five types of fire are also related to the five sheaths (*kosas*) in the human body, the five types of breath, the five senses, and the five elements. They are, in turn, connected to the five dimensions of the universe. In the act of creation, which is a sacrifice in itself, these fires are said to manifest as the world of the sun, the moon, the earth, man, and woman. According to the Upanishads, the ascetics who meditate upon Brahman in the forests and realize their true nature go to the world of the gods, then to the sun, and finally to the world of Brahman. They never return. Those who make sacrifices and practice charity and austerity go to the world of ancestors and from there to the moon. There, they become food to the gods and pass into space, from where they return to the earth through rain. From the earth, they enter the bodies through food. From food in the body, they enter into the semen, and finally, through semen, they assume a new life to restart their lives all over again.

Vaisvanara Vidya: Vaisva means universal, omnipresent, etc. Vaisvanara means the god who is present everywhere, a reference to Brahman in His aspect of universal fire and the sun, or Savitur, who spreads sunlight in all directions and illuminates everything. It also refers to the internal fire, especially the all-consuming digestive fire. The Upanishads describe Brahman as the devourer of all. Hence, it also refers to Brahman as Shiva, Death or the destroyer of all. The Upanishads declare that by contemplating upon Vaisvanara as one's own Self and as the universal Being, one comes to know about it. In the Brihadaranyaka Upanishad, Vaisvanara is referred to as the digestive fire and the internal sound that one hears by covering the ears. Vaisvanara is also the individual Self. According to the Chandogya Upanishad (5.18.1), if you meditate upon Vaisvanara in your own heart as your own Self, which is of the size of a thumb, you become one with it. The Upanishad also describes the universal form of Vaisvanara, which is akin to the Cosmic Male (*Purusha*). Its head is said to be light (sun); eye the universal form; breath its various currents; body fullness; bladder wealth; feet the earth; chest the sacrificial place; hair the sacred grass; heart the Garhapatya fire [1]; mind the Anvaharya fire [2]; and mouth the Ahvaniya fire [3]. In the Mundaka Upanishad, we find a similar description of the universal Self in relation to fire. "Fire is His head, His eyes are the sun and the moon, the quarters are his ears, His speech reveals the

Vedas, the air is His breath, His heart is the world. The earth is born out of His feet. He is indeed the Self of all beings." Vaisvanara also refers to the Self in the body, which is described in the Katha Upanishad as a flame of the size of the thumb that shines brightly. It illuminates the body and all the organs in the body. When it departs, the presiding deities of all the organs accompany Him to the mid-region, from where they return to their respective abodes. Thus, Vaisvanara Vidya involves contemplating upon Brahman as different types of fires that illuminate His creation and keep it alive and dynamic (*chaitanyam*).

Sandilya Vidya: The knowledge taught by sage Sandilya, which is mentioned in the Chandogya Upanishad (3.14), goes by the name of Sandilya Vidya. The teaching focuses on four important aspects of liberation: the nature of Brahman, the nature of Atman (Self), the nature and consequences of actions, and the importance of self-restraint in becoming one with Brahman. According to the doctrine, the whole world is Brahman. It comes out of Him and dissolves into Him. A man's life here and hereafter depends upon his actions. So, one should carefully choose one's purpose. The individual being is made up of both subtle and gross bodies, desires, and sensations. Hidden within it, in the heart, is the minute inner Self, smaller than a grain of rice or millet. Restraining speech, without attachment and desires, one should meditate upon it as greater than the earth, the atmosphere, the sky, and the worlds. He who believes in the Self as Brahman and contemplates upon It will have no doubts and will not return after death.

It is not possible to write here in detail about all the 32 vidyas. I have therefore presented a brief description of each. If you want to study them further, please refer to the respective Upanishads, which are mentioned below in the brackets in conjunction with each vidya.

1. **Akasa Vidya**: Knowledge or study of the element ether or space (*akasa*), from where all beings are produced (Chand. 1.9.1)

2. **Akshara Vidya**: Knowledge or study of the imperishable Brahman (Brihad. 3.8.8)

3. **Aksharapara Vidya**: Knowledge or study of the absolute Brahman as the imperishable from whom arises the universe. (Mundaka. 1.1.7)

4. **Akshi Vidya**: Knowledge or study of the all-seeing Person (Akshini Purusha) who is present in the eyes (Chand. 4.15.1)

5. **Anandamaya Vidya**: Knowledge, study, or the contemplation of the Self as the eternal and infinite bliss by which one may attain eternal bliss (Taitt. 2.8.1, 3.6.1)

6. **Angushta-paramita Vidya**: Knowledge or study of the Self, which is of the size of the thumb residing in the middle of the body like a flame without smoke (Katha. 2.1.12-13)

7. **Antaraditya Vidya**: Knowledge or study of the golden person, who is hidden in the sun as an Aditya or a solar deity (Chand. 1.6.6)

8. **Antaryaami Vidya**: Knowledge or study of the inner controller, as described by Yajnavalkya to Uddalaka Aruni (Brihad. 3.7)

9. **Balaki Vidya**: Knowledge or study of the progressive definition of Brahman, which leads to the knowledge of the deep sleep state, as taught by King Ajatasatru to Gargya Balaki (Brihad. 2.1.1 and Kau. 4)

10. **Bhuma Vidya**: Knowledge or study of the progressive worship of Brahman (Chand. 7)

11. **Dahara Vidya**: Knowledge or study of the innermost Self in the heart, as taught by Brahma to Indra (Chand. 8)

12. **Gayatri Vidya**: Knowledge or study of the significance of the Gayatri mantra (Chand. 3.12)

13. **Isavasya Vidya**: Knowledge or study of Isa, the Lord of the Universe, as taught in the Isavasya Upanishad (Isa)

14. **Jyotishaam JyotirJ Vidya**: Knowledge or study of the light of the lights (Brihad. 4.4.16)

15. **Madhu Vidya**: Knowledge or study of the Sun as the honey of gods (Chand. 3)

16. **Maitreyi Vidya**: Knowledge or study of the teaching of Yajnavalkya to his wife Maitreyi that everything is dear because of the Self (Brihad. 2.14)

17. **Naciketa Vidya**: Knowledge or study of the eternal Self as taught by Lord Yama to Naciketa (Katha. 1.2)

18. **Nyaasa Vidya**: Knowledge or study of Brahman as one's own Self or by identifying oneself with Him (Taittiriya Narayana Upanishad 49-52)

19. **Paramajyoti Vidya**: Knowledge or study of light, which is high above, and which is also in the person (Chand. 3.13.7)

20. Paramapurusha Vidya: Knowledge or study of the Purusha (the cosmic Being) (Katha. 1.3)

21. **Paryanka Vidya**: Knowledge or study of Brahman as the highest God in the Supreme Abode (Kau. 1)

22. **Pratardana Vidya**: Knowledge or study of Indra as the immortal Self, as taught by Indra to Pratardana, the son of Divodasa (Kau. 3)

23. **Sat Vidya**: Knowledge or study of Sat, the primal Being, the one without a second (Chand. 6.2)

24. **Samvarga Vidya**: Knowledge or study of the all-absorbing nature of the transcendental states as taught by Raikva (Chand. 4.1-3)

25. **Sarvantaratmaa Vidya**: Knowledge or study of Brahman as the inner Self of all (Birhad. 3.4)

26. **Satyakama Vidya**: Knowledge or study of Brahman as the four quarters, as taught to Satyakama Jabala by Gautama. (Chan. 4.4)

27. **Upakosala Vidya**: The knowledge that breath (prana) is Brahman, Kama (pleasure) is Brahman, and Kham (ether) is Brahman, as learned by a student named Upakosala from his own internal fires and by his teacher, Satyakama Jabala (Chand. 4.10-15)

28. **Varuni Vidya**: Knowledge or study of Brahman as matter, life, mind, intelligence, and bliss, as taught by Varuna (Taitti.3)

In addition to the above, one may also contemplate upon the following objects and symbols to stabilize one's mind and develop an awareness of Brahman.

The vital breath in the mouth: The vital breath in the mouth is the source of speech and the power that comes from speaking or chanting words or mantras. It is comparable to Brahman since the Upanishads compare Brahman to speech and declare Him as the source of all speech, sounds, and vibrations. One should meditate on the throat, on the guttural sound that arises from it when one hums Aum deeply, on how the sounds arising from speech travel through space to reach their objective, and how it connects people and gods, drives away evil, and increases the power of divinities in the body, to realize its source, which is Brahman. (Brihad. 1.3.7)

Food: The Upanishads symbolically extoll the universal energy, matter, or materiality present in creation as food (*annam*), material Brahman, and the food of Brahman. He creates it and devours it as a part of His creation and destruction. In other words, food is another name for Prakriti, the material cause of creation and a source of nourishment for all. One should meditate on the statement that Brahman, indeed, is food (*annam para-brahma svarupam*) and upon its gross and subtle forms and its role in sacrificial rituals and creation as the sustaining and upholding force. Meditate on how food becomes life, and life becomes food. Meditate on the body as the food body and how it can be controlled and attuned through yoga for peace and liberation.

The Sun: Vedic people were essentially sun worshippers. For them, the sun symbolized Brahman. They believed that the immortal world of Brahman was located in the sun, and those who attained immortality traveled to the sun by the Northern Path and stayed there permanently. Therefore, they worshipped the sun daily through prayers and sacrifices. They also worshipped Adityas, solar deities, of whom Vishnu and Savitur were the most prominent. One can meditate on the Sun as the Self, life-giver, nourisher, provider of light, the world of the immortals, the roots of the tree of life (*Asvattha*) or creation, the illuminator of all creation, the all-pervading light, the seer who enjoys through the senses, and the symbol of Brahman Himself.

The Moon: In some verses, Brahman is compared to the moon as the illuminator who shines in the darkness and helps people clouded by ignorance and delusion find their way. The moon is the sphere where the ancestral world is believed to be located and where pious people who performed their obligatory duties traveled upon their death and served the gods to cleanse themselves. Vedic people performed Soma rituals by ritually extracting Soma juice, an intoxicant, from an ancient herb and offering it to the moon before consuming it. Probably, it induced psychedelic experiences and altered states of consciousness, and helped them envision the gods, subtle worlds, and hidden realms of creation. One can meditate on the moon as the white-robed king Soma, as the dream state, as a divine healer and messenger, as the seer in the eye, as the home of the ancestors, as the lord of plants, rivers, and forests, as the illuminator and bestower of life, and as the source of peace and prosperity.

Lightning: Indra's weapon is lightning, which denotes that the source of Indra's might and majesty is Brahman only. Some Upanishadic verses compare the lightning that occasionally appears in meditative states to Brahman only. Just as lightning flashes in the dark clouds before it rains or during storms, Brahman appears momentarily like a flash of lightning in the minds that are clouded by ignorance, egoism, and delusion during deep churning or intense meditation. One can meditate on lightning as Brahman or the power of Brahman hidden in the natural phenomena, which manifests in heaven as the power of Indra, as the power that drives away darkness, as the light that illuminates the mind and intelligence, as the flashes of intuition, premonition, or random messages that descend from beyond deep sleep into dream or wakeful states, and the power that descends to the earth from the heavens, illuminating everything in its path.

The elements: Brahman is the source of the five elements—fire, water, earth, air, and space—and is responsible for the whole diversity of creation due to their permutations and combinations with the triple modes, Sattva, Rajas, and Tamas. This process is explained in the Kausitaki Upanishad. The elements are a part of the Prakriti tattvas. Together, they represent the objective reality or the not-self. Therefore, the body is also called the elemental self (bhutatma). It has both gross and subtle aspects. Each of the elements also personifies several deities and their powers (*Shaktis*). They are also used in invocations and sacrifices. The five elements are said to arise in creation from the perceptions of the five senses. Hence, they are associated with the five senses and their objects of perception. One can meditate upon the five elements, their origin from perceptions, their role in diversity, and their different manifestations, representations, and associations in creation and the human body.

The senses: The senses are fifteen: the five organs of actions, the five organs of perception, and the five sense perceptions (*tanmatras*). The status of the jivas in the comic hierarchy depends upon the number of senses they possess. Thus, the jivas with no senses or one sense represent the lowest rung. In humans, they develop fully. Each of the senses is presided over by a deity who corresponds to a deity of the macrocosm. They depend upon the breath (prana) for their nourishment and upon the Self for their support. The mind is their lord. They work for him. When the Self departs from the body with the breaths, they follow Him to the mid-region and disperse to return to their respective abodes. The senses are restless and responsible for the restlessness and modifications of the mind. They are also vulnerable to evil thoughts and intentions. Hence, they must be withdrawn into the mind and restrained with intelligence and resolve to achieve self-control, stability, and equanimity and practice detachment, sameness, and renunciation. One should meditate upon the senses as the sources of afflictions and disturbances of the mind (*vrittis*) and the cause of desires, attachments, suffering, and bondage. Meditate upon their role in our bondage, ignorance, and suffering.

Sound: Brahman is the source of all sounds. Creation itself is said to arise from sounds only. Brahman is also the power that moves these sounds from one place to another. He is hidden in the hymns and chants of the Vedas as sound only. Hence, he is called Sound-Brahman (*Shabda Brahma*). However, through sounds alone, one can never attain Brahman because they do not allow the mind to settle in meditation to reach Him, who is beyond all sounds and objectivity. One may take refuge in Him or the sacred sounds He personifies to withdraw the senses, stabilize the mind, and reach the pure and soundless state of self-absorption. Meditate upon sound as the power of Brahman is hidden in the Vedic prayers and chants and upon the subtle sound that yogis hear within themselves in intense states of meditation.

Sleep: Of the four states of consciousness mentioned in the Mandukya Upanishad, the deep sleep state (susupti) represents the tamasic state of complete ignorance, the chasm that exists between our objective reality and the transcendental, eternal, indestructible, and self-existent reality. Due to ignorance, one may mistake the deep sleep state for the transcendental state of self-absorption or Nirvana and fall into delusion. It is the state in which neither the knower nor the known exists, and one experiences neither duality nor nonduality. It is an indeterminate state that needs to be transcended to attain the pure state of Brahman. One should, therefore, meditate on sleep as an obstacle to self-realization and to overcome the delusion and ignorance induced by tamas. In meditation, one should also try not to fall asleep, which is a common problem for novices. One should try to establish the mind in the Self and let the mind and senses rest in sleep without losing sight of the Self so that one reaches the state where the Self alone remains without any duality or otherness.

Mental states: The mind is subject to different states of consciousness and is seldom stable. The Mandukya Upanishad identifies four states of consciousness: the waking state, the dream state, the deep sleep state, and the transcendental state. According to the Upanishad, he who knows these four states enters into the Self and becomes one with it. Apart from this, we can identify three layers of consciousness: the surface consciousness, which is highly unstable and entirely made up of the objects, feelings, and sensations arising from the perception of objective reality; the middle layer, which is relatively stable, detached, attentive and mindful with a heightened sense of awareness and discernment, a deeper state that is completely free from modifications and perceptions and is absorbed in itself in which one becomes a witness to all that happens within and without, without any reaction, identification or involvement. These are aspects of manifested Brahman or the Field of Prakriti. One can reach Brahman and attain His pure state by meditating on them and transcending them.

Aspects Brahman: The one absolute, supreme Brahman manifests numerously by activating Prakriti, His dynamic principle and primal energy. The numerous manifestations of Brahman are all around us. He is hidden in the best and brightest aspects and qualities of creation. All the worlds and divinities are His manifestations only. They all manifest from Him at the beginning of creation and subside into Him at the end. He is the Cosmic Purusha, Isvara, Brahma, Vishnu, and Shiva. He is Shakti and all the manifestations of Shakti. His manifestations are well described in the tenth chapter of the Bhagavadgita, in which Lord Krishna states, "He who truly knows my divine manifestations and powers becomes absorbed in steadfast yoga state. There is no doubt about this." One can meditate upon Brahman's numerous forms and manifestations to reach His absolute, formless, and infinite state. One can also meditate upon His divine qualities, such as wisdom, truthfulness, forgiveness, self-control, equanimity, contentment, etc., to cultivate them and attain purity and perfection.

Udgita: The hymns of the Samaveda are known as Samans. They are composed according to specific meters, which produce melodious rhythms when they are sung loudly. For this reason, Lord Krishna states in the Bhagavadgita that of the four Vedas, Samaveda is his best manifestation. The Samans are praised highly and compared to Brahman and His manifestations in several Upanishads. In the Vedic sacrifices, some of the Samans are sung at the beginning as the introductory songs. They are called Udgita, or high chants, which are meant to awaken the worshipper's minds and set the right tone and atmosphere for the divinities to descend and grace the sacrifices. The birth of jivas, the sunrise in the morning, and an intense desire to achieve liberation are comparable to Udgita only. Aum is also compared to Udgita, which is said to be highly beneficial and produces a soothing effect on the mind and the body. One can meditate on the mystic symbolism of Udgita and its significance in ritual and spiritual practices.

The body: The body represents the not-self, objective reality, the Field of Prakriti, perishable creation, and what the Self or Brahman is not. It is the shadow self, presided over by the ego, and is subject to aging, sickness, and death. Deluded and ignorant people consider it the real Self and become bound by their desire-ridden actions and attachments. However, for the jiva, the body is the support. The Upanishads compare it to a temple or a city of nine gates, in which the embodied Self resides. No one can achieve liberation without a body. Therefore, even though it is impure and the source of bondage and suffering, for the sake of liberation, one should keep nourishing it and controlling it with detachment and renunciation. One can meditate on the human body and its various tattvas as the not-self or as the city of God with nine gates where the individual Self resides. By meditating on the body as a not-self and knowing what the Self is not, one can cultivate discernment and withdraw the mind and senses into oneself to experience peace and equanimity. One may also meditate upon it as a world in itself, comparable to the world outside, and why it is necessary to nourish it and purify it to achieve liberation.

The individual Self: The Self is either an aspect of Brahman or Brahman Himself. Like Brahman, it is eternal, indestructible, infinite, pure, and remains immutable even when bound to Samsara. Meditate upon the individual Self (*Atman*) that is hidden in all the jivas. Meditate upon its essential nature as Truth, Bliss, and Consciousness, as the witnessing Self, as the source and support of the body, as breath, as the lord, and as the light that illuminates and supports all the organs in the body, including the mind and intelligence. Meditate on the Self that resides in the cave of the heart, in the area between the eyebrows that shines like a flame the size of a thumb.

The cosmic phenomena: One can meditate on Brahman anywhere and everywhere. There is no place where He does not exist. By constantly remembering Him everywhere, you can cultivate exclusive devotion, which, according to the Bhagavadgita, is essential to achieving liberation. All the cosmic phenomena, both gross and subtle, are aspects of Brahman and a part of His material projection or creation. Meditate upon Brahman as the creator and sustainer of various phenomena such as Time (*Kala*), the divine order (*Rta*), Truth (*Satyam*), Justice (*Dharma*), Universal Laws (*Niyamas*), dualities (*dvandva*), illusion (*maya*), bondage (*bandha*), and liberation (*Moksha*). Meditate on the phenomena that manifest in our lives due to our actions (*karma*), those caused by others, and those that arise due to fate or providence. Meditate on how they influence your thinking, actions, and destiny.

Footnotes

1. The Garhapatya fire is the central fire in the middle of the house, kept burning continuously by those who perform Vedic sacrifices and adhere to the Vedic way of life. It belongs to the master of the house. As per the Vedic injunctions, it should be kept alive at all times. The other fires kept in the house should be kindled from it.
2. The Anvaharya fire is the fire located in the southern part of the house where certain rites for ancestors are performed during every new moon day.
3. The Ahvaniya fire is located in the east, where offerings to the deities are made. Together, the three fires are known as the triple fires (Tretagni). In the Vedic period, these fires were used to kindle the sacrificial fires for making offerings to Agni.

The Creator God of the Upanishads

The Upanishads declare Brahman as the creator, who creates the worlds out of Himself by sacrificing a part of His body (matter) as an offering in the sacrificial act of creation. Most of the verses, which deal with the subject of creation, describe creation symbolically, using Vedic terminology associated with the performance of rituals or the structure and composition of human personality. The creation hymn from the Rigveda reflects the enigma of creation. It suggests that in the beginning, there was neither non-existence nor existence; neither the realm of air nor the sky; neither the mid-region nor the heavens; and neither the days and nights nor death. Everything was indiscriminate chaos. There was only "that One Thing, which was breathless, and which breathed by its own nature." In the Upanishads, that One Thing is identified as the undifferentiated (*avyakta*) Brahman or Brahman in a state of deep sleep (*turiya*).

In our case, either we create things continuously or creation happens to us continuously. Waking, cooking, eating, cultivating, harvesting, solving a problem, texting a message, thinking, dreaming, writing a poem, giving birth to a baby, imagining or visualizing something, all these are acts of creation only. It is even more appropriate to say that in this impermanent phenomenal world, creation begins and ends constantly as each moment appears and disappears like waves in the ocean. In the case of gods and Brahman, that moment may stretch into millions of years as they have different timeframes. The days and nights of Brahman span billions of years. Unlike us, He is never subject to aging, decay, or death. What He creates is a projection or extension of His will, which He withdraws at the end of the day and goes into a long sleep. In modern terms, it is like a vast amount of intelligent information exists in Brahman and manifests according to set processes into objective reality consisting of numerous gross and subtle forms. The whole universe and all the intelligence inherent to it may arise from the same processes that help us in creating things or manifesting our thoughts.

One of the fundamental questions concerning creation is whether things manifested out of nothing or from an eternal, indestructible, ever-present, and constant reality. If it arises from the latter, how does it happen? Does that reality undergo any change to manifest things out of itself, or does it merely project things without undergoing any change? The Vedas generally concur with the second opinion that creation arises from the eternal and indestructible Brahman like a spider web. However, those who disagree with the assertion that Brahman is the creator also find evidence in the same Vedas to support their arguments. According to some Upanishads, creation is essentially an act of transformation or differentiation (Brihad. 1.4.7). It happens due to the division, multiplication, and intermixture of preexisting primordial things (gunas and tattvas) and their transformation from one state to another. That One Thing, self-existent, becomes many to manifest the worlds and the beings by means of expansion, dispersion, division, and evolution. Like the rays that scatter from the sun, the world manifests as emanations of one essential reality. Since, in their final essence, all things emanated from one being and one source, there is a fundamental unity hidden in them, which threads them together, and eventually, at the time of dissolution, all things will resolve themselves into that one indivisible reality.

Parallel to this interpretation is another explanation that creation is not only an act of transformation and differentiation but also superimposition of multiple realities upon the essential truth of Brahman, which may either arise from faulty perception and ignorance or from the act of creation itself. It means one eternal reality becomes superimposed by several other impermanent realities, whereby truth becomes hidden, and the apparent reality passes off as the real. Just as the same earth appears differently at different times during day and night and during different seasons, the same reality of Brahman becomes superimposed by many layers of appearances, whereby we develop mistaken notions of what we see and experience. It may also happen because we may make a mistake for one thing for another, such as mistaking a rope for a snake. This is what the scriptures call maya or illusion. Maya is so powerful that it camouflages everything and makes truth very hard to ascertain. Therefore, if we want to know the truth of our existence, we have to resolve things into their fundamental or original state and remove the layers of illusion behind which their source is hidden.

Since the one became many, we consider Brahman as the cause and the manifestation as the effect. With regard to the cause of creation, the various schools of Hinduism speculate on whether Brahman is the essential cause, the material cause, or both. Some Upanishads concur with the opinion that He is both. According to them, creation is not a random or chance event without a purpose, intent, or intelligent source. Brahman creates it for a specific purpose: to keep himself occupied, to create the 'other' for a company, or to enjoy it as a witness. Since He manifests different worlds and classes of beings wailfully, He is the essential cause and the Lord of all. Secondly, the material that He uses as the sacrificial food to manifest them in the sacrifice of creation comes from Him only. He is both Purusha, the Cosmic Self, and Prakriti, the Cosmic Nature. The former is pure consciousness, and the latter is primal matter and energy. As Purusha, He uses his bodily parts (Prakriti) since there is nothing other than Him to sacrifice. Hence, He is the source of all, the hub of the Wheel of Creation (*Brahma Chakra*) or the Wheel of the Mother (*Matrka Chakra*), with Prakriti serving and supporting it as its spokes. Since He is also Prakriti and the source of all the material, He is not only the efficient cause of creation but also its material cause. Although He is without support, He is the supporter of all. Although uncreated, He creates everything.

The Upanishads list two primary reasons why Brahman manifests the world, namely desire and enjoyment. According to Brihadaranyaka Upanishad, when Brahman awoke, He found Himself alone, and He was afraid. The fear passed away when He realized that there was nothing other than Him, and he should be afraid of what. Once that fear passed, he felt lonely and desired companionship with another. Therefore, He created another form of Himself, His other half, with the materiality of His Primal Nature (*Mula Prakriti*). They played hide-and-seek for some time and produced male and female versions of numerous species. It resulted in the creation of numerous jivas.

Most of the verses in the Upanishads dealing with creation are shrouded in deep symbolism. They describe the process of creation using the analogy of rituals and human nature. In them, we find two main ways by which the cosmic order and various cosmic phenomena manifest. According to one version, creation happens because of a sacrificial ritual Brahman performs on a cosmic scale at the beginning of each creation cycle with the help of ancient gods [1] serving as divine priests. They perform the sacrifice, with Brahman (*Purusha*) serving as the host of the sacrifice (*yajamana*) and His bodily parts serving as the sacrificial material. The Creation Hymn from the Rigveda describes this event poetically. It states that Purusha, the Cosmic Being who manifested from Brahman, summoned the ancient gods and requested them to perform a grand sacrifice using parts of Himself as the sacrifice. The ancient gods who presided over it as divine priests obliged and performed the sacrifice, from which emerged everything.

According to the second version, creation happens when Brahman (*Purusha*) engages in austere meditation (tapas), a form of internal sacrifice. A verse (1.8) from the Mundaka Upanishad [2] describes it. " Brahman expands by the heat (*tapah*) generated from penance (tapas), and then from Him, food (materiality) is born; from food life (*prana*), mind (*mana*), truth (*satyam*), the worlds (*loka*), obligatory duties (*karma*), and immortality (*amrtam*)." In other words, Brahman unleashed His transformative universal energy through an internal sacrifice (tapas) and created within Himself numerous parts (tattvas), forms, worlds, order, and regularity (*Rta*). All names and forms which characterize the creation arise from Brahman's penance.

In a sense, we all are creators with infinite capacities and possibilities because the Self and the creative energies of Brahman are hidden in each of us. Although much of our creative potential remains concealed and suppressed due to the impurities and limitations of our natural faculties, yet, within those limitations, we can still create many things and realities. With the limited resources at our disposal, we can still create beautiful forms out of lifeless materials, awaken our hidden energies to perform extraordinary tasks, control many aspects of our lives and destinies, or create conditions and circumstances according to our dreams, desires, knowledge, intelligence, and effort. We can direct our minds to achieve difficult goals, reinforce them with affirmative thoughts and emotions, realize our dreams and desires through persistence, or use our thoughts, dreams, desires, and actions to create our lives and destinies or our future. There is no limit to what our minds can conceive or imagine. In infinite ways, we can use our imagination to create and destroy whatever we can think of without the constraints of time, space, or ability. We create our karmas through actions, and through them, we create our current and future lives, our joys and sorrows, or our suffering. All these potencies, possibilities, and faculties point to our inescapable connection with Brahman and our inherent divine nature. If Nature has clouded our consciousness and imprisoned us in physical bodies, we have the power to break free from Her control and escape from our bondage to the cycle of births and deaths.

The Upanishads describe how the one eternal formless Self (*amurtam*) differentiated Himself into many names (*nama*) and forms (*rupa*). The differentiation happened at many levels. While we are not certain of the order in which it happened, the Upanishads contain some vague references to it. They suggest that in the beginning, everything was either in balance or restful. There were no movements or activity. Then, Brahman (*Purusha*) manifested from Himself and differentiated the five elements (*mahabhutas*). He produced Water (*apa*) first. The froth of the water solidified and became the Earth. While He was resting on it, his essence of brightness came forth as Fire. Next, He divided Himself into three: the Earth, Mid-region (*antariksham*), and Heaven. Then, He differentiated names and forms (*nama rupa*) and bodily parts. He became the vital force in breath, the voice in speech, the seeing in the eye, the hearing in the ear, and the thinking in the mind. Next, He differentiated beings of different kinds: asuras, gods, humans, animals, and other creatures. He created gods of virility (*kshatra*): Indra, Varuna, Soma, Rudra, Parjanya, Yama, and Isana; He created gods of commonality (vis): Vasus, Rudras, Adityas, Visvadevas and Maruts; and He created the earthly god Pusan (Brihad 1.4.4 and 1.4.11-14). He differentiated various things from Himself, such as Time (*Kala*), Order (Rta), Divine Laws and Obligatory Duties (*Dharma*), Karma, and Samsara (the cycle of births and deaths). He also differentiated people into various classes (varnas) according to their modes (*gunas*) and natures into Brahmanas, Kshatriyas, Vaishyas, and Sudras. He established Dharma (duties), Karma, and Rta (order, regularity) to ensure that life and creation progressed as intended and that all the jivas lived and acted according to their essential nature.

The Aitareya Upanishad presents a slightly different version. It states that in the beginning, the Self was alone. He thought, "Let me create the worlds." He created the space above (*ambha*) with heaven as its support, the world of light (mariachi) with mid-region as its support, and the mortal world (mara) with the earth as its support. Beneath the earth are the waters (*apah*). After creating these worlds, He thought of creating the Guardians of the Worlds. From the waters, He drew forth a person (Purusha) and gave him a shape. As He brooded upon him, the mouth, the nostrils, the eyes, the ears, the skin, the heart, the navel, and the generative organ were separated. From them again, speech, fire, breath, air, sight, the sun, hearing, the quarters of space, the hair, plants and trees, mind, moon, out-breath, death, semen, and water were separated. When He created the divinities, He made them the abode of hunger and thirst and made the human beings the abode of the divinities. He created food (energy) and established breath to support the human body and its various functions. Finally, He made the Self enter the body through an opening in the skull known as the suture (*vidriti*). Much of what is stated here is symbolic. In summary, we may say that Brahman manifested out of Himself as the Creator, the Cosmic Being, and differentiated numerous things from Himself, from the lowest to the highest worlds and from humans to gods, to manifest the whole existence.

What we have described so far about the nature and process of creation is just a fraction of the knowledge hidden in the Vedas, taken from a few verses in the Upanishads. There can be other views and interpretations. The Upanishads are not well-organized scriptures. Those who are familiar with them know that they contain fragments of superlative knowledge about various metaphysical subjects and concepts, which require considerable effort to make sense of. They are also incomplete and probably incongruous since what we have today may be parts of what has survived from much larger texts that were lost. Our interpretation of them may not necessarily be correct since we cannot be definitive about the true meaning of the ritual symbolism found in them. The Vedas belong to a period about which we know but little except what we can glean from the literature of that period. Even their dates are uncertain. We may find in them a progressive development of speculative philosophy and a gradual enfoldment of a Vedic worldview on creation and the origins of the universe. The earlier views might have subsequently developed into various schools of philosophy (Darshanas), which discuss the spiritual and material aspects of creation or existence. Therefore, we must be careful about whatever conclusions we draw from them and consider them with an open mind.

The Vedas, especially the Upanishads, are foundational to the six schools of Hindu philosophy (*Darshanas*). Based on them, they present their arguments and theories about the nature of reality and various worldly phenomena. If we want to understand them and draw conclusions and inferences, we must study the Vedas and develop an insight into their ritual and spiritual aspects and their hidden symbolism. The Upanishads constitute the end parts of the Vedas. They belong to various ancient teacher traditions, composed at different times, and cannot truly be considered as authoritative and inviolable as the Samhitas, Brahmanas, and Aranyakas. However, they contain profound knowledge and, in a way, reflect the maturity of the Vedic thought or, rather, the culmination of it. The most ancient Upanishads most certainly complement the ritual knowledge of the Vedas to which they are attached, offering spiritual insights. At least, that was the plan or the intent they were meant to serve. Hence, they are known as the Vedanta, the end part of the Vedas. Since they contain fragmentary or constricted knowledge. for proper understanding, they should be studied in the context of the entire Vedas, which is not the case today. We study them as independent texts without any reference to the other parts of the Vedas to which they belong.

Therefore, we do not see the whole truth they represent and their correlation with the rest of the knowledge found in the Vedas. Vedanta without the knowledge of the Vedas is like knowledge without a rudder. Indeed, any interpretation or commentary on the Upanishads must be done in the context of the other three portions of the Vedas to which they are attached. Unfortunately, this is not the case. We study them as independent texts, and in doing so, we miss the true meaning of many verses and, thereby, their mystic significance. The Upanishads themselves suggest how important it is to know both the higher knowledge and the lower knowledge. As the Chandogya Upanishad (5.24.1) states, performing the sacrificial rituals without having the right knowledge of the Self and Brahman is like removing the coals and pouring the oblations on dead ashes. The Isa Upanishad states that those who study only the ritual or the spiritual knowledge found in the Vedas, ignoring the other, enter sunless worlds. However, those who study both attain Brahman with the help of each. The instruction is clear. The Vedas must be studied as a whole to understand their parts correctly and put them into practice to attain the ultimate end, Moksha.

According to the Vedas, God is the cause and source, and creation, consisting of all the worlds and beings, is the effect. Their relationship is the subject of much speculation in Hinduism. The answer depends upon whether a cause is different from the effect or effects it produces or in any way related to the latter. V. Raghavan [3], a noted Indian scholar, described three different theories of causation found in the six schools of Hinduism, namely "origination (*arambha*), transformation (*parinama*) and transfiguration (*vivarta*). According to the first theory, known as Asatkaryavada, effects originate from the cause as new because they do not exist until they manifest. The Nyaya and Vaishesika

Schools hold this view. This theory ignores that causes may transform into effects. According to the second theory, known as Satkaryavada or Parinamavada, effects are preexistent in their causes and manifest differently when they are activated. In other words, effects do not arise without causes, have the same nature as causes, and manifest when causes transform or evolve (parinama) into them when the right conditions or circumstances are present. This theory presupposes that effects pre-exist in their causes and become separated when external or internal factors activate the causes. The Samkhya and Yoga Schools approve it. According to the third theory, known as Vivartavada, an effect is only a transfiguration of the cause, whereby it appears differently. The Monistic Schools (Advaita) uphold the third view and acknowledge the world as an appearance, a dreamlike condition, which presents itself differently to different beings according to their states of mind, desires, and levels of consciousness. When the illusion is removed, one realizes that Brahman alone is real, and one is Brahman. As we hear from the Brihadaranyaka Upanishad, "Whoever knows thus, 'I am Brahman,' becomes this all." This is in contrast to the Satkaryavada, which holds that both Brahman and this world are real, and bondage arises due to ignorance of one's true nature.

Footnotes

1. In the Vedic cosmogony, there are hierarchies of gods. The ancient gods are usually unknown and remain in the background as deities of remote regions of heaven. They are the most ancient divinities, hailing from the previous creation cycles and ready to take up greater responsibilities in future creations as the highest gods. We may compare them to the Bodhisattvas of the Buddhist religion.
2. Mundaka Upanishad, Section 1, Verse 8, From the Selected Upanishads Edited and Translated by Jayaram V, 2013.
3. Part III, Hinduism, Chapter 13: Moksha, The Fourth End of Man, from the Sources of Indian Tradition, which is part of a Three Volume Series on Introduction to Oriental Civilization, edited by Wm. Theodore de Bary, Columbia University Press, 1958.

The Attributes of Brahman

The Upanishads abound in Brahman's descriptions. They explain His majesty, mystery, glory, and absolute state, using various symbols and ritual terms that are difficult to understand unless one is familiar with the Vedic tradition and symbolism. The verses reflect the difficulties of reducing an absolute and universal reality into concrete and relative terms to express the inexpressible and present them to people who are rather conditioned to see reality relatively and objectively as what their minds present to them according to their knowledge, ignorance, and intelligence. In some Upanishads, we notice the patience of seers like Uddalaka Aruni, Angirasa, Pippalada, and Yajnavalkya trying to translate the universality and infinity of Brahman into familiar terms and explain them to their disciples who were not familiar with the subject. From the same Upanishads, we come to know that even the gods were not very familiar with the knowledge of an unknown, mysterious, and unfathomable Brahman, and they were not very pleased if men tried to know Him before them.

The Upanishads also explain the dangers of not knowing Him correctly. According to one of the stories found in the Chandogya Upanishad, Vairochana, the leader of the demons, once went to Brahma to learn about the Self. From the initial teachings of Brahma, as the story was narrated, he hastily drew the wrong conclusion that the body was the Self. Satisfied with that incomplete knowledge rather thoughtlessly, he returned to his world and taught the same doctrine to other demons. As a result, the demons fell into delusion and lost an opportunity to transcend their limitations and become immortal. To this day, they delusionally believe that the body is the true Self and live accordingly, pursuing passions and pleasures. Indra, the leader of the gods, on the other hand, was not content with Brahma's initial teaching that the reflection one saw in the water was the Self. Doubts assailed him since he could not reconcile with the fact that if the body were the Self, then it would be subject to death, suffering, aging, and sickness, which was not the case. Therefore, he went back to Brahma and requested him to teach him further. Eventually, after Brahma used a series of misleading analogies to teach him what the Self was not, he eventually understood the true nature of the Self and attained self-realization. What it means is that one should overcome misconceptions and delusional thinking to discern the Self from the not-self.

Vedic seers, the knowers of Brahman and masters of Brahma Vidyas, envisioned Brahman both as an impersonal universal Self (*amurtam*) and as the Lord of the Universe (*murtam*), who was to be feared as well as revered. They regarded Him with both awe and fear. In the Katha Upanishad, Lord Yama, the Lord of the underworld, explains to Nachiketa that the world moves in fear of Brahman. He says, "In fear of Him, the fire burns, the sun shines, the clouds rain, and the winds blow. In fear of Him, death stalks about to kill." We find a familiar emotion in the Svetasvatara Upanishad, where the seers address Rudra with devotion as well as fear (Sevta.4.22). The fear in this context is not the ordinary fear arising from feelings of insecurity or anxiety but the fear arising from reverence, awe, and humility. It is the respect that masquerades as fear.

The attributes of Brahman are useful not only for intellectual speculation but also for regular contemplation. According to the Brihadaranyaka Upanishad (2.4.5), by seeing (*darsana*), hearing (*sravanam*), thinking (*matyam*), and understanding (*vijnanam*), one comes to know about the Self. The Advaita school recommends three main approaches to knowing Brahman: Sravanam (hearing), Mananam (remembering), and Nidhidhyasanam (contemplating). One may follow any method, but what is important is establishing the mind in the Self with devotion and reaching a stage where the duality between the subject and the object or the Self and the not-self disappears, and one dwells in the Self without distinction. Yoga Upanishads recommend contemplative methods such as the chanting of mystic syllables and mantras, withdrawal of the mind and senses, concentration on an object or a small dot (trataka), contemplation, and contemplation with control and balance (*samyama*).

We may use the various names and attributes of Brahman to establish the mind in Him or know Him, using all such methods recommended by the scriptures, seers, and sages. Meditating on the attributes of Brahman is a proven technique followed by the various traditions and sects of Hinduism to purify the mind and the body, overcome delusion, and develop an insight into the essential nature of things and reality. Most of the attributes also apply to the individual Self. Hence, it also helps us discern the distinction between our true and false selves and between our higher and lower natures so that we can see the reality about ourselves. The following attributes of Brahman are collected from various Upanishads. Some of them are positive, while some are negative. The positive ones describe what Brahman is, His powers, and His supremacy. They throw light upon His particular powers and aspects by which He is known. The negative attributes denote what Brahman is not or does not mean. They are useful for practicing the not-this-not-this or the neti-neti technique recommended by the seers to know Brahman through a process of elimination.

Positive attributes

- Amrtamaya: The immortal
- Anekarupam: Of diverse forms
- Atman: The individual Self
- Atmantaryami: The Inner Controller
- Avyapyadesyam: Not nameable
- Bhagavan: The Lord
- Bhavabhavakaram: Maker of existence and non-existence
- Bhavagrahyam: To be grasped by feelings
- Bhokta: The Enjoyer
- Bhutadhipatih: Lord of beings
- Bhutapalah: Protector of beings
- Bhuta-yonim: Source of beings
- Brahman: Brahman
- Daivatam: Highest god

- Devadhipa: Lord of the gods
- Devatmanam: Self of the gods
- Dhruvam: The Constant
- Divyam: Divine
- Drsta: The Seer
- Eka Deva: The one God
- Eka Devam: One God
- Guhacharam: Mover in the secret places
- Gunesah: Lord of qualities
- Guni: Virtuous
- Hara: The Lord
- Hiranmaya: Resplendent
- Hiranyagarbha: The Golden Egg
- Isam: The Lord
- Isana: The Ruler
- Isata: One who rules
- Jalavan: One who spreads the net
- Jyotisman: The Luminous One
- Kalakarah: The Author or Creator of Time
- Kalasargakaram: Maker of arts and sounds
- Kapilam: The Red Seer
- Karmadhyaksha: Ordainer of all deeds
- Kevalah: Alone
- Krsnam: Black
- Kshetrajna: Knower of the field
- Lohitam: Red
- Loka Adhisritha: In whom the worlds rest
- Mahad Yasa: Great Glory
- Mahan: The Great
- Mahantam: Great
- Maharsih: Great Seer

- Mahatma: The Great Self
- Mahesvaram: The Great Lord
- Mantri: The Thinker
- Mayinam: Wielder of Maya
- Narayana: The Lord of waters
- Niskalam: Pure
- Nitya: Eternal
- Param: Highest
- Paramam: Supreme
- Parameswara: Supreme Lord
- Paratparah: Higher than the highest
- Pati: Husband
- Pavitram: Pure
- Prabhu: The Lord
- Prakasavan: The Shining One
- Prapanchopasamam: Into which the world ends
- Prathamaja: The First-Born
- Pratyagatma: Witness Self
- Preritaram: Mover of all
- Puranam: The Ancient
- Purusha: The Person
- Rudra: The Red One
- Rudra: The Terrible
- Sad: Being
- Saksi: Witness
- Samanhitam: Well fixed
- Sambhu: Beneficent
- Santam: Peaceful
- Santamaya: Filled with peace
- Sarvabhutaadhinivasa: Established in all
- Sarvabhutantaratma: Indweller of all beings

- Sarvagatam: Omnipresent
- Sarvajnaj: Knower of all
- Sarvasya adhipati: Ruler of all
- Sarvasya vasi: Controller of all
- Sarvasyesanah: The lord of all
- Sarvatmanam: The Self of all
- Sarvavyapi: All Pervading
- Sarvesvarah: Lord of all
- Sasvata: Permanent, everlasting
- Satyakamah: Whose desires are pure
- Satyam: Truth
- Savitr Varenyam: Light of Savitr
- Setuh: Connecting Bridge
- Shiva: Lord Shiva
- Sivam: Auspicious
- Srota: The listener
- Subhram: Pure
- Suklam: White
- Sukram: Pure
- Suksmati-suksmam: Minute of the minutest
- Susuksmam: Very subtle
- Tantunabha: Spider
- Tejomaya: The Shining One
- Trayam: The Triad
- Vaivasyanaram: The Universal Self
- Varadam: Giver of blessings
- Varishtam: The Greatest
- Vibhum: All Pervading
- Vijnantr: The Knower
- Viraj: The World
- Vishnu: Lord Vishnu

- Visvadhipa: The ruler of all
- Visvakarma: The maker of all
- Visvarupa: Universal Form
- Visvasvadharini: The supporter of all
- Visvatobahu: Hands-on on every side
- Visvatomukha: With a face on every side
- Visvayonih: The Source of all
- Vyaktam: Manifested

Negative descriptions

Negative descriptions suggest what Brahman is not. These descriptions are useful to know Brahman by knowing what He is not. The context in which they are used is also important. For example, when we say Brahman is Abahyam, it does not mean that Brahman is not external to us. This description refers to Atman, which is always internal to the jiva.

- Abahyam: Not external
- Abhayam: Without fear
- Achaksuh: Without sight
- Achaksuksam: Without eyes
- Acchayam: Not shadow
- Achintyam: Unthinkable
- Adirgham: Not long
- Adisa: The ancient Lord
- Adresyam: Not perceptible
- Adrstam: Not seen
- Advaitam: Nondual
- Advitiyam: Without a second
- Agandham: Without smell
- Agotram: Without lineage
- Agrahyam: Not graspable
- Aghoram: Not terrifying
- Ahrasvam: Not short

- Ajah: Not born
- Ajaram: Not decaying
- Akarta: Not active
- Aksaram: Not perishable
- Alaksanam: Without distinctive marks
- Alohitam: Not glowing red
- Amanah: Without mind
- Amatmam: Without thought
- Amatram: Without measure
- Amtratah: Not mortal
- Amukham: Without a mouth
- Amurtam: Formless
- Anadi: Without beginning
- Anakasam: Not space
- Anantam: Without an end
- Ananu: Not small
- Anidakhyam: Without body
- Apanipadam: Without hands and feet
- Apapakasini: Showing no evil
- Apranam: Without breath
- Arasam: Not tasty
- Asabdam: Without sound
- Asad: Non-being
- Asangam: Not attached
- Asariram: Without body
- Asiryah: Not destructible
- Asneham: Not bonding
- Asparsam: Without touch
- Asrotram: Without ears
- Asrutam: Not heard of
- Asthulam: Not gross

- Atamah: Not darkness
- Atejaksam: Without radiance
- Avac: Without Voice
- Avarnam: Without color
- Avayu: Not air
- Avijnatam: Not known
- Avyaktam: Not manifested
- Avyaktam: The unmanifested
- Avyaya Jyotih: Never diminishing light
- Avyayam: Not decaying

Brahmopasana – The Paths To Liberation

The various traditions and sects of Hinduism identify many paths to Brahman which leads to liberation and immortality or freedom from samsara. The most important ones are the Path of Duty or Action (*Karma*), the Path of Knowledge (*Jnana*), the Path of Devotion (*Bhakti*), and the Path of Renunciation (*Sannyasa*). The Bhagavadgita combines these to suggest a holistic approach suitable for both householders and ascetics alike. It also prescribes a few additional methods, such as the Yoga of Self-control (*Atma Samyama Yoga*) and the Yoga of Intelligence (Buddhi Yoga), which help seekers practice these yogas more effectively with purity and discernment. It also suggests that one can realize Brahman by contemplating Him in three ways: "Aum, Tat, Sat." Aum is the sacred syllable, Aum; Tat means 'That,' the transcendental Self, in contrast to this, the world or the body; and Sat means truth, goodness, virtue, any good action, and reality in contrast to the untruth, any desire-ridden action, evil deed, or passion, or the illusory nature of this world.

We find aspects of these yogas or methods in the Upanishads also. For example, Maitri Upanishad recognizes the importance of knowledge, duty, and meditation in the realization of Brahman. Self-purification or cultivation of virtues, which leads to the predominance of sattva (purity), is a part of the duty. According to the Upanishad (4.3), the solution to resolve the problem of the elemental body (*bhutatma*) is acquiring the knowledge of the Vedas (*Veda Vidya*) and practicing the obligatory duties that arise from one's essential nature (*svadharmanucharanam*), which is in turn determined by the triple modes (gunas) namely sattva, rajas, and tamas. The duties are determined by the Varnashrama Dharma, which prescribes specific duties for each phase of human life (*svāshrama*), namely life as a celibate student (*Brahmacharya*), householder (*Grihasta*), hermit or forest-dweller (*Vanaprastha*), and ascetic (*Sannyasa*). One must respect these Ashrama Dharma or the obligatory duties that pertain to these four phases. Performing austerities (penances and sacrifices) without performing one's duties in the four phases (Ashramas) is improper. At the same time, one should not ignore austerities also. They must be performed at the right time without ignoring the duties. By performing them according to the Ashrama Dharma, one obtains purity (sattva), and from purity, one gains a tranquil mind (manas), and from a tranquil mind, one realizes the Self. Realizing the Self, one never returns to the mortal world. The Upanishad (4.4) also identifies three ways to attain knowledge of Brahman (Brahma vidya), namely right knowledge (vidya), austerity (tapas), and contemplation (chinta). Collectively, they are known as the triad (trikena) and together constitute the worship of Brahman (Brahmopasana). Whoever worships Brahman with the triad declares the Upanishad, goes beyond the world of gods, and reaches the state of supreme divinity (adhidaivatam). He attains inexhaustible happiness and freedom from death and achieves union with the Self.

With regard to the question of who should be worshipped, the Upanishad suggests that one may worship any divinity to whom one is devoted. One may worship fire, air, sun, time, breath, food, Brahma, Vishnu, Rudra, or whatever deity it may be because Brahman is all (sarvam). By worshipping any of them, one moves higher and higher, and in the end, when things perish, one attains Brahman only. The same Upanishad identifies Brahma, Vishnu, and Rudra as the three deities (trinity) and suggests that one may worship Brahman outwardly by following the sun or inwardly by following the vital breath or energy (prana). The Upanishad is averse to the practice of image worship (5.3). Unlike some scriptures, it states that Brahman is both with form (murtam) and without form (amurtam). The formless Brahman is real (satyam), while the one with form is unreal (asatyam). The formless Brahman is the light and the sun. Therefore, one should meditate on the sun as Aum and become one with it. This makes sense because the absolute state of Brahman is real and eternal, whereas all his manifestations (murtis) are temporary and cease to exist with each cycle of creation.

The same Upanishad refers to the six-fold yoga (*sadanga yoga*) for achieving oneness, which consists of breath control (*pranayama*), withdrawal of the senses (*pratyahara*), meditation (*dhyana*), concentration (*dharana*), contemplation with self-inquiry (*tarka*) and mental absorption or the absorption of the mind in the Self (*samadhi*). The key to samadhi is the vital breath. When the flow of energy, which is the source of all, is controlled or suspended within oneself, yogis enter into the fourth state, Turya or the transcendental state, and merge their thought with the non-thought (*achittam*) to attain that subtle being (*lingam*) that is unthinkable (*achintyam*), hidden (*guhyam*) and the highest (*uttamam*). Yoga is described in the Upanishad as a very effective method for self-realization, but it is useless without detachment. If a person practices yoga for six months with constant detachment, he accomplishes the purpose of yoga and becomes eternally free (*nityamukta*), but if he is driven by modes of rajas (passion) and tamas (ignorance and delusion) or if he is attached to his children, wife or family, he will never be successful in yoga (6.29).

Purity (*sattva*) and virtue play an important role in the realization of Brahman. Without them both knowledge and meditation are useless. The Subala Upanishad states that the way to liberation is cultivating the six means: truthfulness (satyam), charity (*danam*), austerity (*tapas*), fasting (*anasaka*), chastity (brahmacharya), and complete indifference to the worldly objects (*nirvedana*). One should also remember the three Da's: Dama (self-control), Daya (compassion), and Dana (charity). These three principal virtues are also referred to in the Brihadaranyaka Upanishad (7.2) in an allegory in which Brahma, the father of all the beings of the three worlds, prescribes self-control for gods, compassion for the demons, and charity for humans, knowing their chief weaknesses.

The Isavasya Upanishad identifies two types of worlds: the radiant worlds of gods and celestial beings (*Surya lokas*) filled with the purity of sattva and the sunless underworlds of demons and evil beings (*asura lokas*) that are covered in blinding darkness filled with the impurities of rajas and tamas. This is in line with Hindu cosmology, according to which creation consists of seven upper realms of light (*sattva*) and seven lower realms of darkness (*tamas*), with the earth in the middle serving as the bridge between light and dark realms and as the battleground between good and evil forces (gods and demons). Because of their peculiar status in the cosmic hierarchy, human nature contains both divine and demonic qualities and propensities, and depending upon which way they learn, their karma and future are determined. They can ascend to the worlds of light or descend into the worlds of darkness according to their actions and desires. The gods and demons always look to the world of mortal beings for their nourishment to satisfy their hunger and increase their strength and support. If humans follow demonic ways and nourish the demons with their selfish thoughts and actions, they will gain strength and spread their influence in this world, and emboldened further with renewed vigor and strength, they will invade even the higher worlds. However, if they engage in righteous actions selflessly, nourish the gods through sacrifices, and uphold the Dharma, the gods will gain strength and protect the humans from the demons.

Maitri Upanishad also identifies two types of knowledge: avidya and vidya. Avidya means ignorance or that which is not vidya or the right knowledge. However, the type of ignorance that is referred to here is not intellectual ignorance but the ignorance of the Self. It also refers to the worldly knowledge that is devoid of spirituality and purity and is used for purely selfish and materialistic purposes. According to Shankaracharya, avidya refers to the knowledge of Vedic rites and rituals (*karmakanda*), and vidya refers to the knowledge of meditating on the Self. However, not all scholars agree with him since Bhagavadgita clearly states that performing obligatory duties (such as daily sacrifices) also leads to self-purification. Avidya is the knowledge that increases our ignorance and illusion and, thereby, our suffering and bondage. Vidya is the knowledge that makes you spiritually self-aware and reminds you of the need to work for your salvation by simplifying your life and cultivating dispassion and detachment towards worldly enjoyment. The Vedas themselves are structured into two main parts based on this division. However, the divisions are not precise and sometimes overlap. For example, the Brihadaranyaka Upanishad forms part of the Satapatha Brahmana.

Different results are expected when people pursue these two branches of knowledge. If people pursue avidya (worldly goals) by performing sacrifices and obligatory duties for selfish ends, they may please the gods and obtain material wealth, power, and happiness. However, those temporary gains strengthen their desires and attachments, prolong or increase their suffering, and delay their liberation. If they pursue the knowledge of the Self and Brahman (*vidya*) and engage in spiritual practice or nishkama karma (desireless actions), they have greater chances of attaining liberation. By cultivating virtues, detachment, sameness, and equanimity and overcoming desires and attachments, they become equal to the pairs of opposites, withstand suffering, attain freedom from karma (*naishkarmya siddhi*), and become absorbed in the Self. However, for liberation, both types of knowledge are important. In the initial stages, one must perform sacrifices and obligatory duties and pursue knowledge with an eye toward liberation. As they advance on the path of karma yoga and perform their obligatory duties as a sacrifice without desiring their fruit, they advance further and quickly progress towards liberation. This is the essence of karma sannyasa yoga, which culminates in knowledge, devotion, self-control, renunciation, and liberation.

Hence, Isavasya Upanishad emphasizes the importance of both vidya and avidya because both are necessary for success and fulfillment in this life and liberation here. The good deeds one performs in this life are equally important since they are necessary for the continuation of life and the transmigration of souls. For discerning yogis, both are knowledge only but with different implications in the four phases of their lives. Therefore, the Upanishad suggests that one should pursue both to attain eternal life, crossing the ocean of Samsara. It even suggests that suffering is inescapable for those who pursue one and ignore the other. Householders must perform their obligatory duties to uphold God's creation and do their part. At the same time, they should not ignore the ultimate purpose of life, which is liberation. Hence, it declares, "Those who worship avidya alone enter into blinding darkness, but those who worship vidya alone enter into even a greater darkness." For a holistic and fulfilling life, one must pursue both the path of knowledge (*Jnana Margam*) and the path of action (*Karma Margam*). With spiritual wealth, one attains immortality, and with material wealth, one serves God and His creation. The rites of passage (*samskaras*), such as the sacrificial ceremonies associated with one's conception, birth, initiation, marriage, pregnancy, death, etc., are especially useful for the embodied souls when they depart from this world or return to it.

Early Vedic people believed in the existence of two upper worlds: Pitr Loka, or the world of ancestors in the sphere of the moon, and Amara Loka, or the world of Brahman in the sphere of the sun. The Vedas declare that when embodied souls depart from here, they go to either of these worlds according to their actions (karma) and the time of the year in which they died. Those who attain liberation go to the immortal world of Brahman by the Northern Path and will never return. Those who die without resolving their karma go to the world of ancestors, where they stay until they are let go by gods and allowed to return to take another birth. As time went by, Vedic people expanded their vision of the Cosmos and included other worlds. One of them is the underworld or hell, to which sinners are said to depart when they die to suffer from the consequence of their evil actions. Yama, the teacher of the Katha Upanishad, who is said to personify Dharma, is the lord of this world. He ensures that no one escapes from their evil deeds. Even the pious souls must pass through his court and pay for their intentional or unintentional transgressions before they move on to the ancestral heaven. Those who attain freedom from karma and whose karma is squared off go directly to the immortal heaven.

The early Vedic tradition identified three heavens: the ancestral heaven, Indra's heaven, and the immortal and highest heaven of Brahman. Subsequently, we see a further evolution of the thought according to which our world is just one of the several worlds in the universe of Brahman (*Brahmanda*) ruled by several Brahmas and inhabited by beings of different types. The immortal heavens also became several, such as the heaven of Brahma, Vishnu, Shiva,

Shakti, and warriors' heaven, a special upside-down heaven called Trishanku created by Vishwamitra with his spiritual power in a star constellation.

The Upanishadic seers knew the value of sacrificial rites and rituals in human life, but they had deep reservations about overindulgence in them or about their significance in life and liberation or achieving immortality. For example, Mundaka Upanishad declares that rituals are like "unsafe rafts for crossing the ocean of Samsara or the world of births and deaths. Those who try to cross that ocean with those poor rafts are doomed to suffer from shipwreck." The argument continues," Ignorant of their ignorance, yet wise in their estimate, these deluded people proud of their learning go round and round like the blind, led by the blind. Living in darkness, lacking in knowledge and discernment, unaware of any higher good or goal, they fall again and again into the sea."

Isavasya Upanishad, just as the Bhagavadgita, identifies two methods of worshipping Brahman (*Brahmopasana*): worshipping the unmanifested and the formless (asambhuta) and worshipping the manifested with form (*sambhuta*). Shankara identifies asambhuta with Prakriti (undifferentiated Nature) and the Cosmic Being (*Purusha*) with Hiranyagarbha (the cosmic germ or universal soul). This is in line with the basic belief that Brahman is immortal, indestructible, and immutable and contains within Himself Purusha and Prakriti in their undifferentiated aspects. In other words, the absolute state of Brahman will always be asambhuta and cannot become manifested (*sambhuta*) at any time. What manifests or becomes sambhuta is His materiality or Prakriti. In His original and absolute state, Prakriti remains undifferentiated and inactive. When creation begins, she becomes differentiated from His absolute state and manifests with her parts (*tattvas*), modes (*gunas*), and dynamism (*chaitanyam*). Containing the pure and absolute Brahman within herself as her pure Self, she manifests the whole creation.

Isvara, the Cosmic Being, is the first evolute in that process. He becomes the Creator God (*Isvara*) with Prakriti as His creative force. He is the Supreme Lord of the Universe, who goes by many names and forms, and whom we worship as Brahma, Vishnu, Shiva, Krishna, and so on. All the living beings (jivas) are His replicas only. Higher than Him is Brahman Himself, the pure, absolute, and unmanifested Universal Self, who cannot be seen and difficult to worship. These two aspects of Brahman, the Manifested and the Unmanifested, are also known as Saguna and Nirguna Brahman or Brahman with and without Nature's modes (*gunas*). The two are also called in some texts as the Being and the Non-Being. According to the Isavasya Upanishad, different results accrue from the worship of the unmanifested Brahman and the manifested Brahman.

The Bhagavadgita states that worshipping the unmanifested or formless Brahman is difficult. Therefore, one should worship Isvara, the Supreme Lord, who alone can liberate people with His grace according to their faith, purity, and devotion. He also says that those who worship gods, demigods, etc., go to them, but those who worship Brahman go to Him only. Hence, in the devotional traditions of Hinduism, devotees worship the manifested Brahman, and in the ascetic traditions, seekers of liberation may initially meditate on both aspects but eventually settle with the formless and infinite Self. However, Maitri Upanishad declares that meditation on the formless Brahman is superior. It makes sense because only the adepts, the conquerors of their minds, senses, and bodies who excel in complete self-control (*vijitatma*), can successfully meditate on the formless Brahman without distractions and disturbances. That in itself is a great accomplishment.

Worshipping gods through sacrifices and domestic rituals is an integral aspect of Hinduism. According to the traditional Vedic model, which is now a part of Hinduism and which we have briefly discussed before, a householder must pursue the four ideals (*purusharthas*) of human life: Dharma (righteous duties that are obligatory and morally imperative), Artha (righteous wealth), Kama (righteous pleasure), and Moksha (final liberation). Dharma is important in the first phase of human life when one pursues religious and vocational knowledge as a student (*Brahmachari*), living righteously. Dharma, Artha, and Kama are important in the second phase of life when one performs obligatory duties as a householder (*Grihasta*) on the path of righteousness. However, one should perform them, keeping the ultimate aim, Moksha, in mind, which means one should live virtuously and avoid unlawful conduct. In the third phase, as a forest dweller or hermit (*Vanaprasthi*), Dharma and Moksha become priorities as one prepares for the next phase of renunciation. In the last phase, as an ascetic or renunciant (*sannyasi*), one must renounce all other aims and every preoccupation and pursue Moksha only. The Vedas approve of this basic model of righteous living, which several Upanishads, such as the Isa Upanishad, also echo.

Two paths are open to the devotees who worship Brahman or His highest manifestations. One is reserved for the householders who perform their obligatory duties to fulfill their desires and live righteously, serving the aims of creation. The other is reserved for the ascetics, who renounce worldly life and dedicate themselves to realizing Brahman. The Upanishads refer to them as the gray path and the radiant path, respectively—the former leads to rebirth and suffering, and the latter to liberation and immortality. In the Katha Upanishad, Lord Yama explains to young Nachiketa about these two paths, saying one is the pleasant (*preya*) and the other is the preferable (*sreya*). They serve different purposes. Those who follow the first one fail in their aim to achieve Moksha, and those who follow the second do well in resolving their karma and escaping from samsara, the cycle of births and deaths. Endowed with discrimination, the wise ones (dhiras) choose the auspicious path, while the shallow-minded (*manda buddhis*) choose the easy, pleasant, or convenient path.

People choose these paths according to their knowledge (*vidya*) and ignorance (*avidya*). Therefore, Katha Upanishad further states (1.2.6) that they lead to divergent results. Brahman is difficult to attain. One can know Him neither by hearing nor by reasoning. By practicing Adhyatma Yoga (establishing the mind in the Self), one comes to know the primal God, who is difficult to be seen (*durdasam*), well-hidden (gudham), and dwells beyond reach in the cave of the heart (*guhatitam*). Adhyatma yoga is an inward process in which one withdraws the mind and the senses from the objects and enjoyments of the world into oneself and remains fully established in the thoughts of the Self with unwavering concentration and devotion. However, to achieve perfection in this, one must overcome the obstacles created by the senses, the mind, intelligence, desires, and attachments. In short, one must overcome Prakriti, the Great One, and all the distractions she creates to keep the beings bound to the world. When one overcomes them and attains the Cosmic Lord (Purusha), who dwells inside, one reaches the end of the journey and realizes that there is nothing else to attain. Yogis reach this auspicious state by restraining their speech in their minds, their minds in their intelligence, their intelligence in Prakriti, the Great One (*Mahat*), and Prakriti in Brahman or the pure Self (*Atman*).

A seeker of Brahman, according to the same Upanishad, does not take pride in this effort or consider it to be a proud achievement. He knows that self-realization does not arise from egoistic effort but from selfless effort by giving up egoism, desires, and delusion. It is a graceful effort attained through resolve, endurance, and stoical indifference to the dualities and hardships of life. For the seekers of liberation, success and failure are the same. They engage in practice without desires, leaving the result to God. As the Upanishad declares, the Self is known neither by instruction nor by intellect nor by hearing but only by those whom the Self chooses (1.2.23). Right conduct, self-control, and equanimity are important in this journey.

The Katha Upanishads also refer to the use of Aum in meditation. The Tantric texts refer to the use of other sacred syllables and seed (*bijakshara*) mantras. Aum is the best among them since it is Brahman in sound or seed form, which can germinate into a deep longing for liberation or open the doors for transcendental states. According to the descriptions found in several texts, it contains within itself the four states of Brahman (Mandukya), and by contemplating upon them, one can reach the highest state of self-absorption. Mundaka Upanishad suggests that a yogi should use Aum as the bow, the Self as the arrow, and Brahman as the target and hit it diligently without making a mistake. Then, becoming the arrow, he becomes established in Brahman and attains Him.

Desire, attachment, and passion, especially evil passions like anger, lust, pride, etc., are the main obstacles on the path. They cloud the mind and lead to suffering and rebirth. Faith, resolve, purification, and renunciation are the means by which one must overcome them. The ascetics, who have ascertained their knowledge of the Self or Brahman from the Upanishads (Vedanta) and cultivated purity (*suddha sattva*), by means of detachment, dispassion, and renunciation, enter the world of Brahman and become fully liberated.

The Svetasvatara Upanishad describes how one should practice meditation. To restrain the senses, yogis must choose a clean and secluded place, free from pebbles and protected from wind. They should hold their bodies steady, keeping the three upper parts (chest, neck, and head) erect, and withdraw their senses into their minds and their minds into their hearts. Having controlled all the movements, they should restrain prana in their bodies and breathe through their nostrils. With diminished breathing, they should enter tranquil states and become self-absorbed. When yogis practice this sincerely, they may see visions of certain objects in their meditation, such as fog, smoke, sunrise, golden images of deities, hills, mountains, sky, etc., and finally, when those images and modifications subside, they realize the true nature of Brahman in the deepest state of non-duality.

From the various descriptions found in the Upanishads, it is evident that there is no one sure method or approach to realize Brahman or achieve self-realization. As the Bhagavadgita states, the paths to God are numerous, and they all lead to Him only. The various methods and practices to achieve liberation found in the Vedic tradition or the Vedic scriptures are alternatives that suit different human personalities, temperaments, and essential natures. The Upanishads contain many streams of enlightened philosophical thought and fragments of valuable knowledge and wisdom about the Self, Brahman, purification, and liberation, drawn from the findings and teachings of numerous ancient seers and spiritual gurus who might have had their own teacher traditions and family lineages of great repute. Since the knowledge formed part of the secret teachings of the Upanishads and was meant for the most qualified and deserving students, they naturally guarded them until they found highly evolved souls ripe for liberation like Uddalaka Aruni, Yajnavalkya, or King Janaka.

Brahman as Isvara, the Personal God

The Upanishads are fragmented pieces of transcendental knowledge that survived the ravages of time, interspersed with mystic symbolism, which is sometimes difficult to decipher. They also abound in poetic expressions and superlative metaphors about Brahman and his vast dimensions. Although Upanishadic seers of great wisdom were dispassionate and lived austerely in secluded places, at times, they expressed their devotion, amazement, and joy at the thought of Brahman. In the following verse, we cannot miss the depth of emotions experienced by its composer upon seeing a vision of Brahman as the creator and destroyer of innumerable forms. *"Imperishable is the Lord of love, as from a blazing fire thousands of sparks leap forth, so do millions of beings arise from Him and return to Him."* These words also remind us of the thrill experienced by Arjuna upon seeing the universal form of Time (Kala), the Lord of Death, in the Bhagavadgita. Again, in the Katha Upanishad, we come across a very poetic and emphatic description of Brahman, similar to the previous one in devotional exuberance, *"In His robe are woven heaven and earth, mind, and body...He is the bridge from death to deathless life."*

Vedic people in ancient times worshipped Brahman both ritually and spiritually in at least seven different ways: by reciting the Vedas and other sacred literature, chanting sacred mantras, performing sacrifices as ordained by the Vedas, acquiring knowledge of Brahman through learned teachers, remembering His name, spending time in the company of pious people, and contemplating upon Him. They also engaged themselves in debates and discussions to prove their intellectual superiority or acquire new knowledge from others. At times, they were humble enough to admit their ignorance and approach enlightened masters like Ajatashatru or the sage Raikva to know the secrets of Brahman. Caste was not an important factor in those days, at least in the sectarian and ascetic traditions. The ascetics (*sannyasis*) came from different backgrounds. Many Kshatriyas taught Upanishads. Even low-caste people possessed knowledge of

Brahman, the Self, and liberation. However, a vast majority arrived at the knowledge of Brahman through a gradual enfoldment of their religious thought, having mastered the Vedas, the essentials of ritual worship, and knowing their value as well as their limitations. If they were lucky, they met learned masters and had the good fortune to learn from them. Otherwise, they remained ignorant. As a result, Brahman remained confined to spiritual practices and internal worship, while in the rituals, He remained in the background, known to a select few as the uplifting, facilitating, and joining power.

Brahman consumed the minds and hearts of the seers and ascetics who lived mostly in the forests and secluded places, away from worldly people and the humdrum of worldly life. They looked upon the body as a sacred field (*kshetra*), a playground of Prakriti, or an outer shell that embodied the individual Self, just as the whole world contained Brahman as its shining light and living embodiment. The body was the ground or the sacrificial altar where one would come face to face with the resplendent Self that was hidden behind the golden sheath (bliss body). Since the body was the temple of Isvara, it meant one had to spend considerable time purifying the mind and body; just as in ritual practices, the officiating priests paid attention to the purity and sanctity of ritual places and kept them free from impurities and evil influences out of respect for the deity.

The seers relied upon many practices and approaches to find Brahman in their own hearts, whom they referred to as Isvara or the Lord. The Upanishads reflect the diversity of these methods. For example, Subala Upanishad speaks of the six ways to attain the state of Brahman: truthfulness, charity, austerity, fasting, chastity, and complete indifference, in addition to the practice of self-control, charity, and compassion. Vedic meditation techniques and austerities are grounded in the belief that one can generate spiritual power or energy internally in the body as heat (*tapas*) and preserve it for future use, for removing the grossness of the body and cultivating sattva or for developing spiritual powers and perfections (*siddhis*). We do not know much about the specific techniques they used to accomplish it. The seers gave much importance to morality and conduct on the path of Brahman. They emphasized the need for morality, knowledge, virtue, faith, duty, clarity of thought, contemplation, sacrifice, celibacy, self-restraint, and regulation of breath to practice self-control, suppress desires and attachments, and experience Brahman's absolute state as one very Self. The techniques they used to achieve it might have served as the foundation for the emergence of several yogas that became popular subsequently.

Discipline, devotion, determination, guidance from a self-realized soul, purity of mind, mastery of the senses, self-control, and selfless actions performed without desires are a few qualities and practices mentioned in the scriptures as the prerequisites to reach Brahman. Those with faith, resolve, devotion, and the purity of intention and purpose truly qualify to succeed on the path. Liberation requires unburdening and unwinding all the accumulated thoughts, memories, and karma so that one can become empty, a nobody, and truly achieve the state of aloneness (kaivalya). It may take years of perseverance and several births to dislodge layers of illusion and ignorance that envelop the Self, become practically nonexistent, and see the Truth hidden behind the illusion of forms. True devotion arises only in that emptiness when the mind and body are fully restrained. In the Bhagavadgita (12:5-7), Lord Krishna suggests the importance of devotion in realizing Brahman in the following words, *"Difficult indeed is the path of those whose minds are set on the unexpressed (avyakta), because the goal of the unexpressed is painful to reach by the embodied souls. However, I rescue from the ocean of mortal life those who are solely devoted to me and who worship me and meditate on me with single-minded devotion, surrendering their actions to me."* The devotional approach to realizing Brahman is not well evident in the Upanishads except in some, like the Svetasvatara Upanishad, in which Brahman is compared to Rudra or Shiva as a personal God. He is also described as the wielder of illusion (*maya*) who contains within Himself both knowledge and ignorance. Here, you will find Brahman in personal and devotional terms as a deity with whom devotees can communicate, convey their prayers, and seek favors, unlike the more ancient Upanishads that regard Him in impersonal and neutral terms as Tat (that) who is beyond the mind and senses and cannot be communicated in the state of duality.

Brahman is the central theme of all the Upanishads. Nevertheless, they describe Him mostly in neutral, philosophical, and impersonal terms rather than personal or devotional. The Vedic seers conceived Brahman as the ultimate reality and the supreme power behind all creation. They looked upon Him as the personification of absolute freedom from births and deaths, the ultimate, eternal, and indestructible reality, and the Highest Goal (Parandhama) of human life that could be realized through spiritual effort rather than theorized and ritualized. The Vedic priests, on their part, envisioned Him as the personification of sacrifice and the power hidden in the Vedic hymns, sacred syllables and utterances, gods, beings, and the whole creation that moved by itself, in itself, and by its will, unconditioned and unrestrained by any external or independent cause or agency, and that made possible all actions, existences, and manifestations. In the devotional theistic philosophies, sects, and movements, this vast, esoteric, impersonal, indifferent, and enigmatic Deity became Isvara, the all-controlling, Supreme Lord of the Universe, who would respond to the prayers of His devotees and reciprocate their love and devotion with great compassion and love. We do not know what led to this fundamental shift in the Vedic tradition. Some believe that it happened due to the induction of sects like Shaivism and Vaishnavism, which were essential devotional and theistic traditions that combined the best of all approaches to bring liberation within the reach of a vast number of people without forcing them to turn to ascetic philosophies and practices.

For the deluded mind, Brahman is too universal, transcendental, and remote to relate to Him personally, understand Him intellectually, or worship Him devotionally. Existing beyond all the activities of worldly life, beyond the reach of the mind and senses, He is like a remote star, heard but rarely seen, seen but vaguely remembered, remembered but seldom described in clear and unambiguous terms. Unlike the sun, the moon, or the stars that traverse across the sky, spreading their splendor in all directions, He remains in our minds as an idea or a possibility rather than a tangible reality. Himself invisible, yet He makes possible their movements, appearance, and existence with assuring and predictable regularity. Although said to be fixed and permanent, He ensures the orderliness of the universe, the regularity of the seasons, the progression of time and the epochs, the phases of human life, and the enforcement of laws that establish order and the regularity of life on earth. The ultimate purpose of bhakti is the attainment of supreme Brahman, but through a path that is more concrete, relational, practical, and purely human. Aware of the difficulties involved in worshipping formless Brahman, proponents of the theistic movements suggested the worship of qualified (*Saguna*) Brahman or Brahman with forms and attributes, who is still transcendental and universal but more personal, relatable and responsive to the prayers and calls of His devotees. We know from the Upanishads that the manifested Brahman with forms is unreal and communicable and that the unmanifested formless Brahman is real but uncommunicable, and their worship leads to different results. Traditionally, the consensus opinion is that worshipping the formless and transcendental Brahman is ideal for those who seek liberation by pursuing the ascetic path of knowledge and renunciation. In contrast, worshipping the forms of Brahman is ideal for those who seek liberation by pursuing the path of action with exclusive devotion but without desires and attachments and the desire for the fruit of their actions. Bhagavadgita recommends the practice of karma-sannyasa for both while discouraging people from worshipping the formless, impersonal, unmanifested Brahman.

Even today, the Brahman of Upanishads attracts the attention of contemplative and spiritual minds rather than worldly people who are drawn to the attractions of worldly life. Until the emergence of the modern publishing industry, Brahman was relatively unknown even to the educated followers of Hinduism. They had fewer opportunities to know Him unless they studied the Vedas and the philosophies based on them or received initiation from enlightened gurus. It is doubtful how many

Brahmanas of the medieval period knew Him unless they extended their study of the Vedas to the Aranyakas and Upanishads, which was a slim possibility since only a few had access to written manuscripts. During the Islamic rule of India, when the monotheistic Islamic beliefs challenged the polytheistic and ritual practices of Hinduism, the saints of medieval India focused on exclusive devotion to personal God (*Isvara*) rather than abstract notions of Brahman because devotionally, it was easier to relate to an objectified personal Deity rather than to a transcendental, enigmatic, and formless deity.

Worshipping a personal God devotionally has never been alien to Hinduism or the Vedic tradition, as some scholars erroneously suggest. Devotional sects and movements of Hinduism might have gained popularity in the medieval period, but the concept of Bhakti yoga as a direct path to liberation is certainly pre-Buddhist and may have existed for a long time before the Buddha. The Bhagavadgita, which is part of the epic Mahabharata, validates it. It might have even influenced the birth of the Mahayana and Vajrayana Buddhism and the Tantra traditions of Hinduism. The Nayanars and Alvars (500 C.E. – 100 C.E.) worshipped Lord Shiva and Vishnu, respectively, with great devotion. They sang devotional songs and worked tirelessly to spread the idea of devotion to God as the best way to achieve liberation. Even Shankaracharya (9th century C.E.), who preached and practiced Advaita Vedanta (nondualism), declaring Brahman as the only reality, encouraged devotional worship, composing numerous devotional prayers to the gods and goddesses. He wanted to attain the formless, supreme Brahman by engaging his mind in the devotional contemplation of His forms. The devotional (bhakti) movements encouraged the worship of various divinities with devotion and surrender, treating them as Brahman in their ultimate aspect. As a personal God, Brahman acquired names and forms, but as the formless and invisible universal Self, He remained largely outside the devotional practices of the common people. Even after these developments, the knowledge of Brahman is mainly confined to those who study the Upanishads or pursue the teachings of Vedanta.

Brahman and Brahma Prajapati

That which is imperceptible, undecaying, inconceivable, unborn, inexhaustible, indescribable; which has neither form, nor hands, nor feet; which is almighty, omnipresent, eternal; the cause of all things, and without cause; permeating all, itself unpenetrated and from which all things proceed; that is the object which the wise behold, that is Brahma, that is the supreme state, that is the subject of contemplation to those who desire liberation, that is the thing spoken of by the Vedas, the infinitely subtle, supreme condition of Visnu. Vishnu Puranas [1]

Hindus worship many gods and goddesses rather than Brahman. Only a few people know Him by name. The priests in temples do not worship Him directly because tradition does not support the idea of worshipping a formless Deity or a deity who does not require nourishment or depend upon humans for it. However, they worship Him as Shiva, Vishnu, Narayana, Krishna, etc., who accept our sacrificial offerings whether they depend upon them or not. All names and forms belong to Brahman and arise from Him. Yet, they do not chant His thousand names (*sahasranamas*) or his hundred names (*satanamas*), as they do in the case of deities like Shiva, Vishnu, Shakti, Ganesha, etc., who are also His manifestations only, although many worshippers do not remember it when they worship them. Many mistake him for Brahma because the names sound similar except for the letter 'n.' Most likely, in the early Vedic period, the Vedic Kshatriyas worshipped Brahma as Isvara, or the highest, supreme God, and might have regarded Brahman as His Self, or unmanifested or hidden aspect. Just as Atman is the Self of a jiva, they might have regarded Brahman as the Self of Brahma. This is my conjecture, and my intuition tells me this was indeed the case.

Unfortunately, in the later Vedic period, with the emergence of sectarian movements within the Vedic fold, Brahma lost his exalted status as the Lord of the Universe and the highest of all gods and became one of the Trimurthis, sharing his position with Vishnu, the preserver, and Shiva, the destroyer, as the creator god.

The Vedas recognize Brahma as Isvara, the Creator. Vishnu as an Aditya and Shiva as Rudra appear as ancillary deities. We do not know how and why this happened to Brahma in the history of the Vedic religion. It may be due to a lack of patrons as the original Kshatriya clans seemed to have declined and lost their power and their kingdoms. As a result, a clear distinction arose between Brahma and Brahman, so much so that presently, no one confuses Brahma with Brahman. For all practical purposes, Brahman is a deity in the Hindu pantheon, just like innumerable others, although he occupies an exalted place in the hierarchy along with Vishnu and Shiva. At the same time, he does not have many patrons who worship him or look to him for help. Among the Trimurthis, he is the least popular. As a creator god and as one of the three highest deities of Hinduism, he is frequently mentioned in the epics and Puranas as a giver of boons, who, along with Vishnu and Shiva, is ever engaged in protecting and upholding Dharma and all the worlds. Despite these developments, he is still one of the most powerful and awesome divinities of Hinduism. He has all the attributes and grandeur of Isvara Brahman, a fact which is clearly validated by the Vedas. However, for reasons we cannot fathom, he does not have many temples constructed in his name and is not worshipped by many for reasons we explained at the end of this chapter.

According to the Upanishads, Brahma was the first god who manifested during creation out of the waters of indeterminate existence (unmanifested Brahman). No one is said to be responsible for his birth. He arises on his own from primeval waters. Hence, he is called the self-created (*Swayambhu*). This lends credence to the theory that he was apparently the first god and the original Isvara or the Lord of the Universe. He is also the first of the Trimurthis. The Puranas and the epics describe him as lord of creation and lord of all beings (*Prajapati*). The Vedas described him as the cosmic egg (*Brahmanda*), containing within himself the golden germ (*Hiranyagarbha*) extolled in the Vedas as the Universal Self. Traditionally, his name is associated with many auspicious qualities, such as vastness, expansiveness, holy, sacred, scripture, priest, sacred study, celibacy, prayer, etc. That by itself denotes the immense popularity he enjoyed in the Vedic period before the advent of sectarian traditions. Some argue that Brahma and Brahman are the same. That may be true in ancient times, but currently, except for the fact that their names sound similar, they are considered different. In popular Hinduism, Brahma is a god with a descriptive name, form, and specific attributes, whereas Brahman is impersonal, universal, and with no specific form, materiality, or identity. In the past, Brahma might have been the objectified form of Brahman, but today, several other deities also share that distinction. In terms of cosmic hierarchy, Brahman is first, and Isvara is next. As the lord of creation, Brahma comes third or fourth in the hierarchy as the god who arises from the navel of Isvara and manifests worlds and beings. In the Vaishnava tradition, he is believed to have emerged from the navel of Lord Vishnu (the Isvara, according to them) at the beginning of creation. In the Shaiva tradition [2], Brahma is regarded as a foe whom Shiva humiliated by cutting off his fifth head. Such narratives suggest that the sectarian traditions have greatly diminished the aura and importance of Brahma to project their beliefs and promote their deities to a higher position.

In the Vedic literature, Brahman is also referred to as Prajapathi, the lord of the beings, who is identified variously with Purusha as well as with many individual qualities and divinities, such as sacrifice, the year, heaven and earth, father and mother, and the individual self. As the personification of recurring time, his power waxes and wanes, and therefore, gods renew him through sacrifice [3]. No hymns are addressed to Brahma in the Samhitas, maybe because of the belief that he was the ultimate recipient of all sacrifices. Some scholars tend to equate Brihaspati and Brahmanaspati of the Vedic hymns with Brahma. However, they appear as distinct deities in the Hindu pantheon. Historically, the name Brahma appeared in the post-Vedic period in the epics and Puranas. We also find references to him in the Upanishads as Prajapati and the teacher and father of demons, gods, and human beings. Maitri Upanishad (chapter 5) mentions him as the god of passion (*rajas*) and as one of the Trimurthis, who manifested from the Highest along with Shiva and Vishnu. He is extolled in it as

Prajapati and Visva (the universe). This may, again, be due to his relegation in the Vedic pantheon to a lower status due to unknown historical factors as a god of passion despite the fact that he is said to be the god of knowledge, intelligence, and utmost purity, as symbolized by the waters on which he appears seated on a white swan as his vehicle, which is also a symbol of purity. His association with passion or the mode of rajas could be because he is a Kshatriya god who represents creativity and virility with the infinite power to produce countless jivas. They are characteristic of those who possess the predominance of rajas. Undoubtedly, he is the creative power of Brahman and the source of all ritual and spiritual knowledge about Him and the Vedas. Although he is not mentioned directly in the Rigveda, he is mentioned in the hymns of the Rigveda as the second Purusha whom the primal Purusha produced out of Himself for sacrifice. This view is confirmed by some accounts of creation found in the Puranas in which Brahma is mentioned as the deity whom the gods sacrificed.

Brahma personifies many divine qualities of saguna Brahman or Isvara, from whom he arises at the beginning of creation. He is said to be a god of immense proportions and extraordinary poise and grace. Hindu scriptures describe him as the firstborn, golden egg (*Hiranyagarbha*), architect of the universe (*Vishwakarma*), self-created (*Svayambhu*), and creator of destinies (*Vidhata*). He is depicted with four heads, usually seated on a swan, holding the Vedas in one of his four hands. In some descriptions, he is mentioned as the Chief Priest because he is said to have presided over the marriage ceremony between Shiva and Parvathi as the Chief Priest. He is also the original god to whom all the knowledge is attributed, including the knowledge of arts, crafts, law books, music, dance, drama, yoga, etc.

Brahma emerged from the waters of existence before all other gods with the blueprint of creation embedded in his mind. According to some accounts, at the end of each Brahma day, which spans billions of years, he goes to sleep and wakes up the next day. Whatever may be the case, at the beginning of each cycle of creation, he opens his eyes, remembers his purpose, and sets in motion the process of creation using his mind's infinite energies. He creates the worlds, gods, demons, celestial beings, humans, and all other living beings. He also imparts the knowledge of the Vedas to his mind-born seers and establishes the laws (*Dharma*) for humans to guide them on the righteous path and ensure that they perform their obligatory duties for the welfare of all.

According to the Maitri Upanishad (2.6), Prajapati created mortal beings (*jivas*) because he was not happy being alone. Therefore, he meditated upon himself and brought forth all of them. However, when he found them to be lifeless, to bring them to life, he poured into them five kinds of vital energy (five life-breaths). Prakriti is his integral aspect, with which he creates and moves everything that is, that has been, and that will be. He is also described in the early Hindu literature as the golden egg (*Hiranyagarbha*), an epithet that was later ascribed to Lord Vishnu. So is the case with the epithet, Narayana, which is now more popularly associated with Vishnu. According to Chandogya Upanishad (19.1), in the beginning, the world was non-existent (*Asat*). Then, it became existent (Sat). It grew and turned into an egg (*andam*). It lay for a year and burst open. Out of the shell came two parts: the golden world (heaven) and the silvery world (the earth). Symbolically, the cosmic egg represents Nature, the primal matter and energy. The year represents Time (*Kala*), which is symbolically compared to a huge serpent of death that strikes when a jiva's time is due. Hence, Kala stands for both time and death. The division of heaven and earth denotes the division of the cosmos into different planes and realms. It also alludes to the creation of duality.

In the Puranas and epics, we find three or four different versions of how Brahma came into existence and created the world and being. According to one version found in the Manusmriti, which is similar to the one found in the Chandogya Upanishad, which we have mentioned briefly before, Brahma first dropped a seed into the waters of existence. The seed became a golden egg, in which he created himself as the firstborn and emerged from it. He divided the egg into heaven and earth. After creating the mortal world, he created from his mind several mind-born sons (*manasaputras*) and ten Prajapatis to assist him in further creation.

The epic Ramayana provides a different version in which Brahma appeared out of space and created Marichi (sunrays) and his son Kashyapa (a primal human being). Kashyapa, in turn, fathered Vaivasvata and Manu. From Manu descended all human beings. According to another version found in the Puranas, after Brahma divided the golden egg into heaven and earth, he divided himself into male and female, from which emerged Viraj, and from Viraj sprang Manu, who in turn fathered the entire human race. These descriptions match with those found in the earliest Upanishads, which describe how Brahman manifested the worlds. It supports the theory that Brahma was Brahman's direct manifestation as Isvara, the Lord of Creation. According to the most popular account found in the Bhagavata Puranas, which is obviously a subsequent development, at the time of creation, Brahma emerged from the navel of Lord Vishnu, seated on a lotus, and initiated the creation. According to another description, Brahma created Saraswathi, the goddess of learning, and took her as his consort. All the creatures emerged from their union.

Brahma was the first teacher who taught the knowledge of the Vedas to the gods and then to humanity through the Vedic seers. The Mundaka Upanishad begins with this verse: *"Brahma, the maker of the universe, happened to be the first among gods. He taught the knowledge of Brahman to Atharvan, his first son."* Brahma also taught the knowledge of Self to the gods and demons alike. He instructed Indra concerning Brahman and Self. However, the leader of the demons, Vairochana, misunderstood his teachings and was left with the belief that the physical self was the real self. Since then, the demons have been pursuing materialism and denying the Self.

The demons, gods, and humans are all children of Brahma. He knows their weaknesses, loves them in a fatherly way, and wants them to improve their ways. According to one story found in Chandogya Upanishad, once he called them and asked them to practice three "Da's." He wanted gods to practice self-control (*Dama*), demons to practice compassion (*Daya*), and humans to practice charity (*Dana*). Since the gods were pleasure-seeking, he asked them to practice self-restraint. Since demons were cruel and wicked by nature and took pleasure in others' suffering, he asked them to practice compassion. Since humans are selfish by nature, he asked them to give charity so that they could overcome their selfishness. Indeed, the law books declare that for humans, charity is the highest virtue, especially for those who are drawn into a worldly life and perform obligatory duties as householders to fulfill their desires or passions.

While Brahman is eternal, Brahma is not. His lifespan, like that of any other manifestation in creation, is temporary and limited to a certain duration. According to Hindu astronomical calculations [4], in each cycle of creation, He exists for 100 Brahma years, which is also equivalent to 100 cycles of creation. It is said to be equal to one minute (*nimesha*) in the time of Brahman. A Kalpa is half a day in the life of Brahma. It is equal to 1000 Mahayugas (great epochs) or 14 Manvantaras or 4.32 billion years. Each Mahayuga, which spans over 4.32 million years, is again divided into four great epochs (yugas), namely Satyayuga (1,728,000 human years), Tretayuga (1,296,000 human years), Dwaparayuga (864,000 human years) and Kaliyuga (432,000 human years). We are currently in Kaliyuga, the last epoch.

Each Manvantara is equal to one Manu's reign. He presides over all life and events on earth and acts as the progenitor of the human race in each Manvantara. In all, fourteen Manus appear in each Kalpa [5]. Each Manu has a specific name and creates in each of their reigns a new race of humans. Brahma wakes up from a long sleep at the beginning of each Brahma Day and initiates creation. He dissolves it at the end of the day and goes to sleep during the night to wake up again and start afresh. Three hundred sixty days of Brahma constitute one Brahma Year, and one hundred Brahma years constitute his lifespan. Brahman, the highest Supreme Self, is eternal, whereas. The Bhagavata Purana states that innumerable Brahmas manifest and engage in creation in the innumerable creations or universes (*Brahmandas*) of Brahman.

Brahma is said to be the protector of the Vedas and the Vedic knowledge. The Vedas ascribe the early incarnations of the boar, tortoise, and fish to Brahma rather than to Vishnu. They suggest that in the past, he incarnated in these forms to rescue the worlds and preserve the Vedas from destruction. They also suggest that he has four heads facing the four directions, which denotes his omniscience and all-knowing awareness. According to some descriptions, originally, he had five heads, the fifth one facing upwards, in addition to the four facing the four directions. However, he lost that subsequently. Being the father of all, He is said to be easy to please. The demons, who are his eldest children, sometimes take advantage of his generosity and get away with extravagant boons, which results in problems for the gods of heaven and humans of the earth. Emboldened by the boons they secure from him, when the demons become fearless and begin to trouble both worlds, the gods approach the Trinity and seek their intervention to restore order. Brahma is also a prominent deity of Buddhism. He is also considered the firstborn among gods by Buddhists. However, they do not consider him to be the creator [6].

Presently, Brahma is not as popular as Shiva or Vishnu [7]. He also does not have many followers like them. Very few temples exist in his name. We do not know the exact reasons [8]. He may be worshipped in some rituals along with other gods. According to the Hindu temple architecture, a place should be reserved for him in the northern wall of the temple where he should be worshipped regularly with offerings as an important elder of the chief deity's family or entourage (*Parivaradeva*). We will discuss this aspect more in the next section. Brahma is not Brahman in the absolute sense. However, He is an aspect of Him. He personifies Brahman and represents many of His qualities and powers in his capacity as the creator of the heaven and the earth and the creator of all the beings in the whole creation.

Why is Brahma not worshipped regularly?

Brahma is not usually worshipped in Hindu ritual practices as much as Vishnu and Shiva, or even other gods such as Ganesha, Hanuman, Krishna, or Rama. While many reasons are cited for this, the real reasons may be attributed to the decline of the original Kshatriya clans [9] in ancient India due to many social and political reasons and, probably, caste conflicts. The Kshatriyas of the Vedic period seem to have lost their power and influence in the northwestern region where they originally established their kingdoms and republics, long before the advent of Buddhism and the formation of the Mauryan empire. In the earlier Vedic period, they probably enjoyed many privileges and stood higher than the Brahmanas in the social hierarchy. They also rivaled them in their knowledge of the Upanishads, often much to their discomfort, as is evident from the fact that many early Upanishadic teachers were Kshatriyas. They worshipped gods such as Indra, Varuna, Soma, Rudra, Prajanya, Yama, Mrityu, and Isana, who, according to the Vedas, waged heroic battles, were guardians of the earth, and possessed Kshatriya nature (Brihad.1.4.11). Just like Kshatriyas, Brahma personifies the mode of rajas, which induces passions and desires and represents creative and reproductive power. They also worshipped Brihaspati, originally the leader of the gods, and later Brahma, who is also extolled as Prajapati, the leader of the people. In contrast, Brahmanas excelled in ritual knowledge and worshipped Agni, the fire god, and offered daily oblations to Surya, the sun, who is also a Kshatriya deity. They kept different kinds of sacrificial fires burning in their homes and used them to kindle the sacrificial altars. When they performed sacrifices, such as Rajasuya or Ashvamedha, for their patrons, who happened to be mostly kings and members of the royalty, they invoked the Kshatriya gods and made offerings to them on their behalf, seeking their help for peace, prosperity, destruction of their enemies, victory in wars, rains, protection against calamities, etc.

We do not know what happened subsequently or how the Kshatriya clans declined, resulting in a power vacuum and the ascendence of the Brahmanas in the social hierarchy. We have reasons to believe that tensions prevailed between the Brahmanas and the Kshatriyas for some time before the Vedic Varna system became rigid, and the status of each varna in the social hierarchy was fully settled. The Brihadaranyaka Upanishad states that Brahman produced the Kshatra power first. Therefore, there is nothing higher than a Kshatriya, and for that reason, during the horse sacrifice, the Brahmanas sit below the Kshatriyas (probably members of the royal family and ministers of the court). However, the same Upanishad further states that the Brahmana priest who presides over that sacrifice is the source of that Kshatra power. Therefore, even if the king became powerful at the end of the sacrifice, he must always acknowledge the Brahmana as his superiors and pay them proper respects.

The Upanishad also states that Dharma (divine law) personifies Kshatriyas' power. Therefore, they are empowered to act as the guardians of Dharma, which they must protect with their power and authority. Varuna, whom the Vedas extol as the lord of the universe and upholder of justice, personifies that power. They state that in fear of him, rains fall, and laws are observed faithfully by humans. However, Varuna's status declined subsequently, just as Brahma's and Indra's, which might have coincided with the decline of the Kshatriya power. The events associated with Parasurama, an incarnation of Lord Vishnu, prior to the incarnation of Lord Krishna, vaguely point to a possible conflict between Brahmanas and Kshatriyas, resulting in the destruction of the latter. According to the Puranas, as the Kshatriya rulers became arrogant, evil, and drunk with power, they neglected their obligatory duty of protecting and upholding Dharma. Parasurama incarnated to restore Dharma by destroying them all and putting an end to their rule.

Their power and status declined further when many rulers from different social backgrounds gained political power and established kingdoms, principalities, and dynasties in various parts of the subcontinent. Brahmanas, whose livelihood depended upon wealthy patrons, found in this new breed of royalty an opportunity to secure their patronage and ensure their survival. Hence, they admitted them into the Vedic social hierarchy by recognizing them as Kshatriyas and tracing their origins to ancient mythical lineages so that their claim to the throne, connection to the gods, and status as the lawful and divine upholders of Dharma could be legitimized. They served this new class of rulers acting as royal priests and ministers and backed their right to succession as long as they acknowledged their supremacy, sought their advice, and favored them with gifts or land, cattle, etc. As the political fortunes of the ancient Kshatriya clans declined, the popularity of the gods of Kshatra power also declined. Hence, in the later Vedic period, they lost their place of pride in the Vedic pantheon and became relegated to lower levels as lesser and dependent gods and guardians of space (*Dikpalas*).

Indeed, Brahma, who had the title of Prajapati (leader of people), was a true Kshatriya god. He personified royalty, wisdom, justice, and truth. He was the highest god of the early Vedic pantheon and was equated with Isvara, the Lord of the Universe, and Purusha, the Cosmic Person of the creation hymns of the Rigveda and with the decline of the Kshatriyas, his popularity and status in the pantheon also declined. Although he was recognized as one of the Trimurthis, his position became weaker than the other two. His essential nature as a god of purity and intelligence was also compromised as he was identified with the mode of rajas, which is considered an impurity and an inferior mode from a spiritual perspective. In the restructured pantheon of gods, Brahma, the creator god, personifies the mode of rajas, the predominant mode of Kshatriyas; Vishnu personifies the modes of sattva, the predominant mode of the Brahmanas and enlightened spiritual masters; and Shiva personifies tamas, the predominant mode of Vaishyas, Shudras, and Asuras. In fact, the Shaivites do not accept this analogy. According to them, Shiva is Shivam, the purest of the Pure, who is Brahman Himself and the source of all. Prakriti is His inseparable Half. In association with her, He Himself performs the five universal functions in different manifestations as the creator, preserver, concealer, revealer, and destroyer. They are known as the five forms (*Panchanana*) of Shiva.

With the formation of the Varna System and the decline of the Kshatriyas, the ritual practices of each Varna also changed. Brahmanas worshipped radiant gods of sattvic nature, such as Agni and Adityas, foremost among whom was Vishnu, whom they elevated as the lord of the universe, the upholder of Dharma, and the preserver of the worlds. The incarnations attributed originally to Brahma in the Vedas were transferred to him. With their patronage, Vishnu became one of the most popular gods of

Hindus, along with Shiva. Their popularity continues even today. Most of the temples in India are built either in their honor or in honor of their manifestations, incarnations, emanations, and associate deities. With the decline of the Kshatriya clans, the ritual worship of Brahma also seems to have declined. As a result, hardly any temples of Brahma exist today. Interestingly, the most popular and well-known temple of Brahma, the only one of its kind, is located in Rajasthan, which is traditionally known as the Land of the Rajas or Kshatriyas.

Footnotes

Book six, Chapter five, Verse 68, from the Vishnu Purana, English Translation with Sanskrit Text by Veda Vyasa, Internet Archive

1. Skanda Purana, verses 59-69.
2. Chapter, The Growth of the Monistic Conception, From Brahman, A Study in the History of Indian Philosophy by Griswold, Hervey D., 1900.
3. Vishnu Puranam, Chapter 2.
4. The list of Manus are as follows. Svayambhu, Svarochisha, Uttama, Tamasa, Raivata, Chakshusha, Vaivasvata, (current) Daksha, Brahma, Dharma, Rudra, Deva, and Indra.
5. Digha Nikaya 3.28.
6. The most famous temple of Brahma in India is located at Pushkar in Rajasthan.
7. It is one of the mysteries that we might unravel only if we know how the Vedic gods lost their prominence in the later Vedic period.
8. My theory regarding the division of Vedic gods on caste lines and the decline of Kshatriya gods due to the decline in the Kshatriyas' political power is a hypothesis. If the Mahabharata war was a historical truth, it might have contributed significantly to the decline of the ancient Kshatriya clans. However, more research and evidence are required to prove or disprove this theory.

Why Brahman is Not Ritually Worshipped

Whether we consider Him a state, absolute reality, infinite power, or a Universal Deity, Brahman is mysterious and unfathomable. Many Hindus do not know Him, and even those who know Him know but a little. One reason for this is that He has no specific state, form, function, or description and is not ritually worshipped like other gods in temples or at homes. Attempts were made in the past by people like the founders of the Brahmo Samaj in the nineteenth century to promote His worship and oppose polytheism and image worship, but they mostly failed. Advaita Vedanta's main focus is Brahman. However, Shankara himself composed many hymnal scriptures in praise of Hindu deities and, in a way, favored their ritual and spiritual worship.

Those who know Brahman from the Upanishads or Vedas may not know why He is not worshipped like other gods, although they may regard Him in the ultimate and subtlest sense as the essence of all. The fact is that those who worship the numerous gods and goddesses of Hinduism also worship Brahman, although they may not be aware of it. Much of this confusion will disappear if we see Brahman not as a Being but as pure consciousness or as a supreme state or reality (*yogam*). He becomes a Being in creation as numerous manifestations (*vibhutis*) arise from Him and within Him like waves from an ocean. These manifestations contain His essence and power but are different. In his pure and absolute state, He represents the highest reality, which is pure, indefinable, and without names and forms. You cannot communicate with that state or reality because it is beyond your mind and senses and cannot be reached by your speech, thoughts, or intelligence. You can only attain Him through self-purification and become Him or become dissolved in His pure consciousness. For these very reasons, Bhagavadgita affirms that worshipping the unmanifested (*asambhuta*) Brahman is difficult and better avoided.

The highest God of the Bhagavadgita is neither Lord Krishna nor Lord Vishnu, but Brahman only. One may worship Him as Krishna as His devotees do, but Krishna acknowledged Himself as Brahman in oneness. He delivered the entire discourse of the Bhagavadgita in the midst of Kurukshetra as Brahman from the heights of His supreme consciousness in oneness and without duality. So is the case with the Vedas and the Upanishads. They were heard by those who attuned themselves to the supreme state of Brahman. Names and forms are secondary to the One who is without names and forms. Yet, He exists in all and supports all this. Brahman cannot be reached with the mind, intelligence, or the senses. However, he, the unattainable, is attainable through contemplation and self-absorption as oneself in the state of oneness. Yogis who attain Him thus vouch for it. Hence, the Upanishads say that He is near, yet far away. Those who attain Him say that the experience will change you and bring a permanent and everlasting change in you. Worship implies the duality of subject and object. In Brahman, there is no duality. Hence, the self-realized yogis know that one should attain oneness with Him and that He should be realized, not worshipped.

If you are totally absorbed in Brahman, you will see the world differently. You will cease to identify yourself with your physical self, and withdrawing your mind and senses into yourself, you will become fixed in the awareness that Brahman is hidden deep within you as your very Self, which is wonderfully expressed in the Brihadaranyaka Upanishad (1.4.10) as "*Aham Brahmasmi,*" meaning, "I am Brahman." The self-realized yogis do not wish to declare that loudly since they know that the ignorant ones can misconstrue it as a sign of egotism or madness. However, they remain stabilized in that awareness even in the wakeful state, battling against the duality to which the mind is accustomed and the delusion of the ego, which remains active even in the self-realized state, although weakened and subdued. To those who are not familiar with Hinduism, let it be clear that when we say "Brahman," we are not referring to Brahma. We have already explained the difference in the previous chapter. Brahma is a Vedic god (*deva*), a manifested form of Brahman, once revered as

Isvara or the Lord of the Universe and the highest god. Brahman is the supreme, infinite, formless, absolute, indescribable, immutable, and stateless reality. Brahma, the creator god, arises from Brahman at the beginning of creation, just as all other gods. They manifest and unmanifest in the endless waters of existence, like waves and islands in an ocean. They are also Brahman only. As the Bhagavadgita declares, those who worship them as Brahman go to Brahman and attain the highest, immortal world. Those who worship them as individual gods go to them and attain their worlds. In a way, they also worship Brahman but do not attain Him since their focus is elsewhere.

Brahman, the highest God of Hinduism, resides in all as their very Self. He is the Self of all (*sarvabhutatma*), and all exist in Him only. He pervades them and shines through them according to their purity and spiritual growth. However, He is not in them in the sense that he is not a part of their corporeality. He exists in the body of each jiva separately as a pure Self. The same is the case with all the worlds and the universe. The whole creation is His projection or reflection in Nature, which is presided over by Isvara, His highest manifestation. In other words, you cannot attain Brahman objectively or by worshipping Him as an object. You cannot find him in the objective reality because he is not in it or any of its parts, aspects, and components. You may begin your spiritual journey by worshipping His forms, but eventually, you must reach the formless through self-absorption. He is known only subjectively in self-absorption by becoming one with Him or dissolved in Him as oneself. The Upanishads clearly state that Brahman is pure intelligence (*pranjnanam brahma*). He is not a Being but the highest, supreme reality which is described in the texts as kaivalyam (aloneness), parandhamam (highest goal), prasantam (peaceful), atitam (transcendental), advitiyam (without a second), anantam (infinite), aksharam (indestructible), anirvachaniyam (indescribable) and madhuram (extremely ecstatic).

Although He is the highest God, He is not worshipped ritually because He cannot be reached through rituals. Many Hindus do not even know about him. Hence, they worship His manifestations, the lesser gods, demigods, or godmen. However, he is not completely separate from Hindu rituals. He is considered the ultimate recipient of all sacrificial offerings. All the prayers and offerings ultimately reach Him only since He is the ultimate enjoyer and universal witness. In some Vedic rituals, it is customary to engage a Brahman priest whose job is to remain silent and vigilant throughout the sacrifice and correct the priests if they make mistakes. Like Brahman, he participates in the sacrifice as a silent witness.

Since Brahman is remote, indifferent, and unapproachable through objective means, the ritualists of the Purva Mimansa School in the Vedic period literally ignored Him. They believed that there was no need to worship Him or any divinity since the sacrifices (yajnas) possessed all the powers and were inherently equipped to grant worshipers their wishes. Therefore, they focused on performing the sacrifices strictly as ordained by the Vedas. They also believed that the Vedas and all the words in them and their pronunciation and meanings were unchangeable and eternally constant. Therefore, they focused on chanting them correctly with the right pronunciation. They were not concerned about who created the worlds and beings. They were content with the belief that sacrifices by themselves were the source of all manifestation, including creation. According to them, life was created, sustained, and destroyed by sacrifices only. Therefore, they believed that by performing sacrifices strictly as prescribed by the Vedas, one could escape from suffering and attain heaven and a better life in the next birth. Maybe because of them or their influence, Brahman remained in obscurity for a long time. It is even said that the empty space in the sanctum of each Hindu temple surrounding the chief deity symbolically represents Brahman only.

If someone wants to worship Brahman ritually and ignore the deities, there is no taboo. Usually, yogis worship Him mentally by visualizing Him as Shiva, Vishnu, or any god to whom they are drawn. Some worship Him as Shakti or the Mother Goddess, which is a standard practice in many Shakta and Tantra traditions. Let us now examine why Brahman is not ritually worshipped in

Hinduism.

- We need an image or an idol to worship a deity. Brahman is invisible and without form. Hence, it is difficult to worship Him ritually.
- In his absolute state, Brahman is indeterminate, invisible, indistinguishable, equal to all, and indifferent. Therefore, it is difficult to establish a personal or devotional bond with Him and connect to Him emotionally through ritual worship or exclusive devotion.
- In ritual worship, we utter mantras, prayers, and chants that are specific to the deity. Since Brahman is beyond speech, the use of prayers and ritual worship is ineffective in His case. He should be attained in a state of silence and self-absorption.
- Brahman is complete in all respects. He is not subject to hunger or desire and does not depend upon humans for sacrifices or offerings for nourishment. Therefore, sacrifices are not useful in His case.
- The Creator created gods and humans to be interdependent and mutually help each other. Humans should nourish gods through sacrifices, and gods should reciprocate by helping humans in return. The sacrifices are meant for this purpose only. Brahman remains a witness to all the sacrifices.
- Brahman is the highest goal rather than an object of ritual worship. He is to be known internally through the yoga of actions, knowledge, devotion, contemplation, renunciation, etc., rather than through external worship. Ritual worship is preparatory and does not take us far on the path of liberation.
- Vedic hymns, mantras, and prayers have the power and potency to reach the realm of gods through sounds and space. They do not have the power to reach the immortal world of Brahman. Therefore, rituals are ineffective in worshiping Brahman.
- Gods do not like humans who aspire to attain Brahman.

Therefore, worshipping Brahman and the gods simultaneously is counterproductive and better be avoided unless you practice karma-sannyasa and perform your obligatory duties without desiring their fruit.

- There are no known symbols, images, or mantras through which we can invoke Brahman. The best way to attain Him is by meditating on Him as Aum or by fixing the attention on the breath or the point between the two eyebrows.

- In rituals, the mind, senses, and the organs of actions remain active. None of them are helpful to attain Brahman. Indeed, we must withdraw them all into ourselves and fix our minds on Brahman to attain Him. It means the rituals are inherently ineffective and unsuitable for worshiping Brahman.

Brahman, the highest supreme reality, can be realized through self-knowing or self-realization only. Rituals and sacrifices are ineffective in His case. One may know Him intellectually through the study of the scriptures, but it does not count as true knowing. He can truly be known by the Self and through the Self in a state of nonduality. As the Upanishad affirms, by knowing Him through the ultimate union (*yoga*), without duality or distinction, Brahman is attained. By attuning the mind and body to the goal of self-realization or liberation, by attaining nearness and oneness, one can enter the purest and the most auspicious state of Brahman, where all the notions of otherness, disturbance, and duality disappear.

Nidhidhyasana – The Contemplation of Brahman

Contemplation definitely is greater than thought. The earth does contemplate. The atmosphere does contemplate. The heaven does contemplate... Now, the low-minded are quarrelsome, abusive, and slandering. The superior men derive their rewards from contemplation. Meditate on contemplation. Chand.7.6.1)

In ancient times, students learned the Upanishads either to know Brahman and realize Him or to complete and complement their knowledge of Samhitas, Brahmanas, and Aranyakas with special emphasis on Karma Kanda, the ritual knowledge. However, those belonging to various ascetic traditions studied them independently as spiritual texts to know Brahman and work for their liberation. Through their study and contemplation, those who studied them as a part of their study of the Vedas internalized the knowledge of Atman (individual Self) and Brahman and prepared themselves for the occupations they wished to undertake as householders (Grihastashrama), in which they could pursue the four chief aims of human life (Dharma, Artha, Kama, and Moksha) without compromising their spiritual wellbeing. The knowledge of the Upanishads enabled them to view their lives as sacred rituals in which they could become both the sacrificer and the sacrificed, just as the cosmic Purusha was. However, to receive the secret knowledge of the Upanishads, they had to possess excellent qualities and meet the expectations of their teachers. For many, the knowledge of the Upanishads was out of bounds since the teachers were rare, and most of them lived in the forests or sparsely populated areas. While sacrifices were performed publicly in the presence of hosts, guests, attendants, and patrons, the teaching of the Vedas, which contained the knowledge of those sacrifices, was restricted to upper-caste students.

The knowledge of the Upanishads was even more restricted to a qualified few since it was considered the utmost secret. Every day, the gurus taught their disciples a few verses, phrases, or lines from the scriptures, asking them to memorize them and meditate on them until they understood their full meaning and purpose. This went on until they fully mastered the text and satisfied the teacher with their knowledge and understanding. The study, remembrance, and mastery were one part. It ended when the students left their teachers and went their own ways. The practice of the knowledge they gained thus continued for the rest of their lives and helped them in their spiritual journey. Students learned the ritual portions of the Vedas by rote, sometimes without even knowing their meaning or hidden purpose, but as far as the Upanishads were concerned, they had to memorize them as well as understand their true significance because they were meant for their personal use, improving their character and conduct, cultivating discernment and spiritual nature. The knowledge also helped them stretch their minds and see themselves and the world differently, as God's play.

Understanding the Upanishads requires a fundamental shift in thinking and awareness. They are meant for inner transformation through contemplative practices such as concentration (*dharana*) and meditation (*dhyana*) and cultivating knowledge (*vijnanam*) and discernment (*vivekam*) through self-purification. Chapter 7 of the Chandogya Upanishad suggests meditation is better than thinking. However, acquiring knowledge of the Vedas and other scriptures is better than meditation because he who meditates on the learned knowledge as Brahman will have freedom as far as knowledge goes. However, better than meditating on learned knowledge, strength, intelligence, speech, food, fire, water, memory, hope, breath, truth, speech, etc., is meditating on the Self and knowing that it is the source of all. He who, meditating on the Self, realizes thus, does not see death, sorrow, or sickness and obtains everything everywhere. He attains Skanda, the shining one beyond the darkness. In short, the knowledge of the Self sets one free from all bounds.

Much mystic symbolism is hidden in the verses of the Upanishads, which is difficult to understand unless you are familiar with the other parts of the Vedas, namely the Samhitas, the Brahmanas, and the Aranyakas (forest books). Probably, at least six or seven layers of thought are hidden in the hymns of the Vedas. For shallow minds, they present an apparent meaning or content, which is immediately discernible and maybe even misleading, whereas, for awakened souls, it presents a hidden content, which unravels itself according to one's spiritual growth and intuitive awareness. The secrecy of these scriptures is intentional because they are not meant for everyone. Even the seemingly ordinary hymns that are meant for chanting or singing during sacrifices may contain deep symbolism that is difficult to decipher since we have lost the original meaning of many Sanskrit words found in the Vedas due to the passage of time and changes within in the ritual, spiritual and cultural practices of the religion. Indeed, when scholars from Europe took an interest in the study of the Vedas and were trying to decipher the manuscripts they collected, they found many Brahmanas who could recite them by heart but did not know much about their meaning or importance. It may be the case even today. The Vedas mislead the ignorant, challenge the intelligent, and deliver the wise and the pure from bondage.

According to the Vedic tradition, Upanishads constitute the higher knowledge or Vidya, in contrast to the Samhitas or the rituals, which are considered the lower knowledge or Avidya. By contemplating upon the verses of the Upanishads, it is possible to develop an intuitive understanding of the true nature of Brahman. For example, consider the following verse: *"Brahman is above all Gods. None could ever approach Him closely except Indra."* On the surface, it looks like a simple statement with an obvious meaning because those who are familiar with the Hindu pantheon know that Indra is the leader of the gods. Since he stands above all the gods, hierarchically, he is the nearest to the highest Brahman, even if the distance between the two may be truly unfathomable. Nevertheless, it is not what the statement alludes to. Brihadaranyaka Upanishad describes Indra symbolically as the breath (prana) and the mind (Ch. 1.12 & 3.9). They are the highest aspects in the body or the Field of Prakriti and the closest to the

Self or Brahman. Since they are the closest, they are the most illuminated tattvas or divinities.

The eighth chapter of Chandogya Upanishad describes how Indra served Brahma as a student for thousands of years to know the Self and eventually succeeded. He was the first god, and perhaps the only one in the Vedic pantheon, to gain the knowledge of the Self. Kena Upanishad also states that Indra was the first to know about Brahman from Uma Haimavathi after a brief encounter with Him. He also stood closest to Him when He appeared to him as a Yaksha. That very encounter qualified him to become the leader of the gods. The episode is an illustrative example of the typical manner in which many Hindu scriptures present complex religious and spiritual ideas in simple narratives with hidden symbolism. Ordinary people who are not yet free from worldly attachments and not drawn to spirituality or the study of scriptures may find such stories entertaining and informative. However, most likely, they will miss the hidden symbolism and real meaning and purpose they convey unless they acquire the right knowledge, cultivate discernment, and meditate on the deeper aspects of life and the truths of human existence.

The Upanishads are meant to be learned in two ways: one, by sitting closer to the teacher who has a true understanding of them, and two, by moving closer to the Self within oneself. It is in the close proximity of an enlightened teacher or by standing nearer to the Self as Indra did that the knowledge of Upanishads and their statements about Brahman become self-evident. In Hindu teacher traditions, the relationship between a student and his teacher is unique and somewhat similar to the relationship between God and His devotees. The students must spend considerable time in their teachers' company to imbibe their knowledge and wisdom and become true masters themselves. A teacher teaches that knowledge continuously in different ways: by teaching and instructing, setting personal examples, correcting students' misconceptions and erroneous views, providing insight, encouraging them to debate among themselves, and practicing what they learned to find out for themselves their true value and relevance to their lives.

Returning to our main point of discussion, symbolism is hidden in the verses of the Kena Upanishad, which describes the brief encounter between the gods and Brahman. From a psychological perspective, Indra is not just a leader of gods or lord of heaven. He exists in the human body as the lord of the senses and symbolizes the pure mind or mind that is purified and devoid of darkness and delusion (symbolized by the demon Vrta). In the body, he is closest to the Self (Atman), which is but an aspect of Brahman, and is responsible for all the knowledge we gather from study, perceptions, analysis, and contemplation. The senses are the divinities of our microcosm. Like the gods in heaven, they love to indulge in pleasure and are always on the lookout for material things (food) to satisfy their hunger. We know that the minds and senses have an outgoing nature (*pravritti*) and are chiefly responsible for instability, restlessness, and modifications we experience. They also serve as the bridge, connecting us to the world outside and the world within. The mind is subject to different states of consciousness, namely the waking state, the dream state, the deep sleep state, and the transcendental state. In the transcendental state, it comes face to face with the inmost Self, but because it remains asleep and absorbed in samadhi, it does not know much about what it experiences. Therefore, although it encounters the real Self closely, like Indra, it remains somewhat perplexed and uncertain. However, the very fact that it comes face-to-face with the Self in transcendental states makes it divine and superior.

The fact that Indra represents the mind in the body is consistent with Vedic symbolism of Indra as the lord of the senses (the gods) and consciousness (heaven) and his depiction as the slayer of Vrta, the demon who spreads darkness in heaven (in the mind) by keeping it enveloped by rain-bearing clouds. Vrta stands for the ego, and the clouds for the impurities such as egoism and delusion, which are responsible for the mind's chaos and disturbances (*vrttis*). By nature, under demonic influence, the mind is very unstable and restless and acts as an obstacle to attaining peace and higher states of self-absorption (samadhi). When one conquers the (egoistic) mind with the (pure) mind, it becomes stable and serves as the bridge to self-realization.

Thus, Indra (the mind) is his own enemy as well as his best friend, which is also echoed in the Bhagavadgita, which states that the Self is its best friend and worst enemy. The mind's inconsistency and vulnerability to evil desires are well represented in Indra's character and conduct. The Puranas depict him as a spoiler who tries to disturb the meditating yogis and prevent them from transcending their minds. He also entices chaste women like Ahalya and causes them suffering. The symbolism in such descriptions clearly alludes to Indra as the mind. Indra is also known as Purandara. Pur means a fortress or a city with a fortress, and Purandara means invader or breaker of fortresses. Indra breaks our vows and penances with temptations. He breaks the austerity and resolve of seers and sages by sending celestial nymphs to distract them and inflame their sexual desire. Thus, this epithet agrees well with the symbolic depiction of him as the mind. Symbolically, the body is the fortress in which Indra resides as its lord and controls its movements and actions. Since, by nature, he is pleasure-loving, he makes sure that the body is not subjected to unnecessary pain and suffering by penances and austerity. He is a passionate and fickle-minded god who is always looking for an opportunity to derive pleasure and avoid pain, even if it means suffering and bondage for the soul caught in samsara. Just as he is driven by the desire for pleasure and happiness, the mind is always in search of pleasure and happiness, no matter the consequences that may arise from it.

If Indra is the mind, Agni is the inner fire or heat (tapas), and Vayu represents the breath (prana). According to the methods prescribed by the Vedas, both are crucial for self-realization or the realization of Brahman. The spiritual energy generated in the body as heat (tapa) through austerities, penances, and breath control plays an important role in the purification and transformation of the mind and body and building spiritual vigor (tejas) that would eventually enable the seekers to burn away their impurities and latent impressions (samskaras) and achieve liberation. Thus, according to the latent meaning hidden in the verses, self-realization or realization of Brahman is possible if we purify and strengthen our minds and bodies through self-control and channel our energies to stabilize our minds in the contemplation of the Self.

Ancient Vedic schools (*gurukulas*) encouraged students to study the scriptures and develop a deeper understanding of them through questioning, discussions, debates, and contemplation. They wanted them to realize their explicit and implicit knowledge. The Vedas represented Brahman in word form (*Akshara Brahma*) and served as the embodiment of Brahman (Truth). Their study brought them closer to Him and revealed themselves to them to the extent they studied them, understood them, and assimilated them. Hidden within them are numerous existential and transcendental truths. Since they are ancient scriptures, couched in symbolism and archaic expressions, students may derive different conclusions and inferences or understand them differently according to their knowledge, experience, intelligence, and spiritual growth. To them, we also add the accumulated karma of past lives.

However, even a simple study is good for the soul and self-realization. With each iteration, one moves closer to the truths hidden in them and to the truth of the Self hidden within. With continued study, one can find many truths about Brahman, the Self, and liberation, such as the following. They are derived from the Upanishads and serve well for practicing nidhidhyasana, contemplation upon Brahman.

- Brahman is the real and the absolute Truth. All else is a mere illusion, which disappears when true knowledge dawns. Contemplate upon the absolute nature of things and the way illusion may arise on the surface of truth.
- Brahman is eternally stable, permanent, and fixed. He is the unchangeable, immutable, incorruptible, and inexhaustible supreme reality. Meditate on the impermanence of life and the manner in which it affects your life, thinking, and actions.
- Brahman is absolute, eternal, and timeless. Hence, the variations of time do not exist in Him. In his absolute state,

past, present, and future exist simultaneously in equilibrium. Meditate on the timeless Brahman in whom time rests in itself without divisions.

- Brahman is the Creator of all. The world is his projection. He descends into the material universe and subjects Himself to the laws of nature. Contemplate upon the state of Brahman before creation and after creation and the manner in which things might manifest in creation.
- Brahman is the sacred AUM. He represents all states of consciousness that are represented by the syllable AUM. Meditate on the sound of Aum, its relation to breath, and its symbolic significance. Discern the subtle sound that is heard by the yogis in the silence of their minds.
- Brahman is beyond the senses, but He is the mover and enjoyer of senses. Try to discern the Person in you, the enjoyer and witness, for whom senses work and move among sense objects.
- Brahman is beyond the state of duality. In Him, the distinction between the knower and the known does not exist. Choose any object of your choice and meditate on it until you become oblivious of yourself, and the object alone remains in your consciousness without duality.
- Brahman is the first principle. He is the Ancient Purusha. No one truly knows Him, for He is without a beginning and an end. Meditate on the undifferentiated and primal state of Brahman and see what thoughts and images arise in your consciousness.
- Brahman is pure love. He is described as the Lord of Love who reciprocates the devotion of his devotees with greater love. Meditate on the sacred relationship between Him and his devotees, what draws them to Him, and what sustains their faith and devotion.
- Brahman is immortal. He is the Lord of Death and the force that moves the Wheel of Life. Meditate on life and death, the longing for life and the fear of death, and how death and impermanence influence our thinking, actions, and desires.

- Brahman is the source of Dharma (moral duties) and Rta (cosmic order). Contemplate upon Dharma, your obligatory duties, the laws that govern your life, the laws that you must follow, and the order and regularity that depend upon human actions. Think of the ways and means by which you can establish order and regularity in your life.
- Brahman exists in all, and all exist in Him. Yet He is beyond all and different from all. Meditate on the Self that exists in all. Meditate on the not-self and how it is different from the Self. Meditate on what the Self is not and how you can become established in it.
- Brahman is supreme bliss. Your happiness and joy is a feeble reflection of it. You experience it only when you purify yourself and stabilize your mind in the contemplation of the Self. Meditate on happiness and its relationship to peace and fulfillment.
- Meditate on the blissful state of Brahman. Bring the serenity of your mind to the fore and experience peace. Remember the blissful moments you experience and think of the way by which you can prolong it.
- In the body, Brahman is Atman, the individual Self, the silent witness, and the indweller of the city of nine gates. He is the silent and hidden power behind all the movements and actions of the mind and body. Because of Him and for Him, prana, the vital energy moves in the body. Meditate on the Self as the silent witness and how you may identify yourself and dissolve your identity in Him.
- Brahman is above all the divinities. He is the absolute and supreme Lord of the universe. All the worlds exist in Him and draw their support from Him. He is the nourisher of all. Study the hierarchy of the divinities and their respective roles and responsibilities in the creation of Brahman. If you meditate on deities or worship them ritually, what is the best way to do it?
- Brahman is described as the radiant being, the golden one. Meditate on the brilliance and effulgence of Brahman and

how and in what conditions it radiates through us or becomes self-evident to us.

- The state of Brahman is stable and self-absorbed. He is experienced only in the blissful state of Turya, beyond deep sleep. Contemplate upon the transcendental state of self-absorption in which the mind and senses are withdrawn and inactive.

- Brahman is pure intelligence that is independent of the mind and its faculties, including the intelligence (buddhi) of our minds. It is self-existent, self-knowing, and free from the duality of subject and object. It is the state in which there is neither a knower nor the known nor knowing. Meditate on Brahman as knowledge and intelligence. Meditate on the state in which knowledge arises spontaneously and instantly without desire, intention, effort, or purpose.

- Brahman is Isvara, the Cosmic Person (*Purusha*) described in the Vedas as the Being with thousands of hands, feet, eyes, ears, etc.' who manifests worlds and beings and rules over them as their Lord. Meditate on Isvara, His universal form, and the great sacrifice He performed to manifest the four classes of humans.

- Brahman is silence and stillness. Life is full of noise. Meditate on Brahman as the silence that is hidden behind all the noise of existence that reaches our ears. Meditate on how that noise is temporary and eventually dissolves in silence, while silence pervades the whole universe like a never-ending presence and is indestructible and endless despite temporary disturbances.

- Brahman is formless and invisible. Meditate on the formless and invisible state of Brahman and how you can dissolve your name and form in Him and become as expansive as the space around you.

- Brahman is your innermost Self. Meditate on your innermost Self, identify yourself with That, and become established in That.

Mahavakyas for Meditation

The following statements gathered from various Upanishads are also helpful to draw the mind into the contemplation of Brahman.

- One should meditate upon the Self alone as dear. *Atamana eva priya upasita.* (Brihad 1.4.8)
- This Brahman, this is all. *Idama brahma, idam sarvam* (Brihad. 2.5.1).
- I am Brahman. *Aham Brahmasmiti* (Brihad. 1.4.10).
- I am Brahman, I am sacrifice, and I am the world. *Aham brahma, aham yajna, aham loka iti* (Brihad.1.5.17).
- Brahman is lightning. *Vidyut Brahma* (Brihad. 5.7.1).
- That is full, this is full. From fullness, fullness proceeds. *Purnamadah, purnamidam, purnat purnam udacyate* (Brihad 5.2).
- All this is inhabited by the Lord. *Isavasyamidam sarvam* (Isa.1).
- Truly, this whole world is Brahman. *Sarvama khalv idam Brahma* (Chand. 3.14.1).
- This is my Self within in the heart. *Esa ma atamntar hridaye* (Chand.3.1.4.2).
- The sun is Brahman. *Adityo brahmety* (Chand. 3.19.1).
- Brahman is pure intelligence. *Prajnanam Brahma* (Ait. 3.1.3).
- Space is Brahman's body. *Akasa sariram* Brahma (Taitt. 1.7.2).
- Aum is Brahman. Aum is all. *Aum iti Brahma. Aum itidam sarvam* (Taitt. 1.8.1).
- Speak the Truth and follow your righteous duties. *Satyama vada, dharmam cara* (Taitt. 1.2.1).
- By austerity and contemplation, Brahman expands. *Tapasa ciyate Brahma* (Mund. 1.18).
- Brahman is hidden behind the golden sheath. *Hiranmaye pare kose virajam Brahma* (Mund.2.2.12).
- This Self, indeed, is Brahman. *Ayam atma Brahma* (Mandu. 2).

Nidhidhyasana – The Contemplation of Brahman

- The Self is all-pervading. *Sarva vyapinam atmanam* (Sveta.1.16).
- Knowledge of the Self arises from austerity. *Atma vidya tapaomulam* (Sveta.1.16).

Brahman and the Brahman Priest

Truly, that sacrifice inclines to the north, where there is a Brahma priest…with regard to such a Brahma priest, there is this story. Wherever it falters, there goes that man. Chandogya Upanishad (4.17.9).

The importance of rituals

Rigvedic priests focused their energies on securing favors from various gods through sacrificial rituals, leaving the deeper aspects of spiritual life to the Vedic seers and ascetics, who lived in the seclusion of forests, free from the distractions of worldly life. Therefore, we do not find many references to Brahman in the Vedas, except in the Aranyakas and the Upanishads, which were meant for people in the pursuit of liberation. However, as time went by, references to Him began appearing both symbolically and directly in the Darshanas, epics, law books, and Puranas. While Brahman remained the Chief Deity of the Vedic religion from the earliest times, Brahman as the supreme universal Self became public knowledge only in the later Vedic period as several ascetic traditions found a firm foothold upon the Indian soil as they were interested in ritual worship but in realizing the supreme reality or the absolute state of oneself.

For a very long time, sacrificial rituals played an important role in the lives of Vedic people, especially the upper-caste Hindus. Apparently, they believed in their usefulness in directing their prayers towards gods and securing their favors or fulfilling their desires. However, they did not offer much comfort to those who were drawn to the spiritual aspects of life. These enlightened minds did not find much value in them since they were not interested in enjoying worldly pleasure or fulfilling their desires. They were driven by a deep yearning to explore truths about themselves and their liberation from the shackles of their physical nature. Hence, in some Upanishads, we find a noticeable disdain for Vedic rituals. These advanced souls looked for more convincing answers and permanent solutions to resolve the problems of suffering, sickness, aging, death, etc. They were convinced that sacrifices, charms, spells, etc., were not good enough to resolve the problem of human suffering on a permanent basis. At the same time, they realized that sacrifices were still central to the life of an ascetic, which they were supposed to practice spiritually rather than ritually. One might abandon the world and the Vedic rituals as ordained by the Vedas, but not the idea of sacrifice. According to this new understanding, any action becomes a sacrifice if the desires in them are renounced or their fruit is offered to God. Thereby, by renouncing ownership, doership, desires, and attachments and engaging in desireless actions as an offering, one could transform and elevate every action of the mind and body into a sacrifice. By transforming contemplative and ascetic methods and practices into sacrifices, one could achieve the goal of liberation. This was, indeed, a revolutionary idea that led to the development of Vedic philosophical thought and a whole body of spiritual knowledge, beliefs, and practices, such as karma yoga, jnana yoga, and karma-sannyasa yoga, which reduced much of the harshness and negativity associated with asceticism.

It also led to the belief that one might renounce the world but should never abandon actions, whether one lived as a householder and practiced Dharma or as an ascetic and practiced sannyasa. In both approaches, one may still engage in sacrifices, although for different purposes. By performing sacrifices and obligatory duties, householders must realize the four aims of human life and fulfill the aims of creation. By engaging in actions selflessly as sacrifices without desires, ascetics who renounce worldly life must dissolve in Brahman all that separates them from Him and attain liberation. This realization in the ancient world provided the Vedic seers and sages with a better perspective on Vedic rituals and sacrificial actions and their importance to the material and spiritual well-being and progress of humans. They advised householders not to ignore their sacrificial and obligatory duties because they were necessary to serve the Creator and ensure the order and regularity of the world. They instructed the ascetics who renounced their obligatory duties to perform their mundane actions as internal sacrifices to attain Brahman. Thus, whatever path one chooses, the idea of sacrifice remains central to one's life and actions.

The mechanics of the ritual

The success and popularity of Vedic priests in the past depended upon their knowledge of the sacrifices and the results they secured from them for the welfare of their hosts. It meant that if they possessed the right knowledge and adhered to the right methods and procedures prescribed by the Vedas and connected literature, their success was guaranteed. The efficacy of the sacrifices, at least in theory, depended upon ritual purity and adherence to established standards. Therefore, apart from following the ritual procedures and maintaining personal purity, the priests had to ensure that the hosts of the sacrifice (*yajamanas*) also followed strict guidelines and a rigid code of conduct. Everyone who had some role in a sacrifice paid particular attention to the mechanics of the rituals, starting from preparing and cleansing the ritual place, lawfully collecting and preparing the sacrificial materials, and conducting the beginning, middle, and end parts of the sacrifices without mistakes until they were concluded in the right manner. Particular attention was paid to date, time, and place and the proper pronunciation of the hymns to avoid the displeasure of the gods and patrons on whose generosity they thrived. Vedic sacrifices were elaborate ceremonies. Some of them took months or weeks to prepare and an equally long time to complete. Certain sacrifices, like the Agnichayana, were performed in stages at different times in the life of a person. Sometimes, the sacrificial altars took months to build, as the bricks had to be made according to specific measurements and with specific materials to make the altar fit for the sacrifice. For some rituals, the altars had to be built in specific shapes and patterns, laying bricks of different sizes and shapes in concentric layers following strict calculations and configurations. Sometimes, the rules for the sacrifices had to be changed depending upon how many times the patrons participated in them before and to which caste and ancestry they belonged. Such sacrifices could be performed only by the most experienced

Brahmanas. Hence, expertise was very much valued.

The efficacy of the sacrifices also depended upon a few additional criteria, such as the time and place, the purity and history of the ground where the altar was to be built, the type of sacrifice, the source of the sacrificial fire, the number of libations made before and during the sacrifice, the number and types of priests employed, the type of sacrificial fires used, the purpose for which the sacrifice was performed, the faith, caste, and conduct of the hosts, which gods were invoked, and which hymns and prayers were needed to please them. The officiating priests selected the ritual materials carefully and cooked the sacrificial food strictly according to established procedures as specified by the scriptures on domestic rituals (*Grihya Sutras*) since it was meant to be fit for the gods. The sacrificial materials consisted of plant and animal products, such as food grains, milk, ghee, etc., and sacrificial victims or their images. To maintain ritual purity, they were supposed to be collected properly from the right sources, sanctified with appropriate chants, and stored in the right place before the sacrifice began.

Fire occupied a central place in the Vedic rituals. The offerings were dropped into the sacrificial fire under the belief that Agni, the fire god, accepted them on behalf of all the gods and distributed them appropriately among them according to their share. For the hosts of the sacrifice, the rituals opened a celestial door to the heavenly realms through which they could communicate with gods and win their hearts by singing their praise in Sanskrit, the language they understood. The ritual place served as the meeting ground where the divinities joined forces with the mortals below in exchange for sacrificial food and fulfilled their desires or helped them achieve peace and happiness.

Symbolism of internal sacrifice

As we have discussed this topic before, outwardly, Vedic rituals may seem primitive and superstitious. If they involve animal sacrifices, which were common in the past, they may seem even more disturbing. However, Vedic rituals are an integral part of the

Vedic way of life and serve a definite purpose in the lives of Vedic householders. They are based on a complex set of beliefs that are difficult to understand unless you are familiar with the Vedic scriptures, the ritual terminology, and their gradual development from the earliest times. Unfortunately, we know very little about the antecedents of the Vedic people and their beliefs and ritual practices. Whatever we know is based on literary evidence. Even that is not completely reliable since, until its independence, India never had common civil, criminal, or religious laws. We have also lost the original meaning of many archaic Sanskrit words and their hidden meaning, which adds to our difficulty in interpreting the Vedic scriptures. Further, as we discussed before, at some stage in the development of Vedic religion, Vedic seers internalized Vedic sacrifices and added another layer of symbolism to the already complex Vedic belief system. They associated the ritual imagery of the Vedic hymns with their transcendental experiences and created further difficulties in our understanding of them. As a result, even to the most learned scholars, certain passages in the earlier Upanishads, such as the Brihadaranyaka, Chandogya, and Taittiriya Upanishads, present problems in understanding unless they develop an intuitive awareness through their personal experiences.

In Vedic theology, sacrifices symbolized the power of creation or manifestation and showed humans how to follow the example set by the Primal Purusha at the beginning of creation and invoke the divine power hidden in creation to fulfill their desires or ensure their survival, success, peace, and happiness. Vedic people realized that with the help of sacrifices, they could use supernatural powers through prayers and supplications and augment their limited physical and mental powers to engage in acts of creation on a smaller scale for their or the world's welfare. In the sacrificial rituals, they saw an opportunity to manifest their desires and wishes by reenacting creation on a smaller scale. In them, they also saw an opportunity to harness the powers of the Creator, namely creation, preservation, destruction, and regeneration, repeatedly and willfully on a regular and recurring basis. Symbolically and outwardly, they symbolized God's power hidden in the whole creation. Spiritually, they showed them the way to engage in sacrificial actions and attain liberation.

In the inward ritual, which can be any physical or mental action, the ascetic who engages in desireless actions to escape from samsara becomes the sacrificer, the sacrifice, the priest, and the recipient of the sacrifice. Symbolically, his body represents the Field or the sacrificial altar. His head represents the pit into which one pours the oblation of consciousness and the offerings of all the actions of the mind and body and all the joys, sorrows, feelings, emotions, sensations, etc., arising from them as their fruit. The mind represents Indra, the leader of the gods. Digestive fire represents Agni. Breath represents the fuel that keeps the fires in the body burning. Discernment or wisdom represents Varuna, the enforcer of laws. Soma represents passions and emotions (rasas). The Self represents Isvara, the Lord. The senses and organs act as the gods who serve Indra, do his bidding, and accompany him for their share of the offering. When oblations (actions) are poured into that sacrifice with desires, fire (*Agni*) receives them and distributes them among the organs (divinities) in the body according to their share and participation. When such sacrifices are performed with selfish intentions, the karma that accrues from them goes to the one who performs them. He becomes responsible for the joys and sorrows arising from them and remains bound. However, when an ascetic performs them as an offering to the Self without desires and expectations, he does not incur karma and gradually, through such sacrificial actions, purifies himself and sets himself free. This is the essence of karma-sannyasa yoga, which is well described in the Bhagavadgita and several Upanishads.

The growing awareness of Brahman as the highest and absolute God and His presence in creation as the inmost Self of all jivas elevated the originally ritualistic Vedic tradition into a higher spiritual dimension. The purely ritualistic Purva Mimansa philosophy gave way to the spiritual and philosophical Vedanta or Uttara Mimansa philosophy. With the emergence of several ascetic traditions and the inclusion of Shaivism, internal rituals became more significant than external ones, although neither of them was ignored, and each was given due importance in the Vedic way of life. As the meditating seers dwelled upon the supreme Self, they found each human being to be a replica of the eternal Purusha, the Macrocosmic Being described in the creation hymns, and in this reorientation of Vedic thought, the gods now became the inhabitants of the subtle worlds of the cosmos and the subtle planes of human consciousness, nourishing themselves with the energies flowing in them. They are happy as long as beings are engaged in worldly actions and seeking worldly enjoyment. They become displeased if one turns to spirituality, renounces worldly life and enjoyment, restrains the mind and senses, and engages in spiritual practice. Hence, the scriptures advise yogis to take refuge in the Self or Brahman so that these gods cease to be troublesome.

Thus, by internalizing the Vedic sacrifices and recognizing their value in spiritual practice, Vedic seers laid the foundation for transforming the tradition into a holistic system useful to both householders, hermits, and ascetics. Sacrifices became central to all the traditions and sects that subsequently became a part of Hinduism. Vedic philosophies soared high to new heights. The seers deliberated upon the cosmic phenomena using ritual terminology associated with the sacrifices. They saw the idea of sacrifice hidden in all aspects of human life and creation itself. They speculated that life originated on earth due to a sacrifice, humans manifested due to a sacrifice only, suffering arises when humans forget to perform sacrifices, and they can resolve their suffering by transforming their lives and actions into sacrifices. They identified the symbolism hidden in the composition of the human persona and drew parallels between human actions and sacrifices and between parts of the human body and parts of the sacrifice. In the new ritual model, they envisioned that all human actions and their consequences could be elevated into internal or external sacrifices and escape from karma by consecrating them to the all-pervading, absolute Brahman or the Self without desires and attachments. It also led them to envision a divine-centered life in which a devotee could live life as a sacrifice and escape from the cycle of births and deaths.

Brahman, as the priest

Just as the concept of ritual became internalized and the very existence of a human being was attributed to a symbolic act of sacrifice in a much larger sacrificial act of creation by God Himself, the concept of employing a priest in elaborate and complex rituals as a Brahman priest to preside over them as the chief witness, just like Brahman, and supervise them as the head priest became the norm. Usually, a senior priest with considerable knowledge and experience was chosen for this purpose. In Vedic sacrifices, he played an important role both before and during the sacrifice to ensure that it proceeded strictly according to the established procedure. As an overseer, he maintained the continuity, integrity and purity of the sacrifices, helped by the Hotri, Udgatri, Adharvayu, and other priests. The Hotr or Hotri priest initiated the rituals by inviting the gods to the ritual place with the chanting of the Rigvedic hymns. The Udgatri priest sang Samans from the Samaveda and invited the gods to come to the ritual place and accept the offerings. The Adharvayu priest ensured that the sacrifice was conducted correctly according to the established procedures, chanting the hymns from the Atharvaveda and ensuring that the offerings were prepared and made to the gods as ordained. The Brahman priest was responsible for the overall success of the ritual. He carried out supervisory and expiatory functions and acted as the binding thread between the external and internal aspects of the ritual. As an experienced and knowledgeable priest, he kept a watchful eye on the activities of other priests, remaining silent throughout. His silence provided continuity during the official breaks when the priests were not required to chant any hymns. Most importantly, he performed expiatory functions so that any mistakes by the priests during the performance of the ritual were neutralized and the ritual purity was not compromised. Thus, through his detached and silent presence, the Brahman priest played a vital role in the performance of the ritual and its success.

Brahman, the Universal Priest

The silent, watchful, and observant seer, the healer and expatiator who remained in the background in the performance of rituals but without whom the ritual could not be performed or completed, fitted the description of Brahman perfectly and helped the Vedic seers to describe Him in ritual terms. As the silent and ever-watchful witness consciousness, Brahman, in His aspect Isvara, makes possible the ritual of creation on a universal scale. He maintains its purity, continuity, and integrity through the laws (*dharma*) that He creates and enforces and keeps a watchful eye on the gods and other beings as they play their respective roles. At times, As Isvara, He punishes the beings for their lapses and at times, condones them if they repent and mend their ways. In the jivas, Brahman remains hidden as the invisible Self and participates silently in their actions as a witness and enjoyer of the sacrifice of life. In the macrocosm, He makes sure that everyone lives and acts according to their respective nature (*dharma*). Truly, Brahman is the most ancient priest. Every cycle of creation is an act of His sacrifice, and every aspect of His creation is either an aspect of ritual or a ritual by itself. In the Bhagavadgita, we find echoes of the same idea in the following verses:

"He who is free from attachment, who is liberated, whose mind is established in knowledge, whose actions are but actions of sacrifice only, his actions are completely dissolved. His offering is Brahman; his oblation is Brahman; his sacrificial fire is Brahman, and the sacrificer is Brahman. He certainly attains Brahman, who finds Brahman situated in all activities. Some offer sacrifices to gods by performing yagnas, while the mystics worship the Supreme Brahman perfectly by offering the Self as a sacrifice in the fire of Brahman" (Chap. 4.23-25).

"I am Kratu (Vedic ritual), I am Yajna (sacrificial ceremony), I am Svadha (an offering in the sacrificial ceremony), I am medicine, I am the Mantra (the sacred chant), I am Adyam (fuel in the yajna), I am Agni (fire), and I am Hutam (the burnt remains of an offering in the yajna (Chap. 9.16).

The Difficulties of Knowing Brahman

Any attempt to explain Brahman to the satisfaction of a mind that is driven by reason and familiar with the objectification of thought is fraught with enormous difficulties because any amount of reasoning and intellectual deliberation cannot explain that which is inexplicable. Brahman is beyond the senses, the mind, intelligence, and dreams. Then how can we explain the truths about Him to the satisfaction of intellectually curious minds? Rigvedic seers had this problem in their minds when they spoke about Him and referred to Him vaguely in neutral terms such as 'It,' 'This,' or 'That.' They firmly declare that Brahman is incomparable and indefinable. He is both immanent and transcendent. He does not fit into any image or concept that we know of except relatively and conditionally. He does not belong to any gender, although we are accustomed to viewing Him as a Cosmic Male. He does not present Himself to our state of duality except as that which He is not. We may speak of Him vaguely as this and that or as not this and not that, but we are not sure whether such vague references represent the truth about Him and bring us closer to Him. If we logically use the 'neti-neti' (not-this-not-this) approach, the only rational conclusion we ever reach is that Brahman is nothing (*shunya*) or whatever this world or a jiva is not.

The problem of understanding and knowing Brahman is comparable in many ways to our difficulties in envisioning the material universe that stretches far into infinity beyond our most advanced tools or our understanding of its mysteries, distances, and dimensions. With zillions of planets, stars, galaxies, nebulae, and interstellar spaces that span incredible distances, our material universe is a great enigma and beyond our comprehension and imagination. Even with our modern supercomputers, we cannot truly measure its depth or dimensions. Its vastness and immensity stretch our minds and challenge our empirical knowledge. It overwhelms our sense of self-importance and makes us feel humble and tiny. We may envision a part of it or weave beautiful science fiction stories around it using our imagination and scientific knowledge. However, collectively or individually, that does not adequately represent the true dimensions of the universe in which we live. It is sad but true that we may never be able to know the true dimensions of the material universe in which we live. We may never be able to travel beyond our galaxy to know what wonders lie there. If such is our difficulty with the material universe, which is within the realm of our senses, one can imagine the difficulty we have with knowing what lies beyond the limits of our minds and the senses.

The difficulty in understanding and knowing Brahman rationally is well illustrated in Kena Upanishad. Even gods are not free from their ignorance of Him (Section 3). All that we know about Brahman with some certainty is that He is unknowable to our minds and senses. Even after prolonged spiritual practices and meditation, one cannot be certain that He knows Him at all and whether he can ever be known. The Upanishads are very clear about this incongruity. They caution students not to jump to conclusions about Brahman because He does not fit into any definitions or objective notions of reality. If a yogi thinks that he knows Him, he probably does not know Him. Maybe he does not even know that he does not know. If someone thinks that he does not know Him, he probably knows Him but, out of humility, does not want to say it. Hence, the Upanishad (2.2-4) affirms this imponderable situation, "He is not understood by those who think they understand Him and understood by those who think they do not understand Him. He is known only when one experiences Him directly in all states of consciousness. The conclusion is that we can never be sure of our knowledge of Brahman. We cannot be certain about His state or His vast powers. Therefore, we must keep an open mind and keep our egos under check.

Worshipping Brahman incorrectly or ignorantly without knowing the right approach may also result in difficulties for those on the path to liberation. Isa Upanishad warns Brahman seekers not to fall into the trap of deluded notions. Seekers of Brahman must explore all the avenues while approaching Him without jumping to conclusions and should not limit themselves to pursuing specific aspects of Him. If they do, they are bound to create obstacles for themselves. Therefore, one must keep all the options open, remembering that those who worship the unmanifested (asambhuta) Brahman enter blinding darkness, and those who worship the manifested only (sambhuta) enter into still greater darkness. One should discard neither ritual knowledge nor spiritual knowledge to know Him. Both are equally important. One lays the foundation, and the other leads to Him. Knowing this, the wise ones worship Brahman ritually and spiritually with an open mind as the unmanifested and manifested and realize the former through the latter.

Even an enlightened seer like Yagnavalkya had difficulties in explaining the nature of Brahman and His creation to his challengers in a debate in the court of King Janaka. In the Brihadaranyaka Upanishad, speaking to Sakalya, one of the debaters, about the Self, he declares, *"That Self is not this, not this. It is incomprehensible, for it is not comprehended."* When Gargi Vachaknavi continues to question Him about Brahman, not because he is interested in knowing Brahman but because he wants to challenge his knowledge, Yajnavalkya expresses his discomfort, saying, " *Gargi, do not question too much. Otherwise, your head may fall off. You are asking so many questions about a divinity about whom we are not expected to ask many questions."* Elsewhere in the same Upanishad, he tries to explain what Brahman is not by using negative words such as not perishable (*aksharam*), not gross (*asthulam*), not subtle (*ananu*), not short (*ahrasvam*), not long (*adirgham*), does not cast shadow (*achchayam*), not tamasic (*athamah*), and so on (Brihad.III.8.8).

What is the original state of Brahman?

Even self-realized yogis may not have clear answers about the pure state of Brahman. For example, in the Chandogya Upanishad, Uddalaka Aruni informs Svetaketu that in the beginning, the Being was alone. He one only, and one without a second. Unsure of what he just said, he then adds that according to some in the beginning, the Non-Being was alone, without a second, and from That Non-Being the Being was produced. (Chand.5.2.1). Generally, almost all Upanishads convey the difficulty in explaining the pure and absolute state of Brahman. They recommend a deductive process by which one should exclude all that He is not to arrive at some vague idea of what He may be. This is effective only up to some level since there is no limit to what we may know or do not know. Brahman can be neither what we know nor what we do not know since whatever we know represents the objective reality, and Brahman is beyond it.

However, if practiced sincerely, the neti-neti (not-this, not-this) approach may exhaust the mind and lead to equanimity, stability, and self-absorption. For example, Brahman is not the body, not the mind, not the senses, not the intelligence, not the elements, not the matter, not the energy, not the forms, not the reality that we perceive through the senses, not the gods and goddesses, not the dualities of life, not the known, not the destructible or anything else that we know. It may lead to the conclusion that Brahman or the Self is different and distinct from the physical Self and the objective reality. He is not what one thinks He is or what one thinks He is not; He is not the names and forms by which we know ourselves and others, and He is not all the objects in our perceptual reality. This realization is in itself sufficient for some to withdraw their minds and senses from the world and look into themselves for the right answers. Yet, although this deductive process seems easy, it can work differently for different people. For some, it can go on indefinitely since there is no end to the things we know. Some, at the end of an exhaustive inquiry, may conclude that absolute reality or Brahman is nothing or nonexistent, as the Buddha did.

The truth is Brahman is both Is and Is Not at the same time. Brahman contains with Himself all the dualities. He is the Self as well as the not-self. He is both Purusha and Prakriti. He is the whole and its parts. He is here, above, and below. Indeed, all that exists here and elsewhere is Brahman only. There is nothing in the whole creation that is not Him. He is the known and the unknown, what is, what has been, and what will be. Therefore, the neti-neti method should not be taken seriously. It is an aid in our search for truth. When we say He is not the mind or the body, it is to know His essence or His pure and absolute state and realize it within ourselves through spiritual practice. Yet, it is but one aspect of Him.

Aspects of Brahman

Strictly speaking, everything in the universe is a manifestation or reflection of Brahman only in one or more modes (gunas) of nature, namely Sattva, Rajas, and Tamas. Innumerable are his forms and manifestations, but He is one and only, without a beginning and without an end. He pervades everything, conceals himself in everything, and at the same time, envelops all that is here and elsewhere. In the Upanishads, we come across many verses on Brahman, which extol His universal dimensions, inclusiveness, and infinity. However, fundamentally, they allude to His two primary aspects: the unmanifested (*avyaktam*) and the manifested (*vyaktam*). The former is His pure, infinite, primal, indistinguishable state that is devoid of qualities, names, and forms, and the latter is a differentiated state of divisions, distinctions, and diversity distinguished by numerous names, forms, modes, and qualities. In the manifested state, Brahman is subject to certain conditionality, materiality, and modes and contains within Himself an incredible depth and diversity of phenomena, worlds, beings, objects, forces, movements, consciousness, intelligence, illusions, realities, principles, laws, dualities, and manifestations.

Hidden in this manifested aspect are innumerable worlds, planets (*grahas*), and planes of existence inhabited by numerous powers, forces, and beings. Some of them are within the reach of our senses, but most are known only to the gods and beings of celestial planes. Brahman is remote and mysterious, known only to a few divinities, eternally free souls (*nitya muktas*) and liberated souls (*muktas*). Even they do not know much about Him or His manifestations except in a limited way. In each world that He creates, He manifests Himself according to the needs and goals He works out for them. The Upanishads present the immensity of Brahman and His various appearances in the objective world in conjunction with the qualities, energies, and principles of Nature. While His manifestations are numerous, He manifests fundamentally at the highest level in three forms, each of which is

His distinctive reflection in each of the three modes, namely sattva, rajas, and tamas. These, along with His original and undifferentiated aspects, constitute the four Highest manifestations of Brahman, which are listed below.

- The formless Brahman
- Isvara, the Universal Lord
- Hiranyagarbha, the Golden Egg
- Viraj, the World ruler

The last one is the presiding deity (ruler or king) of the mortal world, often described as Brahma, the illuminator. Viraj means king, sovereign, ruler, etc. Brahma is Viraj, the King, and the illuminator. Like the sun, he illuminates all. His creation is Viraji, the illuminated. Hiranyagarbha is the Witness Self, the Holy Ghost. Isvara is God, the Lord of all existence, and the King of kings. He presides over it and performs numerous obligatory duties of creation, preservation, destruction, suppression, and revelation to ensure its order and regularity. In popular Hinduism, Brahma, Vishnu, and Shiva represent the triple functions of Isvara: creation, preservation, and destruction. They have their separate existences and live in their respective worlds. These varied interpretations came into existence due to the historical processes that led to the inclusion of various sectarian traditions into the Vedic religion, which is foundational to Hinduism and subsequently became an integral part of it.

The Formless Brahman

The pure, formless Brahman or the undifferentiated absolute reality is the First Principle. It is variously described as formless (*arupam*), unmanifested (*avyaktam*), without form (*amurtam*), non-existence (*asat*), subtle (*sukshmam*), and invisible (*adrsyam*), unthinkable (*achintyam*), hidden (*nigudham*), etc. Indeed, apart from such descriptions, we know very little about this eternal, imperishable, and indivisible principle that stands above all as the source and origin of all creation. The Upanishads make occasional references to it without actually explaining what it means or what it represents. In fact, they create more confusion in the minds of the readers about the formless state of Brahman, often describing Him in contradictory terms. Maybe they want to convey His universality, inclusiveness, and oneness or they may want to challenge our knowledge and intelligence and know more about Him. The Upanishads also describe Him as "That" to suggest that He is incorporeal (without a body) and genderless. Since He has no objectivity, the best way to comprehend Him is by meditating on what He is not (neti) or cannot be. From the Upanishads we know that the One Eternal Being is beyond all, where the mind does not go, nor the senses, nor our understanding. He is first and foremost and is always ahead of the senses, mind, and intelligence, which means that He eludes us and is beyond our grasp. One may grasp It through personal experience. However, even that, we are not sure.

The undifferentiated Brahman is also often described as the Non-Being, void, nothingness, or non-existence (Asat). We may accept Brahman as non-being because beingness implies formation, individualization, and distinction, and in His essential aspect, Brahman is none of these. However, it is difficult to accept the non-existent state of Brahman as nothingness or the argument that manifestation originated from nothingness. Non-Being means Brahman without any distinct state of beingness or duality. It means the nonexistence of form or active state. If manifestation originated from nothingness, it implies that creation manifested out of nothing, without a cause, as an accidental, unintelligent, and unwilled event, which none of the theistic schools of Hindu philosophy admit. The absolute Brahman, in Its undifferentiated state, contains all the potentialities and possibilities that manifest when He enters into His differentiated state. He is the cause or the repository of all potential causes and effects that can potentially manifest when their time is due, depending upon how effects, situations, and circumstances emerge from causes and creation progresses.

Just as a tree is hidden in the seed from which it germinates, the differentiated Brahman is hidden in a latent form in the unmanifested Brahman as an idea, desire, or concept. Non-being does not mean Brahman is a non-entity. It only means the absence of being or the absence of the awakened state, movements, activities, and processes that lead to definitive outcomes. All the same, it is the source of all because everything is contained in it, enveloped by it, and arises from it. It is the ultimate primordial state to which we can trace every movement, object, and phenomenon that manifests in the creation. It is the soup of primordial intelligence, from which names and forms and the whole diversity manifest as a projection, reflection, alternate reality, or superimposition, depending upon how you may consider it.

Most Hindu schools concur with the belief that creation is essentially a process of separation or projection and transformation or evolution of things (*parinama*) rather than the creation of things out of nothing. The transformation may happen due to the appearance, concealment, or superimposition of effects from their causes. In any case, things undergo transformation and reconfiguration because of inherent factors or self-willed actions. For example, in the material world, things appear or disappear owing to the changes in their constituent principles (*tattvas*) and modes (*gunas*). Their behavior or nature also changes depending upon how the modes (*gunas*) in them are expressed or suppressed by various factors. When the senses are awake, and the mind is active, the perceptual reality is modified or concealed by desires, attachment, and distractions. When they are withdrawn and the mind is restrained and stabilized, truth manifests without discoloration and disfiguration. In that pure and unaffected state of consciousness, one experiences the true nature of one's existence. Therefore, to know the truth, it is necessary to remove the disturbances (*vrittis*) that interfere with our perceptions, thinking, and awareness.

The Creation Hymn in the Rigveda provides a vivid picture of the One that existed before creation. It states that the Primal State was neither existent nor non-existent and neither mortal nor immortal. There was no sky, no earth, no water, and no air. The days and nights were not separated because there was no sun. Apart from that One Thing, there was nothing whatsoever. Enveloped in darkness, all that existed was indiscriminate chaos, void, and formlessness. This is the state of the unmanifested Brahman, the Non-Being. The manifested Brahman personifies order and regularity, while the unmanifested Brahman is portrayed as void, chaos, and absence of duality and division.

It is doubtful whether anyone can really experience something that does not exist and can still speak about it in experiential terms. Every time we return from the deep sleep state, we do not know what happened or where we were. We may remember our dream states but not the deep sleep state in which all awareness becomes temporarily nonexistent. The undifferentiated state of things described in the Rigveda constitutes the Transcendental State (*Turya*) beyond the deep sleep state, which is the same or similar to that of the absolute Brahman or His non-existent state. No one knows what it is. Even Isvara, Hiranyagarbha, and Viraj, the three entities who emerge out of it, do not know what happened prior to their separation or manifestation. According to Taittiriya Upanishad (2.6.1), when one realizes the non-existent Brahman, one becomes non-existent. "Non-existent does one become if a person knows Brahman as Non-Being." It does not mean that one disappears completely when one realizes that Brahman is a state, not a Being. It means that those who enter His transcendental state lose all sense of duality and individuality and enter His absolute, non-dual, pure consciousness in which nothing can be consciously experienced, discerned, or recognized. It is the state in which one's own beingness or corporeality temporarily disappears without a trace.

It is difficult to explain non-existence without a reference to the existence of something. Existence and non-existence are two alternate states of the Self-same reality. The unmanifested Brahman is eternally self-existent, indestructible, and unchangeable but is unknown and imperceptible. He characterizes Purusha's nonexistence and Prakriti's unmanifested state. Both exist in creation and become nonexistent before and after creation, while Brahman, from which they arise, remains unmanifested eternally. Therefore, we cannot say that non-existence is prior to existence because they are interchangeable and different aspects of the same and singular reality. Non-existence becomes existence, and existence becomes non-existence in a cyclical process of projection and withdrawal or renewal and regeneration. They are very much like the sleeping and wakeful states of a jiva. When a person goes to sleep, we do not say whether that person is the same or different. However, we know that the wakeful state is not the same as the deep-sleep state. We recognize both as different states of the same person. Technically, non-existence is also a state of existence but is different from the existential reality with which we are familiar. A part of the unmanifested, absolute state of Brahman becomes active to unleash its creative power. The formless (*amurtam*) becomes the one with form (*murtam*). The one without names and forms (nama rupa) acquires several names and forms to create the appearance of diversity and duality.

Non-existence does not belong to the realm of human experience because it does not happen in the wakeful state of ordinary consciousness. As we have seen before, when we actually experience it, we cease to exist as we are. It is, therefore, very difficult to explain what the stateless state is. There are also other imponderables associated with the subject. For example, the process of creation appears as a transformative process, and the emergence of manifested Brahman from the unmanifested reality is an awakening process. These views seemingly contradict the premise that Brahman is immutable, permanent, eternal, and constant unless we concur with the arguments of Advaita that the changes that seem to take place in the reality of Brahman are actually illusory because of the coming together of certain conditions and phenomena which are in themselves are unreal and insubstantial. The Being and the non-Being always exist in Brahman as the two fundamental dimensions of the selfsame reality, just as different states of consciousness exist in each of us and yet do not qualify us to be treated as different persons in different states. The different aspects of Brahman are His different states of reality. They are relative to one another and yet exist in Him or His absolute state as latent states, ready to manifest in their due time.

Brahman is one and yet exists simultaneously in different states, some of which are subject to change, and others are permanent and absolute. Indiscriminate chaos and nothingness may still exist in some dimension of the universe, and it may still be manifesting alternate realities in other dimensions. Maybe creation is a continuous and never-ending process that may happen in many dimensions and spheres of the same universe or multiple universes, just as renewal and regeneration take place in various parts of our bodies and various beings regularly and recurringly. It may begin in one sphere while it may have ended somewhere else. There may be infinite creations in infinite dimensions, and infinite worlds and universes may exist in infinite states of transformation, evolution, and dissolution.

Shankaracharya interpreted the word asat as subtle and described the undifferentiated Brahman as the subtle being. He considered sat as the gross manifestation of Brahman and asat as the hidden, subtle, and transcendental state of Brahman (Mundaka 2.2.5). Both exist in the universal Self as well as the individual Self. This interpretation refutes the idea that Brahman, or the universal reality, is ever empty or pure void, as the Buddhist philosophers propose. He has a visible aspect, which is perceptible to the mind and senses in duality, and an invisible aspect, which may be perceptible to the internal organ in deep states of meditation but is never registered by the mind since it remains asleep. The undifferentiated aspect of Brahman may also be regarded as the One in which the primal Energy and the Primal Being are undifferentiated and appear as one essential reality. The differentiation begins when a mass of energy manifests as if out of nowhere and begins to undergo separation, division, transformation, differentiation, and formation.

Isvara, the Universal Lord

The word "Brah" means 'to grow, uplift, or extend.' Brahman is that force that continuously expands and is always ahead of everything that manifests within Himself. When He wakes up from sleep and activates His energies (*Prakriti*) to begin a new Day, He manifests as Isvara, the Lord of the universe and the creator of all the worlds and beings. Whether He is a passive witness or the Lord and Controller of all, we leave that to philosophers. Suffice it to say that in His wakeful state, He unleashes His energies and sets in motion the cycle of creation under His inviolable will, His consciousness or intelligence (*prajna*) acting as the seed of the things to be. Thus, Isvara is the creative Spirit, the Being, the awakened Non-Being, the Saguna Brahman, or the Brahman with qualities and state unleashes His creative energies to create the worlds, worlds within worlds, and the world order (*Rita*). He is the combination of truth (*Sat*) and consciousness (*Chit*), beauty and perfection (sundaram), and knowledge and will. As the creator of all, He is also the directing and causative Universal Force who establishes a set of inviolable natural laws and functions (*Dharma*) that are inherent to Nature and necessary to establish control and order amidst chaos and continuity amidst uncertainty. In His aspect as the Cosmic Being, the Purusha (the Universal Male), He activates His creative intelligence and primordial energy (*mula Prakriti*) to bring forth all existence.

Thus, Isvara is none other than Brahman in His awakened and active mode who emerges out of His own sleep with all His primal energies, parts, and modes (*Prakriti*) fully awakened. He is the Lord of the Universe, whom we call by various names: Isvara, Parameswara, Maheswara, Narayana, Prabhu (the Sovereign King), or God. As the creator, sustainer, and destroyer of all the worlds, He is also the Trinity, namely Brahma (the creator), Vishnu (the preserver), and Mahesa (the destroyer). Each of them, in their ultimate essence, is Isvara only, sharing the same consciousness, power, and potency but differentiated outwardly by their functions and roles in creation. As the three gunas, namely rajas, sattva, and tamas, manifest from the primeval Nature, the One becomes threefold and manifests as the Trimurthis (the Trinity), namely Brahma, Vishnu, and Mahesa in their roles as the creator, preserver and destroyer of the worlds respectively. The three-fold aspect of Brahman may manifest as independent entities, but they may be one in their essence. Therefore, they are also worshipped as Isvara and the highest Brahman in their respective sectarian traditions, namely Vedism,

Vaishnavism, and Shaivism. He is also Indra, Varuna, Agni, Vayu, Mitra, Soma, Pusan, Food, Yama, the realms of Bhu, Bhur, Suva, and Maha, Kshara (the perishable) and Akshara (the imperishable). All things exist in Him in many forms for their own ends and according to their natural inclinations. (Maitri. 5.2). As the Bhagavadgita declares, the whole creation is but a minuscule fraction of Him.

Meditating upon the formless, undifferentiated Brahman is useful to break out of the habitual thought patterns of the mind and preconceived and intellectual notions about God and the nature of reality. However, as the Bhagavadgita emphasizes, it is very difficult to stabilize the mind in the formless Brahman with faith and devotion and attain liberation. Hinduism, therefore, places special emphasis on the devotional worship of Isvara, or the qualified and differentiated Brahman, who has names, forms, and attributes. Some Dvaita schools hold that even His form is fixed and definitive. One may choose any god or deity for worship but must worship the chosen one as the highest supreme Brahman. The Upanishads extol Saguna Brahman as the golden-colored Being (*rukma varnam*) who is truth (*sat*), consciousness (*chit*), and bliss (*ananda*). Hence, Brahman is also extolled as Satchidananda. He is also truth (*satyam*), pure (*shivam*), and beauty and perfection (*sundaram*). He is Sahaja (natural) and Vidya (pure knowledge). All these attributes are useful for contemplation. Those who know Him in their meditative states as such and stabilize their minds in His thoughts become free from all sins and travel to the world of immortals upon death.

Classical yoga identifies the individual Self as Isvara or the Lord in the body and recommends devotional meditation on Him (*Isvara pranidhana*) to suppress the modifications of the mind (*vrittis*) and overcome the afflictions (*klesas*). In the Katha Upanishad, Lord Yama informs young Nachiketa how wise men (*dhira*) leave behind both joy and sorrow "by knowing through self-control and contemplation (*Adhyatma Yoga*) that primal Being, who is difficult to be seen, who is very mysterious, who is hidden in the cave (of one's heart) and who is situated deep (within oneself)." According to Maitri Upanishad (6.18), oneness with

Him can be achieved through the practice of six-fold (*sadanga*) yoga, namely breath control (*pranayama*), withdrawal of the senses (*prayahara*), meditation (*dhyana*), concentration (*dharana*), intellectual inquiry (*tarka*) and self-absorption (*samadhi*).

According to the Paingala Upanishad (1.4), the dynamism of Isvara (*Isvara chaitanyam*) arises when the primal nature (*Mula Prakriti*) in Him undergoes changes due to the preponderance of sattva and manifests as His persona with active consciousness (*chaitanyam*) infused with Her energy (*Shakti*). Yet, He holds Maya in His control and directs her to do His bidding. All knowing, He is the root cause of creation, preservation, and dissolution. He gives shape to the world whereby it manifests in Him like a sprout arising from a seed. He emerges from the waters of life because of the previous deeds of the beings and disappears when the deeds are destroyed. In Him alone remains the entire universe like a bundled piece of cloth. In the final analysis, there is no real distinction between Saguna Brahman and Nirguna Brahman. They are the different states of the Over Lord of all (*Parameswara*), who is without a second. When the Non-Being awakens (or goes into hiding since he remains hidden and invisible) with a name and form, He becomes Isvara. At the end of creation, He disappears when He withdraws the whole creation into Himself and recedes into the silent depths of His absolute pure consciousness along with His Primal Nature.

Hiranyagarbha, the Golden Egg

If Isvara is the differentiated cosmic principle and Lord of the universe, Hiranyagarbha is the World Soul (*Mahan Atma*), the Cosmic Egg (*Brahmanda*) that appears in the primordial waters of creation before all. According to the Chandogya Upanishad (3.19.3), the manifested Isvara turns Himself into an egg, from which emerges two halves. The silver-colored half becomes the earth, and the gold-colored one becomes the heavens. The earth differentiates further into mountains, clouds, rivers, and oceans. From the other half, the golden sun rises.

If Isvara is the Lord of Creation, with the preponderance of sattva, who unleashes His inviolable will to set in motion the process of creation, Hiranyagarbha is the active principle, with the preponderance of rajas, who manifests the phenomenal world that includes the earth, the sky, and the immortal world that is hidden in the sun. He is the First Born (*Prathamaja*), who executes the divine will to manifest forms that are already contained in Him. He is the thread (*sutratman*) on which all beings and all the worlds are strung like beads in a necklace. If Isvara is the causative principle (*karanabhutam*), Hiranyagarbha is the implementing principle (*kriyabhutam* or *karyabhutam*). The Paingala Upanishad (1.5) describes him as the power of projection, known as mahat, arising from Isvara, and it manifests both distinctly and indistinctly.

Hiranyagarbha may be none other than Brahma, who manifests from Narayana (Isvara) as His projection. He is the creative and dynamic principle who uses the forms existing in Him to bring forth the beings. The sun that rises from the waters of the ocean every morning like a golden orb and makes life possible on Earth symbolizes Hiranyagarbha. The word "brah" means "bursting out or bringing forth," and "ahm" means ego. Brahma means the one who brings forth many "ahams" or egos or individual entities into this world. Using his divine power and the primordial matter, he pours the life breath, or prana the vital energy, into them. Hiranyagarbha is not an eternal being but the seed of life, objectivity, materiality, and dynamism that comes into existence at the beginning of creation and becomes dissolved in Isvara at the end of creation.

Viraj, the World

Viraj is the materiality, or the world of forms, brought forth by the creative process set in motion by Isvara and manifested by Hiranyagarbha. He is Brahma, or an aspect of Brahma, who represents the world that is illuminated by him and which we perceive in a state of duality or objectivity. Some equate him with the personification of the objective reality or logos, and some with Manu Swáyambhu, the overlord of the world and the ancestor of the human race in each Manvantara. Paingala Upanishad identifies him with Vishnu, the preserver (1.6). Viraj is the manifested aspect of divine will, the seed consciousness. He represents the perceptual world, which, according to some schools, is a formation or an appearance. He also personifies the earth-consciousness and the collective will of the earthly beings. Like Hiranyagarbha and all creation, Viraj is also subject to dissolution. A new Brahma appears after 100 Brahma years or in each universe created by Brahman. Also, at the beginning of each Manu's reign (*manvantara*), a new Manu appears, whose duration, according to the Vishnu Purana, is 71 times the number of years present in all the four major epochs (*yugas*) put together, which is equal to roughly 306,720,000 human years. In contrast to the previous three aspects of Brahman, Viraj is a limited manifestation characterized by the transience of things and frequent disturbances. It is also not self-illuminated but illuminated by the Deity who presides over it.

Indeed, Viraj is not an exception. All three manifestations, Isvara, Hiranyagarbha, and Viraj, arise from Brahman as reflections in the modes (*gunas*) of Nature, with Brahman remaining concealed in them as a distinct reality. They are not real because they are mere reflections of Brahman, the one essential and absolute reality. At the end of creation, they are withdrawn into That. In the microcosm of a jiva or a human being, the inner Self, Atman, is the unmanifested Brahman or the Non-Being, the elemental self is Isvara, Brahma is the ego, and Viraj is the name and form. In terms of human consciousness, the transcendental state is the formless Brahman, the witness consciousness is Isvara, intelligence is Hiranyagarbha, and the mind and body constitute Viraj. We may also extend these manifestations to the Hindu Trinity. Sada Shiva, or the Rudra of Vedas or Svetasvatara Upanishad, is Parameswara, the Over Lord or the formless Brahman. Narayana, or Vishnu, is the Isvara, who appears from the waters of life, resting on the coils of the primal serpent (*Adishesha*). Brahma is the Hiranyagarbha, who arises from the navel of Vishnu, seated on a lotus, and creates the worlds. Siva, the destroyer, is Viraj, the manifested reality, which is subject to constant renewal and destruction. We may also compare them to the Trinity of Christianity: the formless Brahman to the Holy

Ghost, Isvara to the Father, and Brahma to Isaputra (the son of God) or the World Body.

Hinduism and the Belief in One God

Belief in many gods and goddesses is one of the most well-known and fundamental aspects of Hinduism since ancient times. If there is one religion in the world that unhesitatingly embraces the ancient practice of worshipping multiple gods both ritually and spiritually, it is Hinduism. At the same time, Hinduism is not a polytheistic religion in the sense that each divinity is considered either an aspect of the highest Brahman or Brahman Himself. Just as a human being is a father, son, brother, uncle, friend, enemy, stranger, relation, husband, grandfather, and a member of society, in creation, the one God assumes many roles and appears as many to fulfill His obligatory duties and ensure the welfare and orderliness of the worlds. Therefore, Hindus not only worship numerous divinities but also believe in the existence of one Supreme God, whom they call variously Paramatma (Supreme Self), Parameshwar (Supreme Lord), Parampita (Supreme Father), Isvara, Maheswara, Bhagawan, Purusha, Purushottama, Hiranyagarbha and so on. They also believe that each human being (*Purusha*) is a replica of the Cosmic Person (*Purusha*) who manifests in creation.

According to the Hindu scriptures, God is the first, original, and ultimate source of all creation. He is not mere consciousness, as some traditions believe, but a controller and creator who acts as the causative principle to manifest different states of reality and existence in innumerable forms and shapes, which He creates. As Purusha (Universal Male), He expends His energies (primordial forces of Nature) and brings forth the worlds and beings into existence. He upholds the entire creation with His Maya (deluding potency). The Upanishads describe Him as the manifested and the unmanifested, the Being and the Non-Being, and the real and unreal. As the unmanifested, He is meditated upon but not worshipped because Hindu scriptures declare that difficult and painful is the path for those who choose to worship Him as the unmanifested (BG. 14.6).

Brahman exists in all and envelops all. He is without a second, which means there is nothing other than Him, and nothing exists outside of Him. He is Imperishable, inexhaustible, unknowable, immortal, and infinite, without a beginning and an end. Nevertheless, He liberates those who meditate upon Him in their hearts as saguna Brahman and prepares for their liberation those who worship Him or His many forms as saguna Brahman. All the gods and goddesses are His manifestations only. In His female aspect, He is Shakti, the Divine Universal Mother, who activates the guns (qualities) and manifests diversity.

The concept of monotheism is not new to Hinduism. We can trace its antecedents to the Vedas themselves. There are references to the one indivisible and mysterious God in the Rigveda. The Upanishads acknowledge Him as the indisputable and ultimate cause of creation and existence. Brahman, the one God, manifests as many. He is both immanent and transcendent. At the highest level, He manifests as the primal Being, Brahman, Isvara, Hiranyagarbha, the elements, the worlds, the divinities, and the beings. While the seers meditate upon Him as their inner Self, those who are accustomed to the formal methods of ritual offerings accept Him as their personal deity (*Isvara*) and worship Him with faith and devotion. The rise of Vaishnavism, Shaivism, and Shaktism changed the equation between God and His devotees. The tantric worshippers of Shakta traditions identified Brahman with Pradhana (primordial nature) and worshipped the Universal Mother as the controller and creator of all, relegating Purusha (Shiva) to a secondary position as the passive witnessing Self. The Upanishads describe the state of Brahman as truth, consciousness, and bliss (*satchitananda*). He exists in the individual beings as the inner Self (atman), who takes delight in things and bears witness to all the happenings of the mind and body. However, He is not tainted by their activities or the illusions of life which He witnesses. When the senses are quiet, and the mind is silent and restful in equanimity, He emerges from the depths of our own being as the resplendent Self filled with endless bliss. Isvara, the Lord of the Universe, is the all-controlling and all-pervading Supreme Lord. Some believe that even liberation is not possible without His grace. In contrast, Isvara, the Lord in the body, is a passive witness who does not participate in any of the activities of the mind and body.

The Paths to Brahman

There are many paths to Brahman. Just as all rivers lead to the ocean, all paths lead to Brahman only. However, the spiritual traditions of Hinduism identify a few broad-based approaches to realizing Brahman, namely the path of action, the path of knowledge, the path of devotion, and the path of renunciation. They can all be integrated into a holistic approach since there are no rigid rules about how to practice them. One can even integrate the classical yoga of Patanjali into them. Of the main paths, the devotional path is considered superior, the path of action is considered preliminary or preparatory, the path of knowledge is considered difficult to pursue, and the path of renunciation is difficult to practice.

The Bhagavadgita integrates all these approaches into an integrated practice called Karma-sannyasa yoga, according to which one must pursue knowledge (*jnana yoga*) to discern the Self, perform obligatory duties (*karma yoga*) to serve God and uphold Dharma, renounce (*sannyasa*) desires and attachments hidden in actions, including desire for their fruit, and offer them to God, establishing their mind in Him, and surrendering to Him with exclusive devotion and detachment. By practicing it, one attains freedom from karma (*naishkarmya siddhi*) and is no longer tainted by actions. The practice of austerities and self-control (*atma-samyama yoga*), purifying intelligence for discernment (*buddhi yoga*), contemplation, and concentration (*dhyana yoga*) are ancillary practices that lead to self-purification, predominance of sattva and quick progress on the path.

According to Hinduism, God (*Isvara*) is both personal and impersonal. He is with form and without form. As a personal God, He is approachable and adorable, loves His devotees, reciprocates their love and devotion, and grants them liberation. At the same time, as the universal Self, He is indifferent and equal to all. Hidden within each jiva, also as the witness Self, he remains indifferent and passive and does not interfere with the actions of the jiva. He is not God of just one world or a few worlds but contains within Himself and presides over the entire known, unknown, gross, and subtle creation. The material universe is His body. We are indeed his voices and faces and contain within ourselves a miniature version of all that He represents. While the absolute and formless Brahman is worshipped contemplatively by ascetics and pursuers of knowledge, His other forms and aspects are worshipped both ritually and devotionally by householders and common people.

Elements of Monotheism in the Early Vedic Tradition

This discussion is about the origin and development of the concept of God in Hinduism in the context of the Vedas in general and the Isa Upanishad in particular and whether the elements of monotheism entered Hinduism indigenously through prevailing traditions or some external source such as Judaism or Christianity as claimed by some Christian scholars. Vedic people were aware of a single supreme universal God from the earlier days, but they did not mention Him publicly nor made Him any sacrificial offerings directly because of the instructions implied in the Vedas, which encouraged the worship of divinities who needed the ritual food as their nourishment rather than Brahman who was the source of it.

This discussion aims to refute the speculation that the Isa Upanishad of the Yajurveda was composed in the post-Christian era after the Indian scholars came to know about the idea of a universal God from other traditions that existed outside India. This rather erroneous view further holds that ancient Indians had no concept of God or Parameswara prior to the Christian era and that they worshipped only different devas or gods. According to this absurd theory, Hindus copied the idea of Parameswara or God from El Elyon, meaning the highest of the Middle Eastern traditions. In his translation, one of the scholars referred to Isa as Jesus and tried to work around some important concepts of Hinduism mentioned in the Isa Upanishad by imparting to them a rather distorted meaning in support of his speculation. The fact is Isa is a Vedic god, the guardian of the Northeast direction, and equated in the Upanishad with Brahman and Isvara, the Lord of the Universe. The Upanishad is not a tantric text but a Vedic text and contains many important beliefs and doctrines of Hinduism. It even seems to correlate with the Bhagavadgita's teachings.

Whatever the motivation behind such arguments, the scholar who proposed them [1] has done at least a good job by translating the

Upanishad, which is a non-Christian text in origin, and acknowledging it as a sacred and venerable work. In doing so, he ignored the fact that the Upanishad is essentially a Vedic text that speaks about renouncing the ownership of things and doership of actions and echoes the same sentiment as the karma sannyasa yoga of the Bhagavadgita while stressing the importance of performing good actions and remembering them at the time of cremation and the soul's departure from this world. It asks departing souls to remember their good deeds so that they can attain a good life in the next birth. These are essentially Hindu beliefs. The Upanishad also reminds us that all that exists here is inhabited by Isa, the all-pervading supreme God and the source of all actions and their results, including the actions we perform. Therefore, by remembering that one should wish to live here for a hundred years, by performing obligatory duties and without desiring to enjoy their fruit. Thus, we can see that the Upanishad is essentially a Vedic text that embodies important concepts of Hinduism and has no connection with any foreign source.

From a Hindu perspective, there is no transgression if someone identifies Isa with Jesus because names and forms are our temporary illusions that disappear when we realize the transcendental unity or oneness of the whole existence. On the contrary, it may ruffle the sentiments of a few Christians because Christianity does not recognize the scriptures of other faiths and regards them contemptuously as pagan or blasphemous. Comparatively, Hinduism is more tolerant towards other faiths. In Hinduism, one may call God by any name. Name is just a convenience to address 'That,' which is beyond all names, forms, and words.

However, the attitude with which the author tried to justify his theory shows his lack of knowledge of history, his ignorance of the Vedic tradition, and his inability to comprehend the imagery, philosophy, and symbolism contained in the Vedic scriptures. Mr. Ninan conveniently forgot that long before the advent of Christianity, the Zoroastrians worshipped a universal God, and many concepts and beliefs of Zoroastrians found their way into Abrahamic religions. He was probably not aware that

Zoroastrianism was later than the Vedic tradition and that the ancestors of Zoroastrians shared many common beliefs with Vedic people, including Sanskrit as the medium of expression and the sacrificial worship of numerous gods using fire. He ignored the fact that long before the birth of Jesus, the Indian subcontinent witnessed the birth of many theistic traditions and complex philosophies, some of which are still popular today. He conveniently overlooked the opinion of many scholars who think that the ancient Greek philosophers drew richly from the wisdom of the ancient Indian masters. Before misinterpreting the scripture, he should have read the history of ancient religions such as Brahmanism, Jainism, Buddhism, and Zoroastrianism and their connection with primitive Christianity, as pointed out by historians like Arthur Lillie [2]. He should have also followed the advice of Mr. R. Gordon [3], who urged his Christian friends about 200 years ago to recognize some portions of the Hindu scriptures as an ethnic Old Testament because of their value in clarifying certain immanent values of the religion. Gordon wrote:

"Christianity in India needs the Vedanta. We missionaries have not realized this with half the clearness that we should. We cannot move freely and joyfully in our own religion because we have not sufficient terms and modes of expression wherewith to express the more immanental aspects of Christianity. A very useful step would be the recognition of certain books and passages in the literature of the Vedanta as constituting what might be called an Ethnic Old Testament. The permission of ecclesiastical authorities would then be asked for reading passages found in such a canon of Ethnic Old Testament as divine service along with passages from New Testament as alternatives to the Old Testament lessons."

The philosophy and the concepts found in the Upanishads are universal and perfectly fit into any religion as its essential philosophy concerning God. If we ignore the outer and ritual aspects of Hinduism as well as the individual divinities and their outer forms, we can easily incorporate its deeper philosophical truths into any religion. The truths reflected in the Upanishads and the methods and techniques they recommend for one's spiritual practice and transformation in all respects perfectly complement any religion, dogma, or philosophy.

The Sutra literature of Hinduism, especially the Aphorisms of Brahma (*Brahma Sutras*) are very useful to contemplate upon the nature and significance of Brahman and realize Him as the First Cause of the entire manifestation. The Western world would know a great deal about the nature of reality and the essential nature of our consciousness by studying the Upanishads and the Brahma Sutras, also known as the Vedanta Sutras. We know how yoga enabled people in various parts of the world to stabilize their minds and experience different states of consciousness independent of their religious and spiritual beliefs. Yoga is but one of the Darshanas (philosophies) of Hinduism. Its associate philosophy, the Classical Samkhya, is useful for understanding the energies and components of the human body and how they can be aligned for one's physical and spiritual well-being. Vedanta, which is another school of Hinduism and which is based on the knowledge of the Upanishads, has the same potential to help people lead better lives independent of their religious beliefs. One does not have to believe in Hindu divinities to follow its philosophical truths or practice its methods. Beyond names and forms, categories, and distinctions, Hinduism has a universal appeal. It has an abstract philosophy as its essence, which is time immemorial and can be incorporated into any dogma or spiritual practice.

It offers a variety of choices to its followers to practice their faith according to their essential nature or natural propensity. This is one of the advantages of practicing it. It is less dogmatic and encourages free inquiry based on the universal truths found in the Vedas. In an ideal world, followers of other faiths should not have any quarrel with Hinduism because it believes in the divinity of all beings and the possibility of our liberation and immorality according to our faith, devotion, and effort. In this endeavor, religion is just a method, path, yoga, or an approach. Each religion is but a tool. When we become deeply attached to any religion rather unthinkingly and egoistically, it becomes a hindrance rather than a facilitator in our spiritual journey to realizing oneness with the Creator.

Ninan's contention that Indians got the idea of Parameswara from the Semitic expression of El Elyon and then used it to compose the Isa Upanishad is farfetched. In a way, in Christian terms, it is blasphemy because Hindus regard the Vedas, of which the Upanishads are the end parts, as divine revelations (shruti). They believe that the Vedas are eternal and inviolable and that Brahma revealed them to humans for their welfare, unlike the other scriptures, such as the Dharma Shastras (law books) or the Puranas. They are believed to be an authority on universal truths because they exist eternally in the highest realm of Brahman as truths of our existence and are revealed in each cycle of creation to humans for their material and spiritual well-being. Hence, all the philosophical schools of Hinduism to the Vedas for proof to substantiate their arguments and establish their validity. For them, as far as the transcendental truths are concerned, the Vedas are the final authority, inviolable and irrefutable.

The Vedic people did not worship Brahman ritually because they believed that rituals were meant to nourish the gods who depended upon humans to satisfy their hunger, while Brahman was incorporeal, was not subject to hunger, and needed no nourishment or sacrificial offering. They worshipped Brahman internally, acknowledging Him as the inner deity (*antaryami*), practicing austerities (*tapas*), studying the scriptures (*svadhyaya*), hearing (*sravanam*), remembering (*mananam*), and thinking about God's glories (nidhidhyasana) and inquiring rationally into the nature of Brahman or disputing theories that seemed too farfetched (*tarka*). The Vedic scriptures appealed to people differently according to their predominant nature. According to Sri Aurobindo [4], they were conceived and constructed on the principle of providing concrete sense for the mass of ordinary worshippers and spiritual sense for the select ones.

Isa Upanishad identifies Brahman as the highest Supreme Being but places equal emphasis on the worship of both the manifested Brahman (*sambhutam*) and the transcendental, unmanifested Brahman (*asambhutam*). It also speaks about knowledge (*vidya*) and ignorance (*avidya*), the existence of multiple worlds of light and darkness, and the transient nature of heavenly life. These concepts are alien to Christianity. The Upanishad is a pure Vedic text with concepts that are fundamentally aligned with the Vedic worldview and the beliefs of Vedic religion, including the concept of Karma. Though it consists of only 18 verses, its philosophy bears a close resemblance to the Bhagavadgita. It is indeed more aligned with the teachings of the Bhagavadgita rather than the Bible.

Hinduism evolved out of many streams of thoughts, all of which originated and developed in the Indian subcontinent, with little input from outside. By the time the four Vedas took their current format, India was a spiritual center of the world. Seven hundred years before Christ, it witnessed a medley of conflicting thoughts and ideas of profound significance, which in many ways heralded what was to appear later in Greece and elsewhere. It produced many new religious sects, ascetic movements, and independent traditions that reflected upon visionary idealism, passive anarchism, agnostic skepticism, and down-to-earth philosophies of materialism, such as that of the Charvakas or the Lokayatas. Freedom of thought flourished despite Vedic Puritanism, the weight of scriptural authority, and a rigid social structure that rested its foundation and justification in fatalism. Many religious leaders, thinkers, and philosophers appeared on the horizon, who speculated upon the nature of reality and human existence logically as well as intuitively without ignoring the value of scriptural testimony in knowing the truths of life.

If there was an attempt on the part of some to fathom the depth of their own being through ascetic practices and rigorous austerities, there were others who submitted themselves to the vagaries of fate with nihilistic resignation, advocating their beliefs in the predetermined progression of events and encouraged people to lead an effortless and passive life to overcome suffering. Elsewhere, in pastoral communities, ordinary people busied themselves with sacrificial rituals and offerings, while great souls like Yajnavalkya, Janaka, Buddha, and Mahavira explored new paths and alternate belief systems breaking away from existing traditions and worn-out philosophies, seeking liberation and lasting solutions to the problem of mortality and human suffering. Their inquiry was rooted in the freedom of thought that sprung neither from the assurances of constitutional guarantees of a political system nor from the enlightened self-interest of truth seekers but from the faith that rested upon the belief that the eternal reality that existed in the universe outside of oneself also existed within oneself and to know the essential truths about it one must withdraw and look into oneself beyond all the noise and distractions. They were inspired by the idealism of human life and the possibilities of divinizing human nature to transcend the limitations to which the mind and body were subject. They looked for meaning in an apparently meaningless life and permanence in an impermanent world. They had a passion for truth and an abundant curiosity and conviction to fathom the secrets of life beyond the limits of human intelligence and sensory perceptions.

Whether Western scholars acknowledge it or not, in the ancient world, India was an epicenter of profound religious philosophies, ascetic traditions, spiritual movements, and ageless wisdom. It was blessed with mystics, agnostics, religious leaders, spiritual masters, and scholars who possessed great intelligence, knowledge, erudition, and foresight. It has always been, as it is now, an epicenter of the world's spirituality. For a very long time, the ancient seers of India guarded their knowledge defiantly and refused to acknowledge or incorporate alien ideas into their tradition. They even detested the idea of establishing any contact with foreigners and recommended purification rituals for those who crossed the oceans and lived in distant lands. It is hard to believe in the absurd argument put forward by the likes of Ninan that the ancient people of India waited for 2000 years to arrive at the idea of a Supreme Being through an alien tradition with which they had no meaningful contact until modern times.

The Vedic scholars of ancient India were familiar with the concept of an absolute and eternal Being as the source of all as early as 1500 BC, in the development of which neither Christianity nor Judaism played any role either directly or indirectly at any point of time in the history of Hinduism. They were not only aware of Brahman, but they also debated His essential nature and, at times, doubted His existence and His involvement in our lives and destinies. The theistic and atheistic traditions of India existed long before Christianity emerged on the scene as a major world religion. In the early Christian era, when it grappled with its own survival under Roman emperors, Hinduism and Buddhism were the dominant religions of the world, and scholars of both religions frequently debated about the existence or non-existence of a creator God and the source and cause of all.

The Vedic priests did not worship Brahman, the universal Self, ritually but were aware of Him conceptually. They did not worship Him directly because the sacrificial rituals were meant for the divinities, and they believed in the cosmic order, which they did not want to disturb and incur the wrath of the gods. However, they revered Him internally and contemplatively, as is evident from the Upanishads, seeking peace and liberation rather than material wealth. In this discussion, I am not even going to discuss the religious life of the Indus Valley civilization and its possible connection with the Saraswathi civilization, which was believed to have flourished around 5000 BCE. I am content to confine my discussion to the general descriptions of the Vedic religion as mentioned in many standard books of Indian history with its starting point as 2500 BCE or so. I present below my views regarding the monotheistic elements of early Hinduism.

1. The concept of a single universal God as the lord and controller of the world or all the worlds was known to the people of Egypt, Persia, and India long before Christ was born and also before Abraham of the Old Testament. We find traces of monotheism in some of the earliest Rigvedic hymns. Dyaus, the shining god of heaven, and Prithvi, the earth goddess, are "among the oldest of the Vedic deities." [5] Varuna, who is also mentioned in Zoroastrianism and who bears the epithet asura (*ahura*), was the "sovereign of the universe and guardian of the moral law," or Rta. Some of the earliest Rigvedic hymns, such as the following, clearly reflect the elements of monotheism in early Vedic religion [6].

They call him Indra, Mitra, Varuna and Agni;
He is the heavenly bird, Garutmat.
To what is One, the poets give many a name. They call it Agni, Yama, and Matariswan.

In the hymn addressed to Hiranyagarbha (the cosmic golden germ), we find the following expression:

Who is our Father, our Creator, Maker,
Whom every place doth know and every creature;
By whom alone the gods were given their names,
To Him all creatures go, to ask Him.

Hiranyagarbha was a manifestation of Brahman. He brought forth the worlds according to the will of Isvara or the manifested Brahman. The Vedic people did not see the gods as self-born individual entities but as manifestations of one essential power. They speculated upon their origin and their essential unity and viewed them in the context of the larger framework of creation governed by a supreme, universal Lord.

2. In the ancient world, Jesus was not the only person who was recognized as the son of God. It was a common tradition in India, Egypt, and Persia to regard a king as God himself in human form or a direct descendent of God and submission to him and his rule as a mark of devotion and loyalty. The son of a divine ruler was regarded as the son of God and treated with utmost fear and respect by virtue of his birth. Brahma, the creator god, had many sons, some born out of him as his mind born sons (*manasaputras*) and the rest created by him. The list included gods, demons, and humans. Kings and queens often assumed divine epithets to remind people of their special status and their direct equation with gods. It reduced political tensions, ensured the loyalty of the subjects, prevented possible rebellions, and ensured the continuity and survival of the institution of monarchy. These practices were the political ramification of religious beliefs and the clever manipulation of human sentiment to bind people to their states and rulers.

3. Closely related to the concept of God in Vedic religion was the

concept of Rta, or the natural order of things and events. Ancient Indians believed that the regularity of events experienced in life, in the form of recurring days and nights, months and seasons, aging and death, and movement of stars and planets, suggested the existence of an invisible and intelligent controller or regulator who with his unassailable power, ensured their continuity and the predictability (niyati) of the world. They referred to that power as the will of Brahman and believed that things happened predictably out of fear and the power of Brahman.

4. As far back as 1500 BCE, ancient people of the Indian subcontinent had the concept of a single universal God whom they referred to as Brahman, Isvara, Hiranyagarbha, Hiranmayi-Prajapati, or simply as "That." In the words of George Feuerstein [7], "*The nuclei of the oldest Upanishads - Brihadaranyaka, Chandogya, Kausitaki, Aitareya, and Kena Upanishad - appear to date back over three thousand years ago.*" The emergence of Brahman as the single supreme God and Lord of manifest creation happened with the internalization of Vedic rituals and externalization of the human form into cosmic, as is evident in some passages of *Katha* and *Kausitaki* Upanishads. Mr. Feuerstein further adds, "*The idea that behind the reality of multiple forms - our ever-changing universe - there abides an eternally unchanging single Being was communicated already in the Rigvedic times. What was new was that the grand discovery transcended the legacy of sacrificial ritualism.*" Brahman was a mystery even to the gods, then what to say of men! The Kena Upanishad explains how the gods themselves were unaware of the supreme Brahman until they came to know about Him from Uma Haimavati, after a brief encounter with Him, in which they were outsmarted by the mysterious Being. A minuscule knowledge of Him made Indra the leader of the heavens and Vayu and Agni prominent deities. Descriptions such as these and the equation of Brahman with Siva or Rudra support the speculation that elements of monotheism and devotional worship of personal Gods entered Hinduism through ascetic traditions such as Shaivism.

5. Out of the Upanishads that are presently available to us, a few are considered the oldest and the most important. Of them, Isa

Upanishad is one. If we accept Mr. Ninan's argument that Isa Upanishad was composed after the Christian era, we have to predate the oldest Upanishads, which speak about Brahman or the Universal Being, and most of the Samhitas and Brahmanas associated with them by several centuries, which do not agree with the other evidence which point to their antiquity. It also means we have to rewrite Indian history, pushing their dates forward to nearly 600-1000 years after the birth of the Buddha and Mahavira and subsequent to Kautilya, the author of Arthashastra, Chandragupta Maurya, a contemporary of Alexander and Asoka, who converted to Buddhism and organized the Second Buddhist Council. This dating is absurd because many principal Upanishads were composed before the advent of Buddhism and long before the emergence of the Mauryan dynasty. The age ascribed by most historians to the earliest Upanishads usually falls between 1500 BCE and 800 BCE. Some Indian scholars stretch the date back to 2000 BC or so.

6. Brahman is frequently referred to in Upanishads in neutral gender as "That," a concept that is alien to the Semitic religions, which always address God as masculine. The oldest of the Upanishads, the Brihadaranyaka Upanishad, contains the famous saying (*mahavakya*), "Aham Brahmasmi," meaning I am Brahman. Another important statement about Brahman found in them is tattvamasi (you are That). One of the verses in the Isa Upanishad contains the poignant expression, soham asmi, meaning whatever is That, That also I am. These are pure Indian expressions found in no other religious tradition. The Judeo-Christian religions are fundamentally dualistic, whereas several passages in the Upanishads present a monistic view of God as the absolute and ultimate reality and creation as a projection or superimposition upon it. In the Old Testament, when Moses encounters God and asks Him who He is, He replies, "I am I am." In both Testaments of the Bible, we do not find human beings expressing unity with God in such exalted words, whereas, in the Upanishads, we find them frequently and use them as starting points or great statements (mahavakyas) for meditation.

7. The idea of a supreme universal Being as the Creator and

Witness, immanent and transcendent, hidden in every aspect of creation as the subject and object, inhabiting them and enveloping them, developed in the Indian subcontinent indigenously. Through the spiritual and ascetic paths of liberation practiced in ancient India, the vision of such grandeur dawned upon the consciousness of seers and sages as they contemplated upon the mysteries of human existence, looking inwardly for the truth that was hidden within them. In deeper states of meditation, they saw the universe as an extension of themselves projected outwardly and universally upon the visible and invisible reality of the gross and subtle worlds. They saw the universal and infinite form of God in the likeness of their own form (*tattvamasi*), the reality outside as a continuation of the reality within themselves (aham Brahmasmi), and the divinities whom they worshipped in the rituals actually as residing in their own bodies in subtle form, nourishing themselves through their good deeds and acts of sacrifice. They acknowledged His sacred and silent presence, calling Him by different names and honoring His sanctity. However, they were in no hurry to reveal the profound secret to everyone indiscriminately since their emphasis was not on preaching the empty dogma but on duplicating the transcendental states within themselves and others through sustained spiritual practice and intense self-purification. Hence, they kept the secret to themselves, revealing it to a few deserving aspirants. Since the Upanishads were taught selectively and in person, as the master and the disciples sat together in a secluded place, they were known only to a few. Speaking of the singular manner in which the concept of the Supreme Being developed in India, Deussen [8] writes, *"Monotheism was attained in Egypt by a mechanical identification of the various local gods, in Palestine by the proscription of other gods and violent persecution of their worshippers for the benefit of their nation god Jehovah. In India, they reached monism, though not monotheism, on a more philosophical path seeing through the veil of the manifold the unity which underlies it."*

8. The concept of God found in the Upanishads is more complex and essentially different from the descriptions of God found in other religions. The Vedic religion was neither polytheistic nor

monotheistic but had elements of both. It is referred to as Henotheism or Kathenotheism, characterized by a belief in multiple gods, where each god stands out as the highest. The Brahman of Upanishads, in His absolute state, is an impersonal God who does not take sides nor respond to the calls of individuals because there is nothing outside of Him and there is nothing other than Him. He is complete, fulfilled, self-absorbed, and immersed in Himself. He does not communicate with anyone in a dualistic sense because to communicate, you need an object, and no object exists outside of Him. However, one can reach Him and feel Him as oneself in transcendental states. That task is performed by His other manifestations, divinities, and personal Gods, such as Vishnu and Siva, who are worshipped in their highest aspect as Brahman Himself. In Hinduism, the authority of God extends far beyond the earth and heaven to innumerable worlds of light and darkness and multiple planes of existence, from the subtlest to the grossest. The descriptions of Brahman or the Universal Self in Hinduism are not different from those of the universe found in the modern textbooks of quantum physics and astronomy, except that the former is spiritual and the latter purely material. Speaking of the Vedic vision of God, Max Mueller [8] wrote, *"In fact, the Vedic poets had arrived at a conception of the godhead which was reached once more by some of the Christian philosophers at Alexandria, but which even at present is beyond the reach of many who call themselves Christians."*

9. Isa Upanishad is one of the oldest of the Upanishads composed prior to the Christian era. The Upanishad speaks of the universal Lord "Isa" and reflects the growing influence of Vaishnavism, Shaivism, and the Bhakti (devotional) movement. Ancient Indians were familiar with the word "isa" long before the Christian era. The Upanishad does not recognize the concept of the son of God but describes God Himself as the omniscient and omnipresent ruler and dweller of not just one world but the entire universe (Jagat). Some of the concepts mentioned in it are antithetical to the main teachings of Christianity, such as the concept of karma, surrender to God, performance of obligatory duties, impermanence of life and things, detachment, departure of soul,

right knowledge and right actions, sunlit worlds (not just one heaven) and sunless worlds (not just one hell), Agni and cremation. Most importantly, some of its verses are chanted during cremation ceremonies when the deceased is consigned to flames. It advocates neither the blind worship of God nor the unbridled pursuit of material things but a balanced approach to life and liberation and an unfailing commitment to one's obligatory duties. It cautions people not to choose knowledge at the expense of obligatory duties or the ritual knowledge of the Samhitas and Brahmanas at the expense of the spiritual knowledge of Aranyakas and Upanishads to avoid entering the sunless worlds of utter darkness.

10. One of the verses in the Isa Upanishad (15) is a prayer for the departed soul's journey to the world of the sun (Surya or Savitr). The prayer makes an earnest appeal to Surya to grant the soul a passage to the sunlit world, addressing Him variously as Pusan (nourisher) and Prajapatya (son of Prajapati) [9]. According to Vedic beliefs, upon the death of a person, the individual soul travels to the world of the sun or the world of the moon, depending upon in which part of the year the person died. Those who died during the first half of the year (summer solstice) traveled along the northern route to the sun, and those who died in the second half of the year (winter solstice) went by the southern route to the moon. In the world of the moon, their causal bodies become food to the gods, and by that self-sacrifice, they exhaust much of their karma and return to the earth to be reborn again according to the remaining karma. The Isa Upanishad reflects these ancient beliefs of the early Vedic religion before the concept of karma and rebirth took firm roots and the idea of liberation through spiritual and devotional means gained popularity. In no way does the Upanishad refer to either Jesus or the Biblical God of Genesis.

11. The word Isa is a Sanskrit word, neither Semitic nor Aramic nor Persian. It is frequently used in various religious expressions to denote royalty and lordship [10]. There are many derivative and associative words of Isa used frequently in Hindu literature, mostly in a religious sense. Isana, a derivative word, is an epithet

of Lord Siva, Surya (the sun god) and Lord Vishnu. Isanya is the northeastern direction, which is ruled by Isana or God Himself. It has special significance in Vastu sastra, which deals with the construction of buildings and temples. Isita, meaning superiority or greatness, is one of the eight siddhis or perfections of Lord Siva. Isvara, another derivative word, means powerful, capable, lord, ruler, husband, king, and Shiva. In classical yoga, Isvara means individual soul and personal god. Goddess Durga is known as Isvari. Isa-sakha is an epithet of Kubera. The sacred city of Varanasi is known as Isanagari or the city of Lord Siva. From this, one may conclude that Isa is either the root word for Isvara or a short form of Isvara.

12. For more than 4000 years, the priestly families of the Vedic tradition maintained the purity of the Vedas with utmost devotion and dedication. They did it as a moral and an obligatory duty for the preservation of Dharma and in service to God. It was done not by a few but by thousands of Brahmana families for generations in various parts of the Indian subcontinent. As trustees of the sacred knowledge, they assumed moral and personal responsibility to preserve and promote the knowledge of the Vedas and other scriptures for the welfare of posterity, often under testing circumstances and fear of death in the hands of intolerant rulers. They maintained the purity and sanctity of the scriptures to preserve their potency and protect the knowledge from corruption. That the purity of the Vedas and other religious scriptures were maintained in India since the earliest times has been confirmed by the European scholars who studied them in the past. According to A.L. Basham [11], European historians who collected the Vedas from different places in India during the 1780s were amazed to see that "the text as transmitted in Kashmir was scarcely different from that transmitted in Tamil Nadu." This was over 4000 years after the early Vedic hymns of the Rig-Veda were composed.

13. Anyone familiar with Indian religions knows that Hinduism is the oldest living religion [12] in the world. All the religions and religious traditions that thrived in ancient India, including some atheistic and agnostic schools, originated from India indigenously

and shared some basic concepts among them that were peculiarly Indian. Indeed, many religious and spiritual ideas born in India travelled abroad to other countries. Even atheistic schools like that of the Charvakas had something in common with the theistic schools in matters such as determining what constitutes a standard proof (pramana), the nature and categories of substances (*padarthas*), and the elements (*bhutadi*) of the gross material things including the physical body. Christianity did reach the shores of India immediately after the death of Jesus Christ. However, it remained confined to a few areas on the Malabar Coast. Until the Mughal rule in the medieval period (1500 CE to 1750 CE), it remained relatively unknown and almost nonexistent. It had no influence whatsoever until the British, the Dutch, and the Portuguese established pockets of colonial rule in the subcontinent subsequent to the Mughals. Ancient Indians had some knowledge of the Indo-Iranian religions, such as Zoroastrianism, but the relationship between the two was hardly cordial. Even if we assume that some Christian missionaries traveled to India in the early Christian era, their contribution and influence on Indian society and their religious beliefs remained isolated and local.

14. The Bhagavadgita, which is certainly pre-Buddhist, at least in parts, envisions a Supreme Lord and Controller who is the source of everything, including our actions. Whatever happens in our lives, even our liberation happens because of His inviolable will. Those who perform their actions, acknowledging Him as the doer of all actions, renouncing doership, ownership, and the fruit of their actions, will not incur karma. They will attain freedom from karma (*naishkarmya siddhi*) and attain liberation. Lord Krishna, the presiding deity of this scripture, further states that as the Lord of the Universe, He reciprocates the love and devotion of His devotees and speedily rescues them from Samsara. He personally takes care of those who dedicate their lives to Him, serve Him, and worship with exclusive devotion (*ananya bhakti*). At the same, He casts those who engage in evil actions and disrespect His injunctions into evil wombs. Here is a God who is very similar to the God of Christianity in many respects but certainly Vedic in

temperament and nature.

15. The sectarian traditions of Hinduism, Shaivism, and Vaishnavism have a long history and are at least a thousand years older than Christianity. They were also popular in ancient India, first as independent traditions and subsequently as part of Vedism. Each of them recognizes their chief deities, Shiva and Vishnu, as the Supreme Lord and Controller and equates them with Brahman. According to them, all the deities of the Vedic pantheon are their manifestations. These gods are certainly pre-Buddhist and pre-Christian.

15. Until recently, the Brahmana families who safeguarded the Vedas and related knowledge and literature had a deep disdain for foreigners whom they treated with suspicion and avoided as far as possible any personal or social contact with them. In their esteem, they were no better than outcastes (*mlecchas*) and kept themselves aloof from them. Therefore, one can imagine the difficulty one would have had if the idea of God was unknown to Vedic people and someone copied that idea and created an Upanishad. Surely, it would have been noticed by others and criticized. If it were true, the text would have never found acceptance as a legitimate Vedic scripture and regarded it as a principal Upanishad. For over 3000 years, India had an ongoing tradition of scholars writing commentaries on the prevailing texts and debating the finer nuances of their respective beliefs and opinions to settle their differences or clarify their doubts. The religious groups of ancient India competed for attention and membership through devotional and personal means rather than wars and aggression. If they were familiar with the concepts of Christianity, they would have definitely mentioned them in their commentaries, but no such references have ever been found in the ancient texts of Hinduism. The ancient Indian scriptures are strikingly silent about foreign scholars from the West and their ideas.

Conclusion

Although early Vedic people worshipped several divinities, they knew that, above all, there was a supreme, universal, and absolute

Principle or Power that created all this and controlled the order, rhythm, and continuity of all existence. They called it variously That (*tat*), the One (*ekam*), the ancient (*adi*), the eternal (*nityam*), and Brahman. They did not invoke Him directly nor offer Him oblations during the sacrifices because the sacrifices were meant to nourish the gods with the food secured from the creation of Brahman by emulating His original sacrifice. In their hearts, they knew that all the offerings ultimately reached Him only through the numerous deities they worshipped. Secondly, Brahman was an impersonal and absolute God who favored none, desired nothing, and was forever stable and detached. As the silent witness, He took no sides in human affairs. He was beyond the mind and the senses and incommunicable through ritual means. The duality of the knower and the known, the subject and the object, or the process of knowing, did not exist in Him. A gulf separated one aspect of Him from another while He remained detached from the worlds that He created within Himself.

The Upanishads describe two states of Brahman: the gross and the subtle, the visible and the invisible, the apparent and the hidden, the Body and the Self, or the Created and the Creator. They compare them to two birds perched on a tree. Of them, one (the Self) watches silently while the other (the body) enjoys the fruit on the tree (of creation). The gulf between the two could not be reconciled since they are incommunicable. Hence, although Brahman is very near and lives in our hearts, yet, He is far away until we find Him through transcendence. Vedic priests do not worship Him ritually, except as a manifested Deity with a name and form, who is both the ritual and the object of the ritual. However, they know that He is hidden in all the names and forms and witnesses all actions, happenings, rituals, and offerings. For those ascetics who renounce worldly life and seek liberation, He is the goal, the guide, and the liberator.

It was only when the impersonal Brahman became personified as a personal God as the Vedic religion extended into the Gangetic plains of northern India in the later Vedic period do we see a definite shift in their attitude towards the older gods and a gradual erosion of certain ancient practices. During this period, the early Vedic deities such as Indra, Agni, and Varuna yielded their exalted place to a new pantheon of gods such as Shiva and Vishnu, whom people worshipped as their personal Gods alongside the early Vedic gods. The development coincided with the rise of devotional theism (bhakti movement) and the emergence of strong sectarian movements such as Shaivism, Vaishnavism, and Shaktism. In the Bhagavadgita, we see this shift clearly in the words of Lord Krishna, who declares that although He is the unmanifested, supreme, and highest universal God who exists everywhere and in everything, He would respond to the calls of His devotees promptly through His manifested forms. He also explains the difficulties in worshipping invisible and formless Brahman in the following manner [13]. *"Difficult and full of suffering indeed is the path of those whose minds are fixed on the unmanifested for indeed most painful is the path of those whose goal is to reach the unmanifested. But those who are fully devoted to Me, who surrender all actions to Me, worship Me and meditate on Me with unflinching devotion, I speedily rescue them from the samsara that is bound by death."*

Vedic scholars of the ancient world not only envisaged the universal supreme God but also speculated upon the origin of life and the manifestation of all creation, worlds, and beings. The creation hymn of the Rigveda reflects the maturity of thought that characterized the ancient Vedic culture. Even by the estimates of European historians, who tried to fit everything into the framework of the Biblical chronology, the Creation Hymn was composed "no later than 900 BCE [14]." It shows an "incredible sophistication" of the "development of thought," presenting an "imaginative picture of a universe evolving out of a primal condition, where there was neither being nor nonbeing, neither the cosmos nor the chaos." The long hymn, which is a precursor to the Hindu theories of creation, concludes thus.

But, after all, who knows, and who can say
Whence all it came, and how did creation happen?
The gods themselves are later than creation,
So who knows truly whence it has arisen?

Whence all the creation had its origin,
He, whether He fashioned it or whether He did not,
He who surveys it all from the highest heaven
He knows - or maybe He does not know.

Contrast this with the creation theory proposed in Genesis, and you will see the extent to which the two religions differ in their approach to the concept of God and Creation.

Footnotes

1. Isavasya Upanishad, The Doctrine of the Immanence of Jesus, by Prof. M.M. Ninan, April 2007.
2. Lillie, Arthur. India in Primitive Christianity. 1909.
3. Mr. R. Gordon Milburn, the Indian Interpreter 1913. As quoted in the Principal Upanishads by S. Radhakrishnan.
4. The Secret Of the Veda, Chapter I, The Problem and Its Solution by Sri Aurobindo.
5. An Advanced History of India, R.C. Majumdar, H.C. Raychaudhuri and Kalikinkar Datta, Chapter III, The Early Vedic Age.
6. *Ekam vipra bahudha vadanti, agnim, yamam, matariswanam ahuh* - Rigveda 1.164.46.
7. The Yoga Tradition, Its History, Literature Philosophy and Practice by George Feuerstein, PH.D.
8. Outlines of Indian Philosophy, Deussen.
9. The Six Systems Of Indian Philosophy by Max Mueller.
10. Prajapati Brahma is the father of Adityas, the solar deities of whom the Sun is one. Aditi, the universal Mother and the mother of the gods (devas), is also the mother of the solar deities.
11. The Origins and Development Of Classical Hinduism, by A. L. Basham.
12. The word religion is used here and elsewhere for lack of proper expression. Hinduism is not a religion in the Western sense of the word. This fact is well known to all who are familiar with it.
13. The Bhagavadgita, Chapter 12, verses 5 to 7, Bhagavadgita, Unveiling the Gita's Secrets, Translation and Commentary by Jayaram V, 2024.
14. The Origins and Development Of Classical Hinduism, by A. L. Basham.

The Paradox of Knowing Brahman

Brahman, the eternal Being whom the Upanishads described as the Self, the Highest Self, or the Supreme Self, has been extolled for centuries by seers, sages, and enlightened yogis in the sacred land of the Vedas. He is the highest transcendental Truth Being, who manifests as Isvara, the Lord of the universe, to attain whom people renounce everything, prepare themselves for austerity and hardships, and willingly undergo painful transformation. In His thought, thoughts disappear. In His pursuit, all pursuits end. Seeking Him, one leaves behind all seeking. Knowing Him, all is known. He is the most enigmatic Being, whom even gods find difficult to know or explain. Beyond darkness and light, beyond all diversity and visibility, beyond all qualities and quarters, beyond all activity and forms, beyond all imagination and vision, beyond the noise of life and the silence of seers, beyond vistas of life and mysteries of death, is Brahman, enveloping all and hidden within them all. So far away, yet so close, so familiar, yet so detached, no one can explain His mysteries and powers (*vibhutis*) to our satisfaction.

When you find Him, you do not find yourself. When you reach Him, you are lost forever. When you are with Him, you are without yourself. When you see Him, you do not see anything else. Your knowledge does not help you to reach there. Neither your wealth nor your thoughts help you find Him in the silence of your own heart unless you are willing to renounce them. What you build, you have to destroy to find Him who is everywhere. The entrance to the world of Brahman is right in front of you, but your attachments and a thick veil of ignorance stand between Him and you. You are the obstacle. You stand in your way to reach Him. When you realize that and remove yourself from the equation, your journey to reach Him gains pace.

Occasionally, one may get a glimpse of Him in the deeper states of self-absorption. One may find Him occasionally in the recesses of one's own heart and yet may not know. One may think that one does not know and yet may know Him. Like lightning, he descends into our consciousness; that is how the seers of Kena Upanishad envisioned him, but no one can really hold that power with their limited consciousness. That must become empty to fill the Whole. The part must yield to the descent of the indivisible whole. When the part yields to the whole and gives itself up without a trace, does it not cease to be a part? When Brahman is reached, your mind remains asleep, and when your mind is active, you will not find Brahman. To know Brahman, we must stop knowing, striving, and accumulating. To be Brahman, we must cease to be something or anything, subject or object. This is the problem and the paradox of Knowing Brahman.

The state of Brahman

Brahman is the very Self, the "I" ness that is everywhere, in everything, and around everything. There is no dichotomy in Brahman. Brahman is one Supreme, endless unitary feeling of "I" ness. In Brahman, "you" are lost because "you" are not there. You cannot explain your experience to others because, in reality, there is no experience. All is one endless, vast, immeasurable Self, in which, at the highest level, there is one without the other. There is consciousness without distinction and the feeling of separation. Everything is Self, that is "I." There is no "me" or "mine" either because egoism and possessiveness are a part of the separated consciousness.

We possess things because we cannot be the things. We seek things because we cannot escape from the physical feeling of separation and duality and our desire to be complete and secure. We look elsewhere for gratification because we have this incompleteness in us, which seeks fulfillment through accumulation. In Brahman, there is no object and subject; there is no experience, experiencer, knower, knowing, known, or any subjectivity or objectivity. Everything is one endless indistinguishable "I" ness. Brahman is "I am," and "I am" is the eternal reality. "I am," the non-possessive, non-egoistic, non-dualistic "I am," is the Truth, the Whole Truth, the Purpose and the Goal of all life forms that seek and strive upon earth in search of permanence and freedom from fear and sorrow. Brahman is "I am He Who I am." Brahman is "I am" (*Aham*) and "I am" is Brahman. Experience of this awareness of Brahman as Self is what we call Self-Realization. The whole universe is pervaded by this "I am ness." When we become dissolved into it, we achieve oneness. We perceive everything with the eyes and ears of the universe. We speak with the voice of the universe. We become one with the universe, God's universal form.

When we realize that there is nothing else in this vast universe except the eternal Self, who is also the inner Self of all, we reach the end of our journey that actually begins when we are drawn into the process of becoming and being, during which we acquire qualities and identities that are difficult to erase and that keep us distinct from others. We remain in this world because we are bound to our nature, change, and transformation. Craving, competition, striving, passions, and comparison arise in our minds because of the absence of the right awareness that lets us know who we truly are. One seeks things because one feels incomplete and inadequate. One indulges in desire-ridden actions because of the vain hope that by gaining possessions or fulfilling desires, one can become complete and perfect. We know that by pursuing that path, one never reaches fulfillment. It only leads to more craving, seeking, and striving and more disappointments and unhappiness. When we realize that by attaining Brahman or in oneness with Brahman, one attains everything and reaches the end of desire's last frontier, where is the need for any hankering, striving, and struggling? Where is the need for living in insecurity, fear, and anger? When one becomes all and finds oneself in all, with whom should he compete, and for what reason or purpose? The resolve to practice renunciation or pursue liberation arises from such insights. It is further strengthened by profound inner experiences and changes within one's consciousness that lead to the right knowledge, discernment, and awareness about oneself, one's life, reality, and true purpose. Without that realization and discernment, renunciation itself becomes a striving, and in that striving lurks the shadow of separation, delusion, egoism, effort, comparison, the fear of failure, desire, and disillusionment. The following story from a Sufi teaching amply illustrates the point.

A man knocked on God's door.
"Who's is there?" asked God from within.
"It's me," said the man.
"Go away then. There is no room for two," said God.
The man departed and wandered in the desert for a long time until he realized his error. Returning to the door, he knocked once again.
"Who's is there?" asked God as before.
"You," answered the man.
"Then come in," God replied.

Perhaps God would have also let him in if he answered, "I am."

The Duality of Brahman and Atman

Brahman is the universal Self, and Atman is the individual Self. In some Upanishads, Atman is also used to denote Brahman as the Self of all (*sarvabhutatma*). The Upanishads describe Brahman neutrally as "That" or "It" or in masculine terms as "He" or "Him." However, Atman is always mentioned as a universal male with a masculine noun, Purusha. Although we translate Purusha as Person, a neutral noun, in Sanskrit, Purusha is a masculine word. In the following discussion, I followed the same grammatical notations and described the Self in masculine terms. However, it is important to remember that Brahman, or the Self, is without any gender, qualities, or attributes. We impart to them masculinity to make sense of the fundamental duality that exists in creation between Purusha and Prakriti, consciousness and matter, subject and object, creator and the created, and subtle and gross. We identify Purusha as the Universal Male and Prakriti as the Universal Female and recognize them to be the fundamental duality of creation. In a human being, Purusha is the Self, and Prakriti is the body. In the absolute state of Brahman, Purusha is pure consciousness, and Prakriti is the primal force or energy. In creation, they appear together while remaining different. The result is Isvara, the Cosmic Being, and his numerous manifestations from the highest to the lowest, including jivas, the living beings.

Since ancient times, Indian philosophers have been baffled by the question of whether Brahman, the Supreme Self, and Atman, the individual Self, are the same or different. The answer still eludes us. Some Upanishads identify the individual Self with the universal Self in such famous utterances as "Thou art That" (*tattvamasi*) or "I am Brahman" (*aham brahmasmi*). Self-realization is the realization that one is Brahman or the eternal Self. According to them, when we cling to our physical identities and lose sight of our true Self, we become bound and suffer from delusion and ignorance. When we realize that we are pure eternal Selves, which happens after years of intense spiritual effort and may span several lives, and when we become fully established in that realization without duality, desires, and attachments, we attain liberation. While Brahman is addressed in some verses as the transcendental Self (*Paramatman*), the individual Self is described in some as the elemental Self (*bhutatman*) and the living Self (*jivatman*). Brahman is the Lord of the objective reality of the entire universe, whereas Atman is the Lord of the subjective reality of the mind and body. We experience the world objectively (as the other) and our inner world subjectively (as oneself) through our minds, intelligence, and senses. Beyond these two creations is the eternal reality of absolute Brahman or the unmanifested Pure Self, which is beyond our reach. The Upanishads compare the body to a temple or a city of nine gates and the Self to the divinity who resides in the sanctum and receives all the offerings from His devotes (the organs of the mind and body).

The Upanishads abound in the descriptions of Atman. Atman is the transcendental Self, the radiant being who is hidden behind the golden sheath, deep within one's own heart. He is the inner Self, without a beginning and an end, beyond the mind and the senses, and exists in all. Bliss is his essential nature. He upholds the senses, the breath, the mind, and the intelligence. He is devoid of qualities and materiality and, hence, much different from the soul of Abrahamic religions. The individual Self is the microcosmic aspect of Brahman, smaller than the smallest and larger than the largest. The Upanishads describe Him as the golden being, having the size of a thumb, by meditating upon whom one is liberated. Some early descriptions found in them even equate the embodied Self with the jiva, the living being. The Yogasutras describes the Self as Isvara (the Lord) and suggests that one should meditate on Him as Aum. When the seers meditate upon Him with single-minded devotion, they experience stability and self-absorption. Some scriptures describe Him as the passive Self, who remains in the background as the witness (*sakshi*), untouched by the happenings in the objective world. He is the enjoyer, the ultimate recipient of all food, perceptions, and sensory enjoyment.

The Self is pure, inexhaustible, indestructible, eternal, and absolute. He is neither the mind, nor the body, nor the senses, nor the life breath, nor the intelligence, nor any name and form. He is imperceptible to others but perceived by Himself. He is unknown to others but known to Himself. Even when He is subject to the modes of Nature (*gunas*), He is not tainted by the mind and body. The impurities arising from them envelop the Self and hold Him in bondage but cannot stain Him since He is eternally pure and indestructible. In the mortal world, the individual Self is held in bondage by the three main impurities, namely egoism (*anava*), desires and attachments (*pasas*), and delusion (maya). When the Self is held by them as a hostage, the jiva in which He resides becomes subject to the law of karma and the cycle of births and deaths. Even then, while the jiva suffers, the Self remains unaffected.

Bondage, suffering, and afflictions pertain to the domain of the jiva's physical self. By overcoming the impurities of the mind and body and becoming firmly established in the Self through the practice of yoga and austerity, one can resolve the problem of birth, death, and rebirth and attain liberation. When a jiva passes away, the Self leaves the body and travels to the higher worlds, according to the jiva's previous deeds. If the departing Self goes to the world of Brahman, It never returns, but if It goes to the world of ancestors, It returns to the earth after exhausting some of its karma and takes up another life. This goes on repeatedly birth after birth until the jiva is fully liberated. Liberation can take place in different ways, of which devotion is one of the important means. However, in some traditions, knowledge, purity, and discernment or intelligence are considered more effective for liberation than devotion.

Speaking of the relationship between the Supreme Self and the individual Self, the Chandogya Upanishad declares thus: *"Truly what is called Brahman is the same as that space outside a person. Truly, that space which is outside a person is the same as that which is inside the person and that space which is inside a person is the same which is inside the heart. That is fullness. That is the unchanging reality. One who knows this invariably gains full prosperity and unwavering happiness."* Different schools of Hinduism interpret the relationship between Brahman and Atman differently. They all rely upon the Vedas to validate their arguments. Indeed, they interpret even the Bhagavadgita differently according to their beliefs. We summarize below their basic beliefs.

1. Both are the same. Brahman alone is real. The individual Self is a mere illusion. When the illusion is removed, the individual Self disappears, and Brahman alone remains. This view is held by the proponents [1] of the Advaita philosophy, according to which the apparent reality is an illusion created by the mind due to delusion and duality arising from the impurities of the mind and body, karma, perceptions, latent impressions, and other factors. When these impurities are removed, one perceives Brahman everywhere as the only Supreme Reality. After liberation, the Self becomes fully absorbed in Brahman and ceases to exist.

2. Both are eternal, indestructible, and fixed, but not exactly the same. There is a subtle difference between the two, just as there is a difference between an object and its reflection. This is known as the "different but not different" theory (*bhedabheda*). The proponents of Vishistadvaita, or the philosophy of qualified nondualism, hold this view. Sri Ramanuja [2] was its chief proponent. According to this, after their liberation, the liberated souls reach the world of Isvara and live in His company, sharing with Him internally the same supreme consciousness and enjoying eternal bliss.

3. Proponents of the third school, known as Dvaita, or the philosophy of dualism, hold that both are different eternally. According to them, duality exists at every level, not only between the Supreme Self and the individual Self but also between Purusha and Prakriti and between all aspects of creation, including between two types of souls. However, all are real, including our material world. The Supreme Self is the highest and independent principle. He

manifests as Isvara or Paramatman out of abundant love to uphold and support all the worlds and those who reside in them. The individual souls have many qualities of Isvara, but they are different because they are dependent upon Him and are part of His Universal Body. Sri Madhavacharya [3] was the main protagonist of this theory. He proposed that not only was the Supreme Self different from the individual Self but also there were distinct categories of individual souls. Some of the schools equate the jivas with the individual souls.

The dualistic schools, which hold the view that not all souls are the same, distinguish between them according to their essential nature and status of liberation or bondage. The following description is based on the accounts found in some schools of Vaishnavism.

1. The individual Self (atma) represents the dynamic principle (*chetana tattva*), in contrast to the inanimate objects (*achetana tattvas*). It is also known as a being (jiva) or a person (purusha). It is different from Isvara, although it has many of His universal attributes. It is all-pervasive, without modes (gunas) and limitations. Bliss is its essential nature. Some of these souls are subject to bondage and rebirth in samsara.

2. An embodied Self (*dehatma*) in the body represents a living being. Because it is enveloped by the impurities of Prakriti (Nature), it is held in bondage and is subject to the cycle of births and deaths. It is also a dynamic entity, subject to the modes of Nature. The jivas are numerous and fall into three main categories: bound souls (*baddha*), freed souls (*mukta*), and eternally free souls (*nitya muktas*). Bound souls are the embodied souls in all the jivas (living beings), such as plants, animals, birds, insects, and any other beings with corporeality. They are subject to karma, modes of Prakriti, impermanence, birth, death, and rebirth. Some may reside in other worlds, above or below, according to their karma. They keep revolving in the cycle of births and deaths

according to their dominant nature (pravritti) until they are liberated. When they gain knowledge of the Self, they become free. Higher than them are the muktas, the liberated souls who escape from bondage through self-transformation and the grace of God (Isvara). A liberated soul goes to the immortal world of Brahman and lives there forever in a state of bliss, enjoying the company of God and other freed souls. Apart from them, there are eternally free souls (nityas) who live eternally in the immortal world and are never subject to samsara or mortality and rebirth. They never take birth in the mortal world and are never subject to bondage or the laws of karma. Nothing will ever taint them. They serve God directly as His devotees (bhaktas), attendants (Bhagavatas), and helpers who serve His devotees. In some descriptions, we also hear about souls that are eternally bound (nitya baddha). It means they have no chance of attaining liberation in this or any other cycle of creation and will remain forever bound. At the time of the dissolution of the worlds (pralaya), these bound souls are withdrawn by Isvara into Himself to be brought out again as bound souls in the next cycle of creation.

These three schools also vary in their speculation regarding the question of whether the individual Self is eternally self-existent or created by Brahman. According to the Advaita schools, the individual Self is a temporary formation that comes into existence during creation and then disappears through liberation or during the final dissolution of the worlds. According to the Dvaita schools, numerous souls exist eternally in God's creation as distinct entities. They are self-existent but depend upon Brahman. According to the Vishistadvaita school, the souls are brought forth by Brahman as His reflections during creation, and He withdraws them into Himself at the time of the final dissolution.

Brahman and the divinities

Hindus worship several gods and goddesses, not as different entities but as different projections or reflections of Brahman in different material manifestations, aspects (tattvas), and modes (*gunas*). In their essence, they are the same as Brahman, but outwardly, they have distinct identities and qualities, which distinguish them as forms of God. They uphold the cosmic structure (*Srishti*), the divine order (*rta*), and the divine law (*dharma*) and help mortal beings in their pursuit of liberation. Whenever evil gains ascendance, they assist Isvara's incarnations in restoring Dharma and destroying evil. They also reside in the human body to assist the inner Lord or the individual Self during liberation.

From the Puranas, we understand that the gods and their status are not permanent [4]. They may either ascend to higher worlds or descend into lower worlds according to their previous deeds. They allude to the fact that even the gods of the Trinity, namely Brahma, Vishnu, and Shiva, were once ordinary souls in the previous cycles of creation and became the Trinity in the current cycle because of their pious deeds. Devout Hindus worship various divinities as their personal gods, acknowledging them as Brahman or Shakti in their highest and ultimate aspect. In Hinduism, Truth is one but perceived and spoken in different forms [5]. If God has many forms and if they are all the same in their final essence, it logically follows that we can reach Him by any means, as suggested by the following verse [6]. *"Just as the rainwater, wherever it falls, finally flows down into the ocean, so also the worship offered to any god will ultimately reach the supreme God (Kesava) only."*

Life is sacred, and mortal beings exist in different states of bondage. The divinity of each human being is a latent potentiality and a possibility that manifests itself when certain conditions are met. Liberation is a worthy goal that every human being should pursue at some point in their existence on earth. Self-realized adepts are but Isvara in human form. They achieve liberation and the exalted state of Brahman's supreme consciousness by cleansing themselves and earning the grace of God and the help of various divinities, teachers, and attendants whom He appoints for the purpose. Their liberation is permanent, which means they are never born again in the mortal world in this cycle or future cycles. Order and regularity are integral to creation and the whole existence. They, too, are subject to impermanence and transformation and vulnerable to the destabilizing forces of creation. Whenever the worlds are thrown into confusion and disorder, Isvara, the Lord of the universe, incarnates upon earth to restore Dharma, establish order and regularity, and remove chaos.

A yogi stabilizes his mind and body with the practice of yoga. He purifies them by cultivating sattva, practicing virtues and self-control, and stabilizing his mind in the thoughts of the Self. As we find in the Katha Upanishad, restraining the mind and body (*Adhyatma Yoga*) is vital to suppress the modification of the mind and stabilize it in the contemplation of the Self or Isvara. Smaller than the small and greater than the great, the Self is present in the heart of every person. When the mind is tranquil and absorbed, the senses are resting, and all the duality and divisions disappear, one finally sees the Truth hidden behind the golden sheath, the bliss body. We will never be able to know Brahman except through our experience of the blissful state of Turya, which is transcendental and indestructible. Yogis strive to prolong their momentary experiences of Turya by constantly reminiscing about them and making them a part of their wakeful consciousness. Even that is not very helpful in bringing Brahman's pure consciousness totally into our wakeful experiences. The best we can do is to experience the Self in oneness by withdrawing our minds and senses, surrendering to God, and performing our actions with detachment and as an offering to God. This is the path of renunciation of the desire for action (karma-sannyasa) suggested by Lord Krishna in the Bhagavadgita. It must be practiced in conjunction with other yogas described in the scripture to hasten the process. When we dismantle the walls of separation that we build ourselves with our egos and desires to keep ourselves confined to our little worlds, we become one with Brahman.

Footnotes

1. Sri Sankaracharya was the chief proponent of monism or advaita. The earliest reference to it is found in Gaudapada's commentary on the Mundaka Upanishad, which was probably written during the reign of the Guptas around the fifth century CE. According to tradition, he and

The Duality of Brahman and Atman

Sri Sankaracharya, who lived in the eighth or ninth Century CE, belonged to the same lineage of teachers.

2. He lived during the eleventh century CE and played a vital role in the popularity of the devotional (bhakti) movement in medieval India by providing necessary philosophical and theistic justification. He wrote a commentary on the Brahma Sutras and composed eight other works, including a commentary on the Bhagavadgita.

3. He lived between the 13th and 14th centuries CE and authored many works disputing the theories of the other schools, holding God and His creation as separate and distinct entities.

4. For example, the Sivapurana says that Vishnu was chosen as the preserver because of His past good deeds.

5. *Eekam sat viptra bahuda vadanti.*

6. *Akasat patitam toyam yatha gacchati saagaram, sarva deva namaskara kesavam pratigacchati.*

Bhagavan – The Glorious God

In simple terms, Bhagavan means God. It is synonymous with Bhagavat, an epithet of Vishnu, but people use it in conjunction with other gods also [1]. When people see God in gurus and great souls, out of reverence and respect, they address them also as Bhagavan. This is usually done to acknowledge the omnipresence of God and His reflection in every aspect of creation. It is a mark of respect, reverence, and humility. It is perfectly in agreement with the basic tenets of Hinduism, according to which creation is a manifestation of God and His numerous powers (*vibhutis*). The Upanishads proclaim Him as the Self of all, who pervades all and is hidden in all. We have the mark of divinity hidden in us as the Self or Atman. His divinity or divine qualities manifest in us as greatness, purity, power, and many other qualities [2]. Whenever we are in the presence of a great soul (*mahatma*), we feel His presence and aura.

Our hearts know well when we see a truly pure soul who is purified by his knowledge, conduct, self-control, devotion, and austerity. In moments of exalted thoughts, emotions, or awareness, we may feel the presence of God within ourselves. It is the only way we ever come closer to Him in our wakeful consciousness. Some yogis try to extend such experiences using their imagination to bring Him into their wakeful consciousness, who is otherwise transcendental and unknown to the mind's duality in the material world. They believe that through regular practice, they can open their minds to His constant presence and eventually dissolve themselves in Him without duality. Strictly speaking, each living being on earth is a divinity, a sleeping Bhagavan who is ignorant of his transcendental reality and eternal nature. When the Deity who dwells in the cave of our hearts wakes up and spreads His rays in our consciousness, we realize that our bodies are sacred places (*bhaga*) in which He resides as the resplendent Lord (*Bhagavan*)

Etymologically, Bhagavan is a combination of two root words, "bhaga" and "van." "Bhaga" has several meanings: one of the twelve forms of Aditi or Sun God, the moon, a form of Shiva, the divine enjoyer within, wealth, affluence, prosperity and fortune, happiness, dignity, distinction, love and affection, pleasure, pure bliss, female genital organ, virtue, morality, religious merit and so on. "Van" means residence or abode. Thus, Bhagavan means He who resides or abides in the things and qualities mentioned above. In simple terms, Bhagavan means He who resides in the bhaga, the womb or heart of (Nature or the material universe). He is the supreme Lord, the enjoyer of the things in which He resides. In symbolic terms, Bhagavan is represented by many objects and forms, such as the spiral conch (*Saligrama*) and Shivaling.

According to Vishnu Puranas, Bhaga indicates the six properties: wisdom, energy, power or strength, dominion or sovereignty, might or virility, glory or splendor. Va is that elemental Self in which all the beings exist and which exists in all of them. Thus, the great word Bhagavan is the name of Vasudeva, who has these qualities, who is one with the supreme Brahman (*parabrahma*) and of no one else. The same verse also mentions additional related qualities of Bhagavan when applied to the Supreme Lord: righteous fame (*yash*), abundant glory (*shriya*), and dispassion (*vairagya*). This meaning is appropriate when used for the Supreme Being, Vasudeva, or the transcendental Brahman. However, when it is used in conjunction with others, it refers to any person who knows the origin, dissolution, and transmigration of beings and the distinction between knowledge and ignorance [3]. He may possess these qualities, but not endlessly. Thus, according to this traditional interpretation, Bhagavan has the following six primary unending (*asheshatah*) abundances or qualities. This does not mean that Bhagavan, the Supreme Being, has only these qualities. They are His most distinguishing ones among countless others found in all creation.

1. Endless wisdom (*jnana*)
2. Endless energy (*shakti*)
3. Endless power or strength (*bala*)
4. Endless dominion or sovereignty (*aishwarya*)

5. Endless virility or might (*virya*)
6. Endless glory, splendor, or brilliance (*teja*)

The Bhagavadgita uses the word Bhagavan frequently to refer to Lord Krishna, which suggests that it was a popular term in ancient times and was probably used to refer to great souls, divine seers, incarnations, and God's higher manifestations. In the tenth chapter of the scripture called Vibhuti Yoga, Lord Krishna provides a comprehensive description of His opulence, mystic powers, qualities, and attributes found in His numerous manifestations. He says that all qualities, laws, divinities, and beings manifest from Him only, and He is the source and support of all creation [4]. Strictly speaking, even negative qualities, such as anger or pride, arise from Him only when He remains concealed by His own power of tamas and does not radiate His light. While we may like to envision God as only pure, in truth, He cannot be one and not the other. We cannot say that He is only good. Nothing, even evil, can exist without His will and support. Everything exists in Him and is a part of His creation since there is no other place where anything can exist. He resides in everything and encompasses everything without being a part of their materiality or essential nature. Both positive and negative qualities manifest from Him only and find their support in Him only. However, since we cannot conceptualize Him in absolute terms, we ascribe certain qualities to Him for our satisfaction and understanding. "Bhagavan" is one such epithet that reminds us of His greatness and universality. The title also reminds us of the qualities we must cultivate to purify our minds and bodies and attain Him.

Closely related to the word Bhagavan is the word Bhagavat. According to the same Purana, the word Bhagavat is the name of that eternal and supreme God. It should be used in adoration of that Supreme Being, who is almighty and the cause of all causes. It also refers to the one who possesses the holy wisdom, the essence of the Vedas, and fully understands the true meaning and significance of that word. The word is also used to denote the exclusive devotees of Lord Krishna who dedicate their lives to serve Him here and hereafter.

Footnotes

1. It is also used to refer to a devotee of Durga, Lakshmi, Bhagavati, etc.
2. Whatever being is endowed with greatness, purity, and power, know it to be a spark of My splendor. – Bhagavadgita (10.41)
3. Vishnu Puranas (6.5.71), From the Vishnu Purana by Veda Vyasa, English Translation with Sanskrit Text, Internet Archive, 2021.
4. Bhagavadgita (10.8)

Brahman in Advaita and Dvaita Schools

At the most fundamental level, the universe is not just a physical or material entity but filled with the pure intelligence of an unfathomable power that can create, maintain, conceal, augment, and destroy the objective universe at will without effort and intent. We identify this supreme intelligence of infinite capacities and unfathomable mysteries as Brahman. The human mind fails to grasp It because the mind is rooted in sensory knowledge and limited by its own ignorance. It cannot comprehend or estimate the powers (*mahima*) of Brahman beyond the domain of the senses or realize the true purpose of its own existence. The human mind does not belong to the domain of the spirit, although it is modeled on it. It is subject to duality and veiled by the power of Maya, because of which the Self becomes temporarily disconnected from Its source as if a drop of water is lifted from the surface of the ocean and thrown into the ether. For the individual Self, which is caught in the phenomenal world of Nature and the limitations of the body, the available means to return to Its source is through an inverse process of liberation in which what is bound becomes unbound and what is impure because of its association with the elements of Nature becomes purified.

For centuries, Hindu scholars pondered upon the nature of reality and the role of God in creation. They explored the ways and means to ascertain the truth and validate the knowledge one gained through the senses and the intellect, neither of which they trusted completely based upon their experience and insightful observation. They wanted to know what distinguished truth from untruth, reality from unreality, and God from His creation. They observed that our notion of reality changes according to our states of mind, and what appears to be true in one state does not seem so in another. They believed that objects appear or disappear in the mind due to their reflection in the quality of the sattva, and the changes in the mind-stuff (*citta*) create modifications (*vrittis*), which prevent it from seeing the truth as it is. In their transcendental states, they noticed that truth becomes self-evident only when the mind is stable and the senses are at rest. Therefore, they encouraged the practice of yoga and meditation to stabilize the mind and the body and see the world with greater clarity and penetrating insight.

For them, the reality was that which was permanent, indestructible, constant, and free from modifications. Since our world does not meet any of these criteria, it is difficult to accept it or its phenomena as true except relatively. They also probed into the nature of matter, the nature of truth, objectivity, the process of knowing, the experience of duality, the conditions that governed human experience, and the relationship between the Creator and the created. They explored how the cause was related to the effect, how things manifested, what led to human suffering, and what resulted in the liberation of beings. They pondered upon the permanence and impermanence of things and their impact on human suffering. These efforts resulted in the origin of many schools of philosophy, of which only a few survive today. With regard to the essential nature of reality and the relationship between the universal Self and the individual Self, two streams of thought prevailed in ancient India. Both belonged to the school of Vedanta. Both were rooted in the philosophy of the Upanishads, and both accepted the Vedas as the final authority in confirming truth. We have discussed these in the previous chapter. We will explore them further in this chapter.

Brahman in Advaita Schools

According to Advaita Vedanta, or the school of nondualism, Brahman is the one and the only reality, and the rest is an illusion or projection that lacks the consistency or permanency of truth. Whatever you perceive through your senses and whatever your mind can conceive and conjure up in relation to the empirical reality around you is false since it is an extension (or an illusion) of your mind and does not necessarily correspond with what exists outside. In your ordinary state, you will not know it because you are accustomed to experience reality relatively in a state of duality; but, if you experience the state of Brahman (*brahmanubhava*), you realize that there is neither duality nor any distinction between the knower and the known. For example, the sky may appear differently at different times because of the formation of the clouds, the movement of the sun and the moon, and the appearance of several celestial objects. It may also appear differently during different seasons and because of natural phenomena like rains and thunderstorms. However, despite all the drama that happens there, the sky is always the same. It is never truly touched by anything. Even the most devastating storm is just a passing event, a temporary phenomenon. When these things disappear, it seems the sky has returned to its original condition, whereas in reality, it never underwent any change. It is the same with Brahman and the phenomenal world. Just like the sky that acts as a screen for the weather phenomena, Braham provides the support or the surface upon which the world and its myriad phenomena appear and disappear, creating the illusion that we are witnessing great Play. While the world and the objective reality are temporary formations that are fleeing, Brahman remains the same, unaffected by the flux, and so does Atman, the inner witness, and enjoyer. Just as a person who wakes up from a dream realizes that he was dreaming and that his dream was a mere projection of his mind, when a person wakes up from the state of ignorance and delusion in oneness with the Self, he realizes that the world in which he lived thus far was also a mere formation or a temporary construct.

When we do not have the right discrimination, we mistake one thing for another. For example, in the dark, we may mistake a rope for a snake. When truth dawns upon us, we realize that we made a mistake and that the snake never existed, except in our minds or imagination. When we are deluded by ignorance, we mistake the diversity of Brahman for real, whereas in reality, it does not exist at all. Once the veil of Maya is lifted, we realize that everything, including the individual Self, is Brahman. When Brahman extends outwardly, the worlds appear, and when He withdraws into Himself, they come to an end. When He casts His net of delusion, the individual souls become ensnared in it and experience things differently. They become ignorant and identify themselves with their names and forms. This ignorance about one's true nature, which is so characteristic of life on earth, is the cause of duality, desires, egoism, and suffering. One may escape from it by acknowledging Brahman as the supreme reality and overcoming one's delusion and ignorance. In simple words, when you overcome your delusion through knowledge and devotion and remove the formations and impurities from your being, you shed your ignorance and realize who you really are. You also realize that the ultimate reality has always been the same, and what you experienced in your corporeal state was a mistaken notion and a temporary distraction.

The Advaita School attracted the attention of many scholars in the ancient world, including some from Buddhism. Some even believe that Adi Shankaracharya (eighth century CE), a distinguished teacher of Advaita, was influenced by Buddhism. Advaita Vedanta rejects the duality of Samkhya philosophy and believes that Brahman alone represents the absolute reality, and Prakriti is His dependent reality and executes His will. According to the school, one must realize the true nature of the Self or Brahman through self-study, hearing the knowledge from the masters, remembering the knowledge so learned, and contemplating upon it. When the delusion is overcome and truth dawns, one realizes that all is Brahman and nothing else is true. The school also identifies three types of reality: the absolute reality that is eternally immutable, independent, and self-existent; the empirical reality of the world which we constantly experience in our wakeful state; and the reality the mind projects or superimposes because of its impurities and vrittis. The first one is constant; the second one depends upon conditions, circumstances, and factors such as natural phenomena, and the third one depends upon our mental states. Delusion is a state of ignorance (avidya) that arises when the ego-self (jivatma) assumes the ownership and doership of all the experiences and all the possessions, actions, and achievements to itself and assumes the physical Self as Atman or Brahman, the true Self. This ignorance can be overcome by knowing the true Self and becoming a liberated soul in the body (jivanmukta). Then, the world appears as it is, without delusion and distortion, as a play by Maya.

Some monistic philosophies differ in their interpretation of eternal reality and the nature of existence. Most prominent among them is the school of qualified monism (Vishistadvaita). It accepts some of the basic arguments of monism but holds the view that although, in the ultimate sense, everything is Brahman, there is a subtle difference between Brahman and His creation and Brahman and the individual Selves. Besides, it does not agree with Sankara's view that Brahman, in his manifested state as Isvara, is devoid of qualities and impersonal. Therefore, it emphasizes devotion to Brahman or Isvara, the Supreme Lord, as the principal means to attain liberation. It believes that one can relate to God personally and seek His help in liberation. Atman remains distinct upon liberation but remains connected internally to Brahman and His blissful state eternally. In other words, Atman has all the qualities and attributes of Brahman but is a distinct entity spatially, functionally, and essentially.

Brahman in the Dvaita Schools

The dualistic (*dvaita*) schools do not accept the view that Brahman is the only reality and the rest is an illusion. They also do not accept the argument that creation is a superimposition of temporary and alternate realities upon the eternal and absolute truth. They hold the pluralistic view that Brahman is different (*bheda*) from His creation, and there are multiple realities, each true but different from the rest. God wills the creation but does not execute it. It is done by His energy or Shakti. God is, therefore, the efficient cause of creation. According to them, the world in which we live and which Advaita school holds as an illusion is true. It is true and cannot be an illusion because it just does not go away even when we attain liberation. While the nature of their experiences may differ, liberated souls experience plurality and duality as much as bound souls. However, of all the realities, God, whom the dualistic schools identify as Shiva, Vishnu, or Narayana, is the only independent reality. Other realities and entities depend upon Him for their support and continuity. In other words, although individual souls are eternal and indestructible, they cannot exist without God. At the end of each cycle of creation, Isvara, the Supreme Lord, withdraws them into Himself and releases them gradually, according to their purity, in the next cycle.

The dualistic schools not only distinguish God from creation but also perceive distinctions within the various components of creation. Thus, we have a series of distinctions between God and soul, souls and souls, God and matter, matter and soul, one object and another, one divinity and another, and one world and another. In other words, existence is characterized by a plurality of realities and they are all true in their own ways. We may trace their origin to God, but they exist distinctively and relationally by the power of His will. The individual souls are neither equal nor the same. They can be superior souls, inferior souls, bound souls, free souls, eternally bound souls, and eternally free souls. The eternally bound souls never attain liberation, and the eternally free souls are never bound.

According to the philosophy of Dvaita, God is the supreme and the highest reality, endowed with innumerable qualities. He upholds multiple realities as an independent and self-existent Agent of creation. He is their efficient cause, but their material cause is goddess Lakshmi, the universal Mother, who is the first among the dependent realities. She manifests the worlds with the help of the three qualities: sattva, rajas, and tamas. However, she is not independent but serves the Lord by executing His will and assisting Him in the execution of His duties as the Supreme Lord, Controller, and Upholder of Dharma. The dualistic schools do not concur with the argument that upon liberation, one realizes Brahman as formless because, according to them, Isvara, the Lord of the universe, has a specific form. The entire material manifestation is his material body. Unlike the Advaita, the Dvaita school believes that Brahman and Prakriti are eternally different, even when she is unmanifested before the beginning of creation.

The dualistic schools quote verses from the Brahma Sutras in support of their beliefs, the same verses that the monistic schools use to support their arguments. They disagree with the argument of the monistic schools that upon attaining liberation, one realizes that Brahman is formless. Although the form of Brahman is unmanifested [1], as the sutras suggest [2], He becomes directly visible to those who worship Him devoutly. Isvara has a specific form, and within the realm of Brahman, the devotees see other divine manifestations as distinct objects in a city [3]. According to them, the Supreme Lord goes by the names Vishnu, Krishna, or Narayana, and His immortal world (Brahmaputra) by the name Vaikuntha, where the liberated souls live in complete bliss. Although devotion is the principal means to realize Him, it is not easy to cultivate devotion. Devotion arises from the right knowledge, and the right knowledge comes from the study, contemplation, and grace of God. According to Madhavacharya, one of the chief proponents of the school, detachment does not arise from sacrificial effort but from intense devotion to God. Therefore, knowledge, devotion, detachment, and the grace of God are the principal means to attain liberation. When a soul is liberated, it goes to the world of Isvara and lives in His company in total bliss. It never returns to the mortal world.

Footnotes

1. *Tat avyaktam aha,* Vedanta Suta (3.2.23).
2. *Api ca samradhane pratyaksa anumanabhyam,* Vedanta Suta (3.2.24). api=but; samradhane= intense worship; pratyaksa =as directly visible; anumanabhyam=as inferred from scripture.
3. *Antara bhuta gramavat svatmanah,* Vedanta Sutra 3.3.35. antara=inside; bhuta=physical elements; gramavat=like a village; svatmanah= to His own or to His devotees.

The Glossary of Brahma(n) and Related Words

Brahmabhavam: The state of Brahman.

Brahmabhijata: An epithet of the river Godavari, which flows in south India in Karnataka and Andhra Pradesh.

Brahmabhutah: Becoming one with Brahman.

Brahmabhuti: Twilight.

Brahmabhuya: Absorption into Brahman.

Brahmabhyasa: Study of the Vedas or the knowledge of Brahman.

Brahmabijam: The sacred syllable Aum.

Brahmacharin: A religious student, one who has taken a vow to remain celibate, or a Brahmana in the first phase of his life who learns the Vedas while staying with his teacher.

Brahmacharini: A woman who undertakes a vow to observe chastity. An epithet of goddess Durga.

Brahmacharya: The practice of celibacy; a phase, usually as a student, in the life of a human being; study of Brahman or the Vedas; pursuit of Brahman.

Brahmadanam: Gifting away the knowledge of Brahman or the Vedas.

Brahmadhigamah: Same as above.

Brahmadhigamanam: Study or mastery of the Vedas or the knowledge of Brahman.

Brahmadinam: A day of Brahma.

Brahmadveshi: A hater of God or a Brahman priest. An atheist.

Brahmaghnata: Neglecting, disregarding, or ignoring the Vedas.

Brahmaghosha: The loud chanting of the Vedas, the sound of the Vedas, or the sacred word of the Vedas.

Brahmagolam: The universe.

Brahmagranthi: A knot or obstacle located in the first chakra known as the Muladhara Chakra.

Brahmahutam: Hospitality to guests.

Brahmahuti: An offering of prayers.

Brahmaja: An epithet of Kartikeya, the son of Siva.

Brahmajivi: One who lives in the contemplation or study of Brahman. An epithet of Kartikeya and Vishnu.

Brahmajnanam: Knowledge of Brahma; realization of Brahman.

Brahmajyoti: The light of Brahman.

Brahmakalpa: Half a day in the life of Brahma, or roughly 4.32 billion years.

Brahmakanda: The portion of the Vedas, usually the Upanishads, which contain the knowledge of Brahman as opposed to karmakanda or the knowledge of rituals. It's the same as Jnanakanda.

Brahmakanya: Goddess Saraswati.

Brahmakanyaka: Same as above.

Brahmakarah: Fees paid to a Brahmana priest or tax paid to the priestly class.

Brahmakarmana: The religious duties of a Brahmana priest, one of the four principal priests, at a sacrifice.

Brahmakruta: One who prays; also, an epithet of Vishnu used in Vishnu strotras.

Brahmaksaram: Aum, the sacred syllable.

Brahmakurcham: A kind of penance.

Brahmalikhitam: What is willed and written by Brahma on the forehead of each person as his or her fate or destiny.

Brahmalokah: The world of Brahma or the highest immortal world of Brahman, where the free souls reside in the company of Isvara or Saguna Brahman.

Brahmamaya: Concerning the Vedas or derived from the Vedas or Brahman.

Brahmamayam: Filled with Brahman.

Brahmambhasu: Cow's urine.

Brahmamimansa: One of the Darshanas, philosophies of Hinduism. Also known as the Vedanta or Uttara Mimansa, which deals exclusively with the knowledge of Brahman and Atman.

Brahmamuhurtam: Auspicious time presided over by Brahma.

Brahmamurghabhuta: An epithet of Siva.

Brahmamurthy: The form of Brahma.

Brahman: Impersonal Supreme Being; a hymn of praise; a sacred text; the Vedas; the mystic syllable Aum; a priest from the Brahman caste; the power and energy of Brahman; Brahman priest; religious penance or austerities; celibacy, chastity; liberation; theology; Brahmanical portion of the Vedas; wealth; Brahma, the creator god; a Brahmana; a devout man; one of the four Ritvijas or priests employed at a Soma sacrifice; one conversant with sacred knowledge; the Sun; intellect; an epithet of the seven Prajapatis; an epithet of Brihaspati; an epithet of Siva and Vishnu;

Brahmanadi: The river of Brahma; the river Saraswathi; an epithet of goddess Saraswathi.

Brahmanaspati: Another name for Brihaspati. He shares some common features with Ganapati, the Lord of the Shivaganas.

Brahmandam: The infinite universe or the primordial egg from which the worlds and the beings emerged.

Brahmangabhu: Horse.

Brahmani: Goddess Durga, wife of a Brahmana priest, a holy woman.

Brahmanirvanam: Realization of Brahman; unity with Brahman; liberation; self-absorption; absorption into Brahman.

Brahmanishta: Immersed in or intent upon the contemplation of Brahman.

Brahmanjali: Salutations to Brahman, done with folded hands at the beginning and the end of the recitation of the Vedas.

Brahmanubhavam: The experience of Brahman.

Brahmanyam: Respect to brahmanas.

Brahmapada: The exalted position of Brahman or a Brahmana priest; the state or plane of Brahman.

Brahmaparayanam: The recitation of the Vedas; the complete study of the Vedas.

Brahmapatakah: The killer of a Brahmana priest. Same as Brahmaghna.

Brahmapavitra: The kusa grass used in the sacrificial rituals.

Brahmapitr: An epithet of Vishnu.

Brahmapralayam: The great destruction of the dissolution of the worlds.

Brahmaprapti: Attainment of Brahman or the knowledge of Brahman.

Brahmapurah: The city of Brahman; the human body; the heaven. Same as Brahmapuri.

Brahmapuranam: One of the eighteen major Puranas, it deals with creation, the life and deeds of Rama and Krishna, and the importance of Purushottama Thirtha, a holy place.

Brahmaputra: The son of Brahma; the river Brahmaputra.

Brahmaputri: Goddess Saraswathi; the river Saraswathi; daughter of Brahma.

Brahmarakshasah: the ghost of a Brahmana priest who lived a rather impure life. Same as brahmapisacha.

Brahmarambham: The beginning of the recitation of the Vedas.

Brahmarandhram: An opening in the head region through which the soul is believed to leave the body at the time of death.

Brahmarashi: One of the stars in the Hindu calendar, traditionally identified with the Abhijata Nakshatra. An epithet of Parasurama.

Brahmaratah: An epithet of Sukah or Sukadeva, one of the great seers of Vaishnavism who is mentioned in the Puranas. He was believed to be the son of Vedavyasa.

Brahmarishi: A seer well versed in the knowledge of Brahman.

Brahmarpanam: An offering to Brahman.

Brahmasambhavam: Arising or coming from Brahma or Brahman.

Brahmasanam: A particular yogic posture for deep meditation.

Brahmasashtika: Identification with Brahma.

Brahmasati: Saraswathi, the consort of Brahma.

Brahmasatram: Chanting and teaching of the Vedas. Absorption into Brahman.

Brahmasavarnih: The tenth Manu.

Brahmasayujyam: Complete identification and merger into Brahman.

Brahmasruja: Created by Brahma or Brahman. An epithet of Siva.

Brahmasthambah: The pillar of the universe or Sivalingam. The world or the universe.

Brahmasthanam: The center of the house, used in the Vastu Shastra.

Brahmastram: A magical arrow with great catastrophic power, propelled by the power of Brahman.

Brahmasuta: The sons of Brahma. Narada, Marichi, etc. It is also used in reference to Aniruddha, Ketu, and Manmadha. In reality, all beings are children of Brahma only.

Brahmasutram: The sacred thread worn by people belonging to the Brahmana caste. Also, it refers to the Aphorisms of Brahman by Badarayana.

Brahmasutras: The aphorisms of Brahman, also known as the Vedanta sutras.

Brahmatattva: Knowledge or philosophy concerning Brahman.

Brahmatejas: The luster of knowledge and erudition reflected in a Brahmana priest, or a person well versed in the knowledge of Brahman or the Vedas.

Brahmatmabhu: A horse.

Brahmavadin: A scholar or philosopher who argues about the truths of Brahman. Also, a follower of the Vedanta.

Brahmavadyam: Knowledge of Brahma.

Brahmavakta: An exponent of the Vedas or the knowledge of Brahman

Brahmavarchas: The splendor and brilliance of Brahman as reflected in a person because of His knowledge of Brahman, purity, austerities, intellect or holiness.

Brahmavartam: The Indian subcontinent. More specifically, the land to the northwest of Hastinapur, the capital of the Kurus, or between the rivers Saraswati and Drsadvati, as mentioned in the Rigveda.

Brahmavasam: The abode of Brahmana priest.

Brahmavat: Filled with Brahman or the knowledge of Brahman.

Brahmavid: A scholar well versed in the knowledge of Brahman. Knowing Brahman

Brahmavidya: Knowledge of Brahman. There are said to be 32 Brahmavidyas.

Brahmavivardhana: An epithet of Indra.

Brahmavratam: Vow of chastity or celibacy usually observed by a student or yogi in pursuit of the knowledge of Brahman.

Brahmavrikhsam: Palasa or Udumbra tree whose wood is used in the sacrificial rituals. It is said to be the Palasa tree or the flame of the forest, also known as a butea tree.

Brahmavritti: The profession of a Brahmana priest.

Brahmayajna: One of the five daily sacrifices expected to be performed by a householder. It consists of teaching and recitation of the Vedas to pay the debt of gratitude to the seers and saints who uphold the Vedas or the knowledge of Brahman.

Brahmayana: An epithet of Narayana.

Brahmayoga: Union with Brahman by learning or acquiring the knowledge of Brahman or the Vedas.

Brahmayoni: The womb of Brahman or Brahman as the source of all creation.

Brahmi: Goddess Saraswathi; a pious woman; a woman who married according to the Vedic rites; Nature or Prakriti; speech; wife of a Brahmana priest; Durga.

Brahmishta: Proficient in the knowledge of Brahman or the Vedas; a pious person.

Brahmodyam: Explaining the Vedas, the knowledge of Brahman or discussion of theological matters.

Brahmopadesam: Instruction in the knowledge of Brahman or the Vedas.

Brihaspati: A Vedic deity. As lord of magic and prayer, he offers prayers to gods on behalf of the worshippers. He is also known as the teacher of gods (Devguru). In Vedic astrology, he represents the planet Jupiter. Brihaspati is also the name of an ancient Indian scholar who founded the famous atheistic school of the Charvakas, also known as the Lokayatas.

Bibliography

Arthur Keith B., The Religion and Philosophy of the Veda and Upanishads, Volume 1, Greenwood Press, 1971.

Aurobindo, Sri. The Secret of the Veda, Sri Aurobindo Ashram, Pondicherry, 1990. First published in a monthly review Arya 1914-20.

Aurobindo, Sri. The Upanishads, Sri Aurobindo Ashram, Pondicherry, 1972.

Bailey, Gregory. The Puranas: A Study in the Development of Hinduism. University of South Carolina Press, 2003.

Basham, Arthur L., and Zysk, Kenneth G. The Origins and Development of Classical Hinduism, Oxford University Press, 1991.

Brayant, Edwin F. The Yoga Sutras of Patanjali, A New Edition, Translation, and Commentary with Insights From the Traditional Commentators. North Point Press 2009.

Buhler, George. The Laws of Manu in Sacred Books of the East Vol.25, 1886, Online Edition available at Hinduwebsite.com.

Burns, Kevin. Eastern Philosophy: The Greatest Thinkers and Sages from Ancient to Modern Times, Enchanted Lion Books, 2006.

Campbell, Joseph. The Masks of God: Oriental Mythology, Penguin Compass, 1991.

Dasgupta, Surendranath. History of Indian Philosophy, Vol.1, Cambridge, 1951.

Deussen, Paul. The Philosophy of the Upanishads, E.T. 1905

Deussen, Paul. The System of the Vedanta According to Badarayana's Brahma Sutras and Cankaras's Commentary Thereon Set forth As a Compendium of the Dogmatics of Brahmanism From the Standpoint of Sankara. Authorized Translation by Johnston, Charles, The Open Court Publishing Company, 1912.

Farquhar, John N. A Primer on Hinduism, Published by J. Jetley for Asiatic Education Services, London 1904.

Feuerstein, Georg. The Deeper Dimension of Yoga: Theory and Practice. Shambhala Publications, Inc, 2003.

Feuerstein, Georg, The Yoga Tradition: Its History, Literature, Philosophy, and Practice, Hohm Press, 2001.

Gambhirananda, Swami. Brahma Sutra Bhasya of Sri Sankaracharya 1977 (English Translation), Advaita Ashrama, Ramakrisna Order.

Glucklich, Ariel. The Strides of Vishnu, Oxford University Press, 2008.

Bibliography

Griswold, Hervey D. Brahman A Study In The History of Indian Philosophy, The MacMillan Company, 1900.

Gupta, Bina. Perceiving in Advaita Vedanta, Associated Press, London and Toronto 1991.

Hamilton Sue. Indian Philosophy, A Very Short Introduction, Oxford 2001.

Heehs Peter, Editor. Indian Religions, A Historical Reader Of Spiritual Expression and Experience, New York University Press, 2002.

Hopkins, Edward W. The Religions of India, Ginn & Company, 1895.

Hume, Robert E. The Thirteen Principal Upanishads, Oxford University Press, 1998.

Keith, Arthur B. The Religion And Philosophy Of The Veda And Upanishads, Volume 1, Greenwood Press, 1971.

King, Richard. Indian Philosophy, an Introduction to Hindu and Buddhist Thought, Georgetown University Press, 1999.

Macnicol, Nicol. The Religious Quest of India, Indian Theism From The Vedic To The Muhammadan Period, Oxford University Press, 1915.

Madhava, Acharya. Sarvadarshanasamgraha, translation by E.B. Cowell and A.E. Gough, Delhi: Motilal Banarasidass.

Mahadevan, T.M.P. Outlines of Hinduism, Chetana Limited, 1971.

Majumdar, R.C. Ancient India, Motilal Banarasidass, India, 2003.

Miller, Jeanine. Vision of Cosmic Order in the Vedas [Hardcover], Routledge & Kegan Paul Books Ltd, 1985.

Muller, Max F. Six Systems of Indian Philosophy; Samkhya and Yoga; Naya and Vaiseshika. Longmans, Green, and Co. 1919.

Muller, Max F. The Upanishads, Sacred Books of the East Vol.1, Online Edition, available at Hinduwebsite.com.

R.C. Majumdar, H.C. Raychaudhuri and Kalikinkar Datta. An Advanced History of India, The Macmillan Co. Of India Ltd.1976.

Raju P.T. Structural Depths of Indian Thought, South Asian Publishers Pvt. Ltd. New Delhi, 1985.

S, Radhakrishnan. Indian Philosophy, Vol. 1 & 2. Oxford University Press, 1999.

S, Radhakrishnan. The Principal Upanishads, Harper Collins, 1994. First published in 1953 in Great Britain.

Sankaracharya, Adi, Translated by Gambhirananda, Swami. The Eight Upanishads, Vol. One and Two, Advaita Ashrama, Kolkata, 2003. First edition 1958.

Scharfstein, Ben-Ami. A Comparative History of World Philosophy From the Upanishads to Kant, State University of New York Press,1998.

Smith, Vincent A. The Early History Of India From 600 B.C. To The Muhammadan Conquest Including the Invasion Of Alexander The Great, Oxford 1908

The Rig Veda Ralph T.H. Griffith, Translator [1896], Online Edition, available at Hinduwebsite.com.

V, Jayaram. The Bhagavadgita Translation, Online Edition available at Hinduwebsite.com, 2001.

V, Jayaram. The Bhagavadgita: Unveiling the Gita's Secrets, First Edition, Pure Life Vision LLC, 2024.

Vivekananda, Swami. Selections from the Complete Works of Swami Vivekananda, Advaita Ashrama, 1985.

Williams, Monier M. Hinduism, Society for Promoting Christian Knowledge, London, 1880.

Wm. Theodore de Bary et.al. Sources of Indian Tradition, Columbia University Press, 1958.

Credits

Cover Design: by Jayaram V
Front Cover Image: Cris Ramos, SVG, 2017, Modified under Pixabay Content License.
Back Cover Image: Colleen, SVG, 2021, Modified under Pixabay Content License

www.ingramcontent.com/pod-product-compliance
Lightning Source LLC
Chambersburg PA
CBHW061807070526
44586CB00024B/2749